REV. FRANCIS R. DAVIS
ST. PATRICK'S CHURCH
274 DENISON PKWY. E.
CORNING, NEW YORK 14830-2995

UPON THIS ROCK

UPON THIS ROCK

by

Valentine Long O.F.M.

FRANCISCAN HERALD PRESS
Chicago, Illinois 60609

Upon This Rock, by Valentine Long O.F.M. Copyright © 1982, Franciscan Herald Press, 1434 West 51st Street, Chicago, IL 60609.

Library of Congress Cataloging in Publication Data:
Long, Valentine.
  Upon this rock.
  Includes bibliographical references.
  1. Catholic Church—Doctrinal and controversial works—Catholic authors. 2. Popes—Primacy. 3. Modernism—Catholic Church—Controversial literature. I. Title.
BX1751.2.L66   282   82-2412
ISBN 0-8199-0834-7   AACR2

Published with Ecclesiastical Permission

MADE IN THE UNITED STATES OF AMERICA

A Word from the Publisher

The late John Cardinal Wright, in a series of letters from Rome, encouraged the author to write the articles which are now this book. He had meant to do a foreword, but of course God called the great churchman to his eternal reward before he could make good his promise.

What began the correspondence between the two, dates back to an occasion in 1971. The Cardinal in a bookstore in Rome picked up a copy of *The Angels in Religion and Art* and, liking it, not only recommended the book in the *Osservatore Romano* but wrote personally to Father Valentine Long to urge him to do a similar book on the Mother of God, whose prerogatives were also under attack. The chapters in that book, like the chapters in this book, first appeared as articles for periodicals strong for the Faith. Upon reading one of them, "Our Lady Designs a Medal," His Eminence promptly penned his humorous admission, under the date of August 6, 1974: "Dear Father Valentine, this is to record, with gratitude, the fact that I have snitched from your article on Catherine Labouré in a homily prepared for the Rue de Bac!" Upon publication of the completed book, *The Mother of God,* Cardinal Wright wrote an enthusiastic review of it in three different magazines.

He would have done no less for the present book, *Upon This Rock,* for while it was still in the making, the great lover of the Faith by way of encouragement had written the author: "Let me take the opportunity to say how long and with what admiration I have followed your work. In my opinion, you are one of our hopes and by no means the least. Keep it up!" May his noble soul intercede now, before her Divine Founder, for a restoration of unity within the Church he so ardently loved and so faithfully served!

Contents

A WORD FROM THE PUBLISHER 3
Introduction: ABOUT THIS BOOK 7
1. WHAT ADAM DID TO MAN 13
2. OUR TWO-SIDED WORLD 25
3. PHILOSOPHY ITSELF NEEDS GUIDANCE 37
4. THE PRIMACY OF PETER 47
5. THE PRIMACY OF PETER REMAINS 59
6. THE POPE HAS ALWAYS SAVED THE FAITH 75
7. ARIUS — THE "NEW THEOLOGIAN" OF HIS DAY 87
8. ARIUS IN HIS HAUGHTIEST HOUR DROPS DEAD 97
9. TRUTH AGAIN IN CRISIS 105
10. THE NEW "DOGMA" OF PROCESS 115
11. TAKING ORDERS FROM HEGEL 127
12. A FAIRY TALE FOR ADULTS 137
13. ANGELS IN THE UNIVERSE 151
14. SATAN EDUCATES A TEACHER 169
15. THE ICONOCLAST HAS RETURNED 181
16. WHY BEGRUDGE GOD BEAUTIFUL CHURCHES? 193
17. HOW WRONG WAS THE GALILEO VERDICT? 203
18. POPE PAUL LIVED AND DIED A MARTYR 213
19. THAT THEY MAY ALL BE ONE 223
20. POPE JOHN PAUL II: MAN OF THE HOUR 235

Dedication

To a courageous and
tireless champion of
the Faith,
one of the best,
Paul H. Hallett

About This Book

Pope John XXIII opened the Second Vatican Council with a prayer to the Holy Spirit, in high hope.

A week before, he had knelt at the shrine of Our Lady of Loreto to implore her aid. He asked her to beseech the Holy Spirit to soften hearts to his ideal of an ecumenical unity. Not by accident did this General Council open on what was then the feast of Mary's Motherhood, October 11, 1962, and closed under the presidency of Pope Paul VI on her feast of the Immaculate Conception, December 8, 1965. Both pontiffs had planned it so. Both showed the same unfaltering trust in Mary's intercession before the Most High, which our present Pope John Paul II has in his extensive travels no less noticeably shown the world.

Pope John, at the outset of the council, had reason to exude confidence. He had become an instant favorite among Christians the world over. What he did not include in his expression of hope, since it seemed to him already a realization, drew from him the nearest approach to a boast in his long introductory address. He referred to it only once, and with a restrained pride. But he could afford to make such little ado over "the unity of Catholics among themselves" when it stood in no apparent danger of losing its solidarity. It "must always be kept exemplary and most firm," he advised. His Holiness showed no fear of its ever being weakened. It was taken for granted.[1]

Frank Sheed, who in *The Church And I* remembers this Catholic solidarity as a calm before the storm, thinks "we ought to have known that trouble was brewing."[2] Pope John at the council did not know. Or if he did suspect the seething unrest beneath the surface, he kept the suspicion to himself. He voiced no premonition of the forthcoming threat from an influential band of theologians who would hack away at the deposit of faith, not managing to destroy the indestructible, to be sure, yet succeeding only too often in destroying confidence in the changeless truths. Before the council got into its second year, they had begun. They are still at it.

To keep the Faith means nothing more or less than to preserve a firm belief in the sum total of its doctrines, leaving out none. Among these, as a divine expedient for safeguarding them all, is the infallible authority which Christ invested in Peter to be passed on to his successors in the Roman See. Dean Milman in his historic treatment of the subject went into a rapture of wonder that the Bishops of Rome, in the excitement of every great doctrinal controversy, had the acumen always to come out of the turmoil on the winning orthodox side. Mere ingenuity? Just plain luck? There is blessedly more to it than that. The explanation lies in the enlightenment which the popes received from the Holy Spirit. Their decisions, their sanction upon the decrees of councils, never failed in the emergency to ensure truth against error.[3]

The truth of which, Pope John well understood. He saw his primacy of authority from Christ, not as a personal honor, but as a benefit to the human race. He was not a proud man who decided to have a council. His keynote address at Vatican II, which only he had the power to convene, reveals him a humble as well as tenacious guardian of the Faith. He proclaimed it. He meant every word of his manifesto to preserve it. He invited the whole world to share it with him.

About This Book

Did not his successor do likewise? Presiding over the council from the beginning of its second year on, Pope Paul promoted to the utmost of his authority the hope of reunion among Christians. However, as with Pope John, it must be a reunion complete. Nothing less would suffice. "It is essential," states the *Decree on Ecumenism,* "that doctrine should be clearly presented in its entirety. Nothing is so foreign to the spirit of ecumenism as a false irenicism, in which the purity of Catholic doctrine suffers loss and its genuine and certain meaning is clouded." With joy Pope Paul signed the document.

He added to it a commentary, in praise of the effort to promote Christian unity, yet again with a caution. It was the familiar caution: a warning against the kind of dialogue that would rashly attempt "to remove doctrinal difficulty by seeking to deprive of their validity, or to neglect or conceal, statements which the teaching authority of the Church declares to be binding and final." The Holy Father concluded his commentary with a breadth of compassion and a dedication to the truth equal to Pope John's. "The fulness of faith is," he said, "a ready benefit which renders us the happier in proportion as we bestow it upon others. We do not call it ours. It is Christ's. It belongs to all men."[4]

This book will have much to say of Pope Paul who bore the brunt of current dissent. If it did not start, it emerged into the open, during his reign and gathered momentum throughout. Valiantly he withstood the onslaught, never cowing before it, never wavering in his convictions. Like Pope John before him, and the whole line of supreme pontiffs back to Peter, Pope Paul VI did not by a single official utterance betray his trust. He confronted without yielding to the pressure upon him to undermine the Rock on which Christ founded the Holy, Catholic and Apostolic Church.

It was during his pontificate that the series of essays which form this book began. Done out of love for the Faith and from a corresponding sense of gratitude to its papal defenders through the ages till now, most of the essays appeared in periodicals of the same bent: *Homiletic and Pastoral Review, Friar, The Wanderer.* The writing, thus seriously motivated, found a secondary and humorous stimulus in the absurdity of a suddenly well-publicized clique of self-appointed dictators of doctrine who talked as if they — and not the duly elected successors of St. Peter — enjoy infallibility. An oddity they are, the modern dissenters who would remake the creed after their own designs while claiming to belong and by some freak of desire wanting to belong to the divinely founded institution they would demolish — if allowed their way. The Holy See, the book brings out, did not and does not and will not allow such people to have their way.

Once let the Vicar of Christ reject a dogma, as process theology would have him do, and what would happen? The Catholic Church through her divinely appointed spokesman would thereby destroy her credibility. By the power of the Holy Spirit, this cannot happen. And what cannot happen is not going to happen. Paul VI saw, as now John Paul II sees, through the *New Theology*: a shameless recurrence of the Modernism which Pius X had condemned, and which itself consisted of nothing more original than an ingenious rehash of ancient errors condemned by earlier pontiffs. How, again, did St. Pius define Modernism? "The synthesis of all heresies." And he found underlying it an atheism which disallows a transcendent God and would have its dupes believe that the Divine Christ of the Gospels lacks reality and must be considered a made-up facsimile of what the primitive Christians wanted their Messiah to be.[5] Arthur Machen, having in mind such of its high priests as Loisy and Tyrrell, labeled the conglomerate "atheism in a chasuble."

Lamentably, three-quarters of a century after their condemnation, Père Loisy and Father Tyrrell have many followers who preach their same variety of errors in a chasuble.

About This Book

This book holds a proportionate variety of essays written in reply and out of love for the Faith, which gives the collection a unity of purpose. The now recurrent denials of God's transcendence over creation, of the supernatural, of the angels good and bad, of original sin and what it did to mankind and to the world, will all receive due treatment. So, too, will the following corollaries be considered: the growing threat of a humanism which takes from the Creator his priority, and the return of an iconoclastic spirit which from a lack of reverence (if not disbelief) would deprive the Blessed Sacrament of suitably beautiful churches, and the delusion that dogmas change from age to age, and, as a cause for the errors, the rejection of papal infallibility, which goes to the heart of the matter. Indeed, the unblemished record of the Holy See in preserving the Faith against the assaults of hell remains from start to finish the dominant motivation of this book, inspiring gratitude, and suggesting the title *Upon This Rock*. All twenty chapters, let it be known here and now, are imbued with the spirit of "thank God for the Popes, from Peter to John Paul II."

* * *

Notes

1. Documens of Vatican II: Appendix: "Pope John's Opening Speech." The Walter Abbott, S.J. Edition.
2. Frank Sheed: *The Church And I*. Doubleday and Company, Garden City, N.Y.
3. Henry Hart Milman: *The History of Latin Christianity*.
4. *The Sixteen Documents of Vatican II*: Commentary on the Decree on Ecumenism. The Daughters of St. Paul Edition.
5. *Lamentabile*: Decree of the Holy Office, July 3, 1907. Encyclical *Pascendi*, September 8, 1907. Cf. Denzinger 2001-2065a and 2071-2109.

1.
What Adam Did to Man

SHE comes to mind as if it were only a year instead of decades ago that her presence edified as well as delighted a college campus. Not a rare beauty, she gave the impression of being one because of an inner force that enabled her to do whatever she did with distinction. It has been said that no lady can sneeze without shattering her dignity: but this girl could. She would cover the act with a handkerchief and with an air of such delicate unconcern over what can't be helped anyhow that her unshaken poise secured her dignity.

She had merely to enter a corridor, a room, the cafeteria, any place, to create a reaction not unlike the stir of interest in a crowded theatre when a favorite actress comes on stage in the first scene. Only, the girl did not show off. Kneeling at prayer in chapel, she didn't seem to care who noticed her — other than the One to whom she knelt. Her more extravagant mannerisms, a pert frown in disapproval, an airy wave of the hand in greeting, the way she would crinkle her nose for the fun of it, none of these characteristics looked to be a pretence. Once she pushed open the wrong door by mistake, flouncing in on a faculty meeting, and it seemed as natural (the dean was afterwards to admit) as a brook running with a song into private property. This *persona grata* could never be an intruder.

She carried her vivacity with a grace that excluded any suggestion of the vulgar, the improper, the indecent. There was nothing cheap about her. She had quality, which brought respect. It was a foregone conclusion that she would graduate, if not with highest academic honors, with a *maxima cum laude* in popularity. And so it turned out. None of her classmates drew an outburst of applause equal to hers, which continued all the while she was walking back to her seat with diploma in hand.

Twenty years later she died a failure. The graduate who had been considered the most likely to succeed did not. Somewhere along the way, after the early collapse of her marriage, she went from bad to worse. The will to resist evil was gone. The prostitute driven to narcotics, made a wreck of the woman she had started out to become. The mortician, who had fixed an unsuitable smile on her emaciated features, could not have imagined the promise which her youth had shown an admiring college. There was nothing left of it. She had shattered it.

This delineation, resorting to fictitious details in order to cover her identity, has not feigned the deterioration of a very real drop-out from society, a refugee from decency, who had been an angel of light. How explain the turn-about? What basic trouble underlay her promise to destroy it? What tendency, of what causing, frenzied the pitiable woman into nullifying her grandeur of person? Any honest handbook of Catholic doctrine holds the answer. But no theologian ever presented it to greater effect than Gustave Flaubert, who only suggests it.

His *Madame Bovary* does more than narrate the decline of a promising woman; it does not stop with her characterization; it would like to get at the source of the trouble. Accordingly, the novelist at every opportunity throws out hints like so many pieces of a jigsaw puzzle that can have no solution without the missing central piece: the postulate of Original Sin. Never naming the doctrine, perhaps not even thinking of it, Flaubert nonetheless asks questions that imply it. "Whence came this insufficiency" in the life of a sensualist who had rejected God, "this instantaneous turning to decay of everything on which she leaned?" The worldling who had all the world could give her could only wonder why "every smile hid a yawn, every joy a curse, all pleasure satiety, and the sweetest kisses left upon the lips only the unattainable desire of a greater delight."

The novelist does not share the poor woman's bewilderment. He supposes, and acts on the supposition, that there is in human nature a natural corruptibility. What is happening to the convent-bred voluptuary seems perfectly clear to him. He may pity but is not surprised. His characterization quite apparently understands what the Fall did to human nature. His suppositions take the doctrine for granted.

The critics, who upbraided Flaubert for no other reason than the demoralization of Emma Bovary, might as well have condemned the Book of Genesis for telling the truth about degraded Eve. The report on neither woman caused her downfall: so why blame the report? As Newman reminded a Dublin audience, you cannot have a sinless literature of sinful man. And the fact is, Flaubert did not invent his scandalous heroine but took her from real life. She was essentially a fictionized copy of the actual Madame Delamarre, the wife of a country doctor who drove him to suicide by her gross infidelities.[1]

What really seems to have vexed the critics of *Madame Bovary* is that, having been shown a budding beauty whom they could venerate as the personification of their wishful thinking, they then had to watch her deprived of a bright future. The air at the time was rife with the theory of man's perfectibility without God, and when the young beauty emerged a promising exemplar of the theory, her credulous admirers were in no mood to forgive a deterioration that insulted their daydream. They denounced it.

The book, from another source and for a different reason than its theme of human corruptibility, drew censure. It got on the now extinct Index. Its choice of scandalous episodes, though delicately treated, got it there. Were the censors, possibly under Jansenistic influence, being oversevere? No lurid details vitiate the descriptions. Nor does the constant portrayal of human susceptibility to vice condone debauchery. Rather it shows a contempt for debauchery. All in all, the novel with its heroine's relentless degradation could supplement the strictest theological tract on the debilitating effect of original sin. The final scene, when the priest stands at the bedside of the dying suicide to administer the last rites, points up the futility of her wasted life. It provokes the conclusion: if lusting comes to this, isn't virtue the wiser course?

This masterpiece of realism, over which Flaubert spent years of labor to get every sentence just right, is a saddening book. It would have to be, having such a theme. The disintegration of a personality, in fiction as in life, produces a sense of loss: we somehow feel that the whole of humanity has thereby been diminished. Mourners at the funeral of that college favorite, who had disappointed them, felt so. Human debilitation in body or soul mocks the original dignity we do not have, but feel we should have and indeed would have inherited from Adam and Eve, had they not sinned.

It has been suggested that, alone of animals, man laughs and weeps because man is the only animal to feel the difference between what things are and what they ought to be. We speak loosely of a horse-laugh, applying the term to the person whose guffaw does not ring true; the connection is self-evident; a horse doesn't have the necessary sense of humor, an awareness of life's incongruities, to produce an

What Adam Did to Man

outburst of genuine laughter. We also speak of crocodile tears, and tears they are, though not of grief. They are the result of a healthy mastication and nothing more. The crocodile does not weep but, when eating, does indeed shed unemotional tears since the pressure of food against the roof of its mouth excites in this reptile the lachrymal glands. The profound observation of Hazlitt still holds: man alone of the animals laughs out of sheer relief and weeps out of genuine sorrow over what things are when he senses they ought not to be what they are.

That there lurks in human nature a pull toward vice to make the practice of virtue difficult, who may deny? That the bright prospects of youth do not stay bright if they stay at all, that the world itself cannot permanently satisfy even the worldling, that the coming on of age enfeebles when it does not completely disable, and that in the end every human life must undergo death, these evils cannot but strike an open mind as undesirabilities which ought not to be. Yet there they are. Madame Bovary does not belie reality. She exemplifies the perverse tendencies of a fallen nature. She suffers its liabilities. And while she did not have to die a suicide, by a curse not of her doing she did have to die.

The discordance of life, only a modicum of which does *Madame Bovary* portray, impresses on the mind a vague sense that something must have gone wrong with human nature, if ever it was right, for to all appearances it labors under a curse. The very continuation of the human race partakes of the tragedy. Except for the miraculous Virgin Birth, no baby born into the world but has come at the expense of its mother. The fact stands undisputed: yet why should it be? Why should this most natural of events inflict upon the unoffending mother so much inconvenience and anxiety and the pangs of parturition when not the alternative of a Caesarean incision? The question, under the impetus of a normal curiosity over life's discrepancies, leads to a hundred similar questions.

In view of such contrarieties, too many to be enumerated here, who would care to brush aside as simply inconceivable the explanation that some primeval damage has befallen the human race to bring upon human nature all this evidence of harm. Who could fail to see, if nothing more, at least the bare possibility? Well, Pelagius could. He failed to see the faintest possibility of it, much less admit it.

This Celtic monk came out of his monastery in Britain into Rome and later into Carthage with his Latin discourses on the perfectibility of human nature from its own inherent resources. It didn't need God's grace to acquire virtue. It had not fallen so as to need help in the first place. There had been no Original Sin. Human nature, therefore, could not be suffering from consequences of what never happened. It was not weakened from its pristine vigor. It retained the vigor in full.[2]

At the same time, with a shiftiness peculiar to heresy, Pelagius did allow that Adam had sinned. But the sin was personal to him, in no way affecting his descendants except by the extraneous influence of bad example. It did not intrinsically harm the human race. Since it was the first sin on record, it might even be called original sin, so long as it be understood as Adam's private affair and not involving mankind.

If this Pelagian explanation looks familiar to readers of certain modernized catechisms, it is because such manuals have adopted the heresy. Long since condemned, it has revived. It is back in fashion with the modernists. They call it new, but it smells of the fifth century monk out of Britain who met his Waterloo in Africa.

Working hard to explain away the doctrine, Pelagius took the curse out of the double decree that Adam would have to win his livelihood with difficulty and that Eve would have to bear her children in pain.[3] Rejecting also the threat of death for mankind in *Genesis,* Pelagius naturally rejected St. Paul's affirmation that "in Adam all die." The Church

What Adam Did to Man

accepted on face value the scriptural statement that "sin came into the world through one man and death through sin, and so death spread to all men."[4] But Pelagius ridiculed this explanation as too literal. His tortuous argument, raising a great fuss about misunderstanding the real meaning, simply wiggled clear of it.

The argument disallows death as a curse and maintains that Adam would have died even had he not sinned, for man was created to live out his natural life on earth and then die and, if he used his ability to overcome sin, he would advance without the aid of grace to the supernatural life of heaven. The text that "one has died for all" meant nothing more to Pelagius than that our dying Savior was thereby offering the human race a good example to counterbalance the bad example of Adam's sin.[5] The fuzzy rationalization went no deeper. It accordingly drew the conclusion that the death of Jesus on the cross did not open heaven to fallen man; it wasn't necessary; man had not fallen. The idea of atonement, the heretic was preaching, had to go.[6]

It obviously had already gone out of his head, if ever it was there. He was sure of himself. He pushed confidenlty on into his labyrinth of errors to another inevitable inference: infant baptism, a common practice in the Church, amounted to an empty formality. And so it did, if the child had incurred no taint of original sin to be purified of.

Pelagianism, if given its way, would have pulled the foundation from under the Faith and one doctrine after another in the integrated structure would have come toppling down. It did not get its way. It looked to be prospering for a while — when it spread into Africa. There its advance suffered a drastic setback. It ran into St. Augustine.

St. Augustine, with the other African prelates whom he roused to action, fought the heresy for the blasphemy it was. They were not going to allow Pelagius, with an accomplice named Coelestius, to travel the land unmolested with an argument that would take the supernatural out of man's life and reduce his Savior to a non-redeemer of no importance whatever to his salvation. A synod of bishops met at Carthage, another at Mileve, to condemn outright the Pelagian denials. From Rome Pope Innocent I sent to each assembly his complete ratification, in the name of Christ Jesus, "without whose Sacrifice fallen man could never gain heaven." It was then that the great Bishop of Hippo made his much quoted comment: "Two synods have written to the Apostolic See about this matter; the replies have come back; the question is settled."

Or was it? For the faithful, surely. But for Pelagius who had meanwhile gone to Palestine, and for his ally Coelestius who remained, the issue was not closed. Neither would submit. Who did that ringleader in Hippo and the hierarchy behind him think they were to order the enlightened to recant? Why didn't the Roman pontiff keep his authority out of this African affair? Did he for a moment believe that his written threat of excommunication would intimidate the threatened? He might as well have thrown it in the Tiber.

After the death of Pope Innocent, both heresiarchs awaited their opportunity to request his successor to withdraw their censure. This, Pope Zosimus would not do. Instead, he reinforced it. He kept the reputation of the Holy See for safeguarding doctrine intact.

The heresy lingered on to provoke a final condemnation in 418 from the Council of Carthage, which St. Augustine by the force of his genius dominated. Its cannons, sanctioned by Pope Zosimus and binding in conscience on the Universal Church, included the following reminders: that Adam died because of his sin and not from physical necessity, and that infants on account of their having inherited the taint of his sin must be baptized, and that justifying grace not only forgives past sins but aids the avoidance of future ones, and that without God's grace it is impossible for fallen man to attain virtue.

The council did not use vague terms in its retort to

What Adam Did to Man

Pelagius. It spelt out in detail, clearly, forcibly, his condemnation. Not a tenet of the heresy escaped. Here, for example, is how the series of eight canons began: "Whoever says that Adam the first man was made mortal, so that, whether he sinned or did not sin, he would die in body — let him be anathema."[7] Such definitive action dealt Pelagianism a staggering blow from which it has time and again tried to recover. Its attempted revivals have had to be put down by future councils under papal guidance, at Orange in 529, at Trent in 1546.

And now, alas, it has revived again. Heaven knows, and Satan too, in how many parochial schools it is being taught to the young who should be learning the true doctrine. The abuse has not gone unchallenged by the Holy See. Pope Paul VI used up all of three paragraphs in his *Credo of the People of God* to restate the dogma of original sin. He quoted from the councils of Orange and of Trent, emphasizing with them the necessity of baptism for all and the duty of parents to have even their babies "who have not yet been able to be guilty of any personal sin" restored to grace through the sacrament.

Pope Paul issued his *Credo* in June, 1968, to mark the closing of "the Year of Faith" which he had introduced in the hope it would prove a restorative of true doctrine to the wavering and a preventive against heresy for the resolute. Under Pope John Paul II, on October 20, 1980, an instruction of fourteen pages went out from the Holy See to the bishops on "Infant Baptism." Therein the necessity of the sacrament is stressed and Pelagianism condemned again for denying original sin and the corresponding need for baptism at all. The instruction warns pastors not to withhold the sacrament from infants, conceived and born as they have been in guilt. The instruction then proceeds to show that the Church has traditionally demanded infant baptism, although at times the practice did wane because of heretical influences. Quotations to prove the point, from councils, from the early witness of St. Irenaeus and St .Cyprian and Origin, and from a considerable array of later authorities, impress by their abundance as well as by their uniformity.

The instruction, like Pope John Paul II who sanctioned it, does not hedge. It comes right out into open to admit what is embarrassing, no less than what is gratifying, in the facts. For example: "Fathers and Doctors, such as Basil, Gregory of Nyssa, Ambrose, John Chrysostom, Jerome, Augustine, even though they had themselves been baptized only as adults (for the reasons just given), nonetheless repudiated this neglect of baptism in strong terms and asked adults not to postpone the reception of baptism since it is necessary for salvation." St. Augustine is quoted, too, as regarding the age-old custom of infant baptism "a tradition received from the apostles."[8]

St. Augustine had the explanation (which Pelagius did not have) for all the manifold sufferings on earth, for hardships of every kind, for sickness, for death, for the constant struggle in our duality between body and soul, for indeed the perversity in human nature that makes being a saint a distinction and being a criminal a common occurrence. The collapse of virtue in a Madame Bovary or in such as that model graduate from college would have grieved but not confounded him. He had from divine revelation the answer. He realized that to stop praying fervently is to close out grace and succumb to vice. He understood the pull of gravity on our nature from experience. He knew what dimmed the intellect, weakened the will, and tempted the passions to an irrational unruliness which made the brothel a normality and jails a social necessity to prevent anarchy. History with its massacres and wars and peace treaties that usually led to worse wars did not leave the expert on Original Sin baffled.

It all saddened. It did not baffle. The author of *Original Sin, The Baptism of Children, Nature and Grace, The Grace of Christ,* was acutely aware of the basic reason for the

What Adam Did to Man

world's ills. The human race, through Adam's abuse of free will, had fallen from its original paradisal state.[9]

In denying which, Pelagius was virtually rebuking the Most High for the sorry mess the world is in: he taught that it had been created so. What a mixed-up heresy! It freed Adam of the blame. It overlooked the malice of Satan's trickery. It put the responsibility for evil in the world upon the All-Holy, the All-Just.

That good and evil exist side by side in the world, but that the evil comes of Satan and the good from God, poses a theological problem. It invites consideration. We shall give it that consideration, making it our next theme. And here again we'll accept aid from divine revelation in reaching an understanding.

* * *

Notes

1. Encyclopaedia Britannica, Vol. 9, *Flaubert, Gustave.*
2. P.L. XXX, 678.
3. Gen. 3:17; 3:16.
4. Gen. 2:17; 1 Cor. 15:22; Rom. 5:12.
5. 2 Cor. 5:14.
6. P.L. XXX, 678.
7. Denzinger 101. Cf. Joseph Pohle: *Pelagius and Pelagianism* in The Catholic Encyclopedia, Vol. XI. Also: H. Daniel-Rops: *The Church in the Dark Ages,* Ch. 1, "The Saint of the New Age." Also: Charles Poulet: *Church History,* Vol. I, Sect. 2, Ch. 3.
    N.B. The name of Pelagius' ally is spelt differently by the three above-mentioned scholars — Caelestius, Celestius, Coelestius, respectively.
8. *The Pope Speaks,* Vol. 26, No. 1, 1981, pgs. 6-19. "An Instruction of the Sacred Congregation for the Doctrine of the Faith."
9. *The Merits of Sinners* and *The Spirit and the Letter* are two more treatises in which St. Augustine demolishes the haughty naturalism of Pelagius and Coelestius.

2.
Our Two-Sided World

FROM a lookout point in the Helderbergs, which a road out of Albany reaches in half an hour's time, the view runs sharply down through a ravine that broadens out into an immense sweep of farmland as far round as the eye can see. I once stood there when October was coming up the hollow in a riot of color, and this sudden rush of gaiety out of that serene background of harvested fields, over which a drift of chimney smoke hung unruffled and no bird flew, was more than anyone could take without a pang of ecstatic bewilderment. There was in the air the hint of something nowhere in sight. The scene by its very grandeur promised more than it could show, so that the promise had in it a tantalizing insufficiency — a strange ache of exile.

The sensation comes with the urgency of a confidential secret to fill the soul as with a foretaste of her native air. That it can happen elsewhere than on a mountaintop outside Albany, N.Y., who needs to be reminded? Who hasn't known the experience in whatever area of creation when the view is of a panoramic amplitude? You cannot in your right mind reject its appeal. You respond to it intuitively, feeling under its disturbing joy that you have never been so much yourself, and never so alien to the world, as now when you cannot drink in enough of its provocative beauty.

The flaming sunrise, the heaving and panting immensity of the sea, the woodland stream, address more than eye and ear. These communications, in satisfying the senses, stir in the heart a yearning and in the mind a frenzy of hope: an intimation which none but the absolute atheist feels without ever catching the hint. "The whole earth is full of his glory," runs the angelic chant that acknowledges in creation its Source of being.[1] The universe does not display its grandeurs to the seraphim in vain. They have quick minds.

But one doesn't have to be an angel to grasp the message. The human mind, if not miseducated, is equal to the attempt. "The world's unfolded blossom smells of God," writes a tramp of London. "From the greatness and beauty of created things," goes a wise saying, "comes a corresponding perception of the Creator." And what Solomon said St. Paul repeats: "His eternal power . . . has been clearly perceived in the things that have been made."[2]

The advice to "look at the birds of the air" and "consider the lilies of the field" invites even the ornithologist and the botanist to see through the freedom of the bird, which neither sows nor reaps, and through the beauty of the flower, which does not spin, to the Providence who feeds the one and clothes the other."[3] "God our Father," the Liturgy therefore pleads, "open our eyes to see your hand at work in the splendor of creation."[4] All creation, in every detail, in its totality, refers to an uncreated Creator. The grape did not learn of itself to fuse the sap of the vine and the warmth from the sun into a delicious juice. Such chemistry, a diminutive achievement on a spinning globe, itself a mere particle of the universe, like the universe derives from their underivative Maker.

But the world presents another aspect not at all good. When Scripture speaks of the world it may praise or it may

Our Two-Sided World

condemn, depending on which of the two aspects it treats: the God-reflecting harmony and immensity and beauty of the universe or, on the other hand, that collective body of men on earth who out of all proportion have turned from their Creator toward evil to constitute a majority and to make society a danger to the soul. In this sense we speak of the world along with the flesh and the devil as being the three sources of temptation. The world in this sense is even identified with the spirit of the age, which in a given period is less prone to evil than in another. Yet at no time does it promote sanctity. It sets the fashion and creates or maintains standards that are hostile to the interests of the soul. In this sense, and in this sense only, does the apostle John record his complaint that "the whole world is in the power of the evil one."[5]

One greater than St. John said it more strongly still, calling Satan "the ruler of this world." Christ knew what had gone wrong with the world of men, and all about its perversity under the diabolic influence, and in the knowledge explained to his apostles that "because you are not of the world, but I chose you out of the world, therefore the world hates you." Having there quoted his blessed Lord, St. John in an epistle has a word of his own to add: "Do not love the world or the things of the world. If anyone loves the world, love for the Father is not in him."[6]

The apostle James of Jerusalem draws attention to the same incompatibility. "Do you not know," he sets up his answer with a question, "that friendship with the world is enmity wtih God? Therefore whoever wishes to be a friend of the world makes himself an enemy of God." As for St. Paul, he speaks under no delusion that catering to the world can ever produce a proper "renewal of your mind." In a composite of texts he warns that "the wisdom of this world is folly with God" and that the true Christian must "not be conformed to this world," for such conformists "with minds set on earthly things" are but chasing phantoms and "their end is destruction."[7]

We live in a damaged world. It had been all good at creation, but "sin came into the world through one man and death through sin," as St. Paul explains, and evil has ever since made its presence felt.[8] Adam in disobeying God turned the world disobedient to himself. He lost his unsullied dominion over it. The harmony between the elements and Adam, between the lower forms of life and Adam, suffered a break, and remains disrupted, so that mankind thereafter has lived under the threat of disease and in danger of the beast, the fangs of the serpent, the sting of the insect, and indeed has had to maintain a livelihood against great odds. The mishaps of draught and floods and quakes and storms and raging fires, and the very obstinacy of the soil, render it difficult to make a living on an earth no longer paradise. The Bible early records God's curse on the world.

And the Bible, as God's word, could not leave the devil out of the account. He instigated the tragedy. With him, contrary to the fuzzy Pelagian notion, the whole divine story of Original Sin opens. The material world, still a magnificent symphony of wonders acclaiming its Creator, owes whatever disorders it has known, and the human race may attribute its own consequent ills, not to Adam alone, nor Eve, but to Satan more than either.

Scripture, knowing all about the world, knows who its evil genius is. "Through the devil's envy death entered the world," is what Solomon has to say of the same ugly meddler whom St. Paul denounces for having incited Ananias to lie to the Holy Spirit. St. John in turn goes to the source of that treachery which sold Jesus for thirty pieces of silver: "the devil . . . put it into the heart of Judas Iscariot, Simon's son, to betray him." St. Paul no less wise to the devil, accuses him of having "blinded the minds of unbelievers to keep them from seeing the light of the Gospel."[9]

The infidel would never of himself suspect the devil's

Our Two-Sided World

influence, not believing in him, but it is nonetheless there. The parables bristle with warnings. "The seed is the word of God," our Lord explains his story about the sower. "The ones along the path are those who have heard; then the devil comes and takes away the word from their hearts, that they may not believe and be saved."[10]

To all of which a correlative truth remains to be added, a happy truth, an important truth. The addict to whatever vice or moral failing, be it lack of faith, immorality, gluttony, avarice, sloth, hatred, pride, can by a cooperation with divine grace resist the natural tendency to evil to become an ardent believer, as did Paul of Tarsus; a model of purity, as did Mary of Magdala; a penitent from larceny, as did the Good Thief; and so on through the whole gamut of converts from every type of sin. Diabolic power has its limitation. And if the widespread evidence of that power so befuddled Manichaeus that in his heresy he divided Omnipotence equally between God and Evil, what of it? The man was heretically wrong.

But didn't St. Paul himself call Satan "the god of this world"? He did, indeed. And having used the phrase in context, in that context the great apostle supplies the clue to its meaning in other epistles. The devil's mastery is not a positive lordship, which belongs exclusively to the Supreme Being, but rather a negative mastery in the sense that the mastered must consent. If drugs are likewise said to hold a mastery over the addict, it is only because the addict chose to submit to their domination in the first place. Accordingly, St. Peter said to Ananias: "Why has Satan filled your heart to lie to the Holy Spirit?" The question, by its very tone of rebuke, implies the guilt of the sinner for having consented to his tempter. The blame was not all Satan's. The human liar incurred a share of it, a sufficient share to have deserved instant death. A proper use of his will would have nullified the diabolic influence, so that in one version the text has been freely translated to read: "Why have you let Satan fill your heart so as to make you lie to the Holy Spirit?"[11]

Satan gained access into the human story through human consent, and through the constant repetition of that consent retains it. With his angelic power of mind and a corresponding malice he knows perfectly well how to exploit human weaknesses and, given the opening, to take control. Addiction to sin, which enfeebles the will, affords him that opening.

The modern world, so predominantly atheistic, thinks that its rejection of God's beneficent law has liberated it from the constraints of the divine order without having in the process subjugated it to another. This is the grand delusion. And the world has been guided into the fallacy by the very devil it would prefer to deny, and has denied, and would continue to deny except that now the horrendous crimes of a rapidly spreading diabolism have shocked an incredulous society into misgivings and have drawn from the diabolists, not confessions of remorse, but obdurate boasts of loyalty to his Satanic Majesty.

Insofar as the world in any age flouts the divine law, and the natural law which comes of the same God, it has gone to the devil. And the diabolists know it. Anton Szador La Vey, the self-styled high priest of hell, founder of the Church of Satan, gloats over the extreme drift of society from the moral code and admits with pride that his religion has led the way by a satanic dedication to "the pleasures of this earth," by which he doesn't mean innocent pleasures, but such deviations from the decalogue as sex orgies. His words, thus understood, are only saying what the inspired writers of God have said: namely, that the collective body of society known as the world, in committing sin, in condoning it, in making it fashionable, yields not simply to an inherited tendency but to the unseen evil exploiter of that tendency. And so the apostle Paul, a knowledgeable high priest of heaven, explains to the Ephesians

Our Two-Sided World

that, before their conversion, they had been "following the course of this world," following the prince of evil, "the spirit that is now at work in the sons of disobedience."[12]

What the inspired writers have had to say on the subject in their day has not lost relevancy for ours, since the devil's hatred of mankind remains. It does not change. It does not weaken. It is immortal, like himself. But its intrusion into the individual soul, the whole tenor of the Gospel shows, can be either prevented or repelled by the soul's reliance on help from the Omnipotent. The person who believes, who prays, does penance, observes the commandments, fosters love of neighbor, doing it all for the higher love of God, obtains the needed help. The devil who enjoys making fools of people is then himself made a fool of; the saint is a terrible frustration to him.

And how the great fighting apostle exults over that! "Put on the armor of God," he urges, defiant of evil, rejoicing that the soul thus fortified will be "able to stand against the wiles of the devil." At the same time let no one underestimate the fury of the combat. The devil has all hell behind his efforts. "For we are not contending against flesh and blood, but against the principalities, against the powers, against the world rulers of this present darkness, against the spiritual hosts of wickedness."[13]

Scripture, besides pointing out the vincibility of evil, sets forth another consideration. If individuals in sufficient numbers try to restore the balance in the economy of grace, God will mercifully withhold his vengeance upon society for their sake. "For the sake of ten I will not destroy it," the Lord replied to Abraham who had been bargaining for mercy on Sodom.[14] But not ten virtuous inhabitants could be found in it, so thoroughly corrupt had the city become. The avenging angel took action. Fire and brimstone wiped it out.

A voice out of heaven, this time the voice of its queen, has spoken similarly to our generation through the medium of three listening children, who relayed the message to the world. Has the world heeded? Have enough souls honored the plea for repentance, for prayer and self-denial and virtue, to bring about peace? The atheist aggression that has since 1917 subjugated half the countries on earth, starved or tortured to death untold millions, provoked wars at will, fomented anarchy, and on the evidence does not intend to give up until it has dominated the world: all this tells louder than words of the failure, on the part of a sufficient quota, to grant our Lady of Fatima her request. She had offered a preventative. It was ignored by too many who should have known better. And the turmoil followed.

What causes such turmoil is sin, which sets loose forces of evil to harass mankind, as is clearly implied in the Fatima message and openly expressed in Scripture. If the world chooses to follow the devil to the rejection of its God, it can; its will is free; but it must take the consequences. On the present generation they have been severe, needless to say. And yet the provision for peace, which God offered the world through his mother, still holds. She has not retracted it.

Worldlings who seek their paradise on earth will never find it. The more that society rejects the supernatural to make this world its be-all and end-all, yielding to the dictates of fallen human nature to the neglect of law, the safeguard of order, the closer will society be moving toward chaos and achieving hell on earth. There is no escaping the result. There is no escaping the final disenchantment, since those who live only for this world still cannot escape their death. Their false paradise will survive them. But how could that be of any satisfaction to them? They will have gone.

We are in this world to get out of it. The world itself, in its vast outlay of sublimities in sky, on sea and land, suggests as much to the thoughtful, the unbiassed. A child looking sadly into a sunset from the window of a cozy

Our Two-Sided World

home, with that unmistakable touch of wonder on its young face, already knows what it is to have pangs of nostalgia even at home. Pity the exile who, having the pangs, does not understand with St. Paul their meaning.

Words can only feel ashamed of their attempt to describe the indescribable; but their honest attempt is better than none. We are surely the better off for the sublime inadequacy of the statement that "eye has not seen or ear heard, nor has it entered the heart of man, what God has prepared for those who love him." The assertion, while it cannot imagine for us the unimaginable, does rejoice our faith, raise our hope.[15]

How long a man or woman remains on earth doesn't matter so long as they reach, after whatever possible delay in purgatory, the right destination. Heaven means as much to St. Cecilia who departed this world in the glow of youth as to St. Raymond Penafort who arrived there after spending ninety-nine years in southern Europe. Heaven cannot be more truly paradise to St. Gertrude of Saxony who died naturally in her convent bed than to St. Lawrence of Rome who died on a red-hot griddle. What matters is, not when death comes, or how it comes, but that it may be said of the departed: "These all died in faith . . . having acknowledged that they were strangers and exiles on earth. For people who speak thus make it clear that they are seeking a homeland. . . . They desire a better country, that is, a heavenly one."[16]

Those rare moments, when the great beauty of nature casts a spell upon us, bring a taste of ecstasy that strains for more and in a delirium of expectancy feels on the verge of attaining it. Always it eludes the grasp. But it is no mirage. It is a genuine foretaste of what awaits the worthy after death, though not the unworthy.

The sublime beauties of earth, along with the complicated magnitude and harmony of the universe, do in truth speak to us of their Creator. Yet many sophisticates to this day remain stone-blind to the message. It has therefore had to be made an article of faith against the denials of heresy.[17] A gorgeous sunset, not to mention a woman of superlative charm, admittedly inspired in Manichaeus and his followers only disgust. They supposed either an evil. They found all matter, everything physical, intrinsically bad and to be despised. From the first uprising of the heresy and during its periods of revival it was always the Roman Pontiffs who set their authority in opposition to it.

Eventually, in the Ecumenical Council of Florence, Pope Eugene IV finalized the traditional opposition of the Holy See by signing the anathema which the assembly had imposed on what it called "the madness of the Manichaeans."[18] Much later, under the leadership of Pope Pius IX, Vatican Council I restated a defense of materiality when it declared that, far from its being evil, "God can be known with certitude by the natural light of human reason from created things."[19] St. Paul, which the document quotes, naturally agrees. "Ever since the creation of the world," the apostolic text says of God, "his invisible nature — namely, his power and deity — has been clearly perceived in the things that have been made."[20] The council did not quote, but might well have quoted, a former Manichaean who converted to the Faith and in a rhapsody of praise advises his readers to open their minds to what the earth and the sea, the air and the sky, the sun and moon and stars, the flying birds and blooming flowers, are all trying to say. And what is that? "Behold and see, we are beautiful." Whereupon the rhapsodist concludes: "Their beauty is their confession of God."[21]

His name? St. Augustine. This genius of a man had been driven to Manichaeism by the evil he saw on earth, thinking it came from a malevolent creator — or, more precisely in the terms of Manichaeus, from the evil and coequal half of God. Surely an impossibility! How could God, if divided into coequally all-powerful opposites, claim on either side a supremacy. Each would cancel the other's superiority. Turning to the sane formularies of the Catholic creed, Augustine discovered the difference at once. Here, while much transcended reason, nothing of the doctrines contradicted it.

He breathed a sigh of relief. He had learnt from divine revelation to put evil in its place, under the dominance of the All-Holy. He knew now, from the doctrine of original sin, how evil intruded into the beautiful world and got mixed up with it with no right to be there and after doomsday would be confined to hell. The satisfied convert felt like a boy who has finally succeeded in putting all the pieces of a jigsaw puzzle together.

Philosophy had failed his questing spirit. It did not have for him the answers he needed for peace of mind. It did teach him the validity of the natural law and did prove to him that the magnificent and complex harmony of the universe could not have happened by accident but had to have an omnipotent Designer who brought it out of nothing. At its best, philosophy does have much to offer — though not enough. At its worst, it runs into a maze of silly contradictions, from which it seems unable to extricate its reasoning. It needs outside help.

* * *

Notes

1. Is. 6:3.
2. Francis Thompson. Wis. 13:5. Rom. 1:20.
3. Mt. 6:26-30.
4. Alternative Opening Prayer for Mass on the 17th Sunday in Ordinary Time.
5. 1 Jn. 5:19.
6. Jn. 12:31. Jn. 15:19. 1 Jn. 2:15.
7. Jas. 4:4. 1 Cor. 3:19. Rom. 12:2. Phil. 3:19.
8. Rom. 5:12.
9. Wis. 2:24. Acts 5:3. Jn. 13:2. 2 Cor. 4:4.
10. Lk. 8:11-12.

11. 2 Cor. 4:4. Acts 5:3.
12. Eph. 2:2.
13. Eph. 6:11-12.
14. Gen. 18:32.
15. 1 Cor. 2:9.
16. Heb. 11:13-14, 16.
17. 1 Cor. 3:18-19.
18. Denzinger 1785.
18. Denzinger 707.
19. Denzinger 1785.
20. Rom. 1 20. :
21. The Liturgy of the Hours, Vol. 1, pg. 1979.

3.
Philosophy Itself Needs Guidance

THE history of philosophy, which shows off the human mind, at the same time shows it up.

One philosopher says this. Another says the reverse. Each in the very act of contradicting the other claims to be right when one of them simply has to be wrong. Parmenides of the Eleatics argued his way to the conclusion that what seems to be changing does not change. He found change an illusion. He stood upon his hard-won conviction that "all is: nothing becomes." But an equally headstrong thinker of the same pre-Christian era, Heraclitus by name, turned the axiom around. He contradicted his contemporary without a misgiving. He would not budge from his counter principle that "nothing is because everything constantly becomes."

The contradictions abound. Among the ancient Hebrews the Sadducees argued down the immortality of the soul whereas the Pharisees upheld it. Guatama Buddha, an implacable foe of materialism, declared the physical world an illusory unreality only to be refuted by the Atomists who under the leadership of Leucippus and Democritus admitted no other reality. Gorgias for his part lost all interest in the wrangling. Since life seemed to him a jigsaw puzzle defying the attempt of philosophy to put the pieces together with any sort of satisfaction, then why bother? The poor defeatist grew desperate. Did his mind possibly break under the strain? Certainly in the throes of futility he came to believe that nothing exists, or if anything were to exist man could not know it. Gorgias had escaped into nihilism.

Confucius, the Chinese sage, held philosophy in equal contempt. While he wrote nothing for posterity to read, we have in the *Analects* a collection of his sayings from his disciples. For all his reputed sagacity, he had this to advise: Don't trouble your head about the reason for things. You are not going to find out anyhow. Be satisfied, then, to curb your curiosity. Refrain from prying into causes. Let your mind mind its business which is not to ask questions but to accept. In other words, Confucius had the murderer's intent to do away with philosophy, stab it to death, and hear no more from it. To him it was a waste of time, promising a knowledge it could not supply.

But Protagoras a century later thought Confucius all wrong. He insisted that man could indeed learn to know reality — by the way he felt about it. What he feels, or desires, determines what truth is. This professional emotionalism anticipated by two thousand years Kant's working principle, what's true for you doesn't have to be true for me. Shakespeare from an urge to mock such nonsense allows Hamlet to reply sarcastically to a tiresome old fool who wouldn't agree that Denmark is a veritable dungeon, a hell of a place. "Why, then," Rosencrantz is told to his face, " 'tis none for you; for there is nothing either good or bad, but thinking makes it so."

Heraclitus the Obscure, who held that nothing is because everything becomes, also featured in his philosophy pantheism. Identifying the material world with its motivating force, without distinction between them, he denied to God

Philosophy Itself Needs Guidance

the necessary attribute of independence. But in direct contrast Anaxagoras strongly affirmed it. This first theist of Grecian philosophy set the tone for that grand harmony of reasoning as developed by Socrates, Plato and Aristotle.

The three proved the existence of one God, an omnipotent, ubiquitous but transcendent Spirit who created the universe. The three extolled virtue, the observance of the natural law, for the wisdom it is. All three reasoned out the immortality of the human soul, but in his deduction Plato went too far and assumed that man's soul before joining his body on earth had a pre-existence elsewhere. Errors there were in their predominant harmony of effort, which must be expected. It was the best that philosophy unaided by divine revelation could do.

Plato and Aristotle took the human mind far in its search for truth: but in the process they disagreed on too many essentials to clear up the confusion. St. Augustine making use of the former, and St. Thomas Aquinas making use of the latter, gave the truth its clearest philosophic treatment. "If we except Aristotle, and perhaps Augustine, the history of philosophy has no name to offer that deserves to stand in the same line with that of St. Thomas Aquinas." So writes an authority on the subject who in fairness to Aristotle adds that he "worked in the night of pagan antiquity while Thomas labored in the daylight of Christianity."[1]

Yet in the broad daylight of Christianity during the twelfth century, the Spanish-born Averroes who made a profession of explaining Aristotle misunderstood his sane principles inexcusably. The Arabian thinker came out with the most un-Aristotelian double standard: what is true in philosophy may be false in theology. Thus, the philosopher in Averroes favored pantheism over theism, determinism over the responsibility of free will, and preferred the soul's mortality to the soul's immortality. But just let Averroes switch from philosopher to theologian in treating these issues, which he did with the ease of changing girdles for his tunic, and he would take the reverse stand. Such a departure from the common sense of Aristotle by one of his expositors did not go unchallenged. St. Thomas Aquinas a century later ridiculed it to death only to have it revive in the modern double talk of Hegel that a thing can be and not be at the same time. The recurrent perversity, if it does nothing else worthwhile, at least offers proof anew of the erratic unreliability of the human mind when alone it goes on search for the really big solutions.

The certitudes of their faith, which threw light on every lesser issue, afforded those Catholic philosophers who thought Catholic a distinct advantage. They started off knowing what Socrates and Plato and Aristotle could not know, that the marvellous ability of the human mind like all the rest of human nature suffered damage from the Fall. Still a powerful faculty, as these pagan thinkers in their use of it have proved, it is a debilitated remnant of what it was created to be; so that now, without enlightenment from a higher source, it must grope for the difficult conclusions and in the process betray a tendency to contribute to the muddlement which has marked man's undirected philosophies down to the present time.

It may come as a shock to be told that, since the golden age of Scholasticism, Christain philosophers have written as if they were not Christian. Rene Descartes, a practicing Catholic, yet founded the modern school of rationalism. He encouraged skepticism with his postulate that a person may doubt everything except his doubting self. He had a formula for it: "I think — therefore I am." Of myself thinking of myself I can have no doubt, but of whatever else, yes: there we have the start of the Cartesian rationalization. From so erroneous a start it got nowhere even in its proof for God. For Descartes, in reasoning that the human mind inevitably thinks of an Infinite Being and in doing so proves his existence as the *cause* of the thought, had in advance under-

Philosophy Itself Needs Guidance

minded his own proof when he subjected the principle of causality to doubt.

Descartes blew up the importance of the mind to an absurd enormity, disallowing so much else of importance. After all, I can be as sure of the world around me as I am of myself, a certitude that Aristotle and Aquinas made capital of. St. Thomas saw without a qualm of doubt that "eggs are eggs", writes Chesterton, because he believed them to be a reality "attested by the Authority of the Senses, which is from God."[2] On the contrary, with a cultivated contempt for the sensory as a source of knowledge, Descartes could scarcely have taken to heart the advice of his God and Savior to learn a lesson from the lilies of the field and from the birds of the air.

And this man, who concocted so narrow-minded a philosophy in a deification of the mind, was the same genius who founded analytical geomtery. Another genius by the name of Leibnitz, who founded differential calculus, did no better as a philosopher. For most of his life a Protestant with Catholic leanings, he saw the world through the eyes of Pollyanna as the best possible world, as though he had never heard of the damage to it from original sin. A denouncer of pantheism and materialism to the end, he yet veered so far from a key doctrine of Christianity as to say of the human will, that it must of necessity always choose what is best. If only Leibnitz and Descartes with their sharp mathematical discernment had kept their reasonings open to the corrective truths of revelation, which they could not but know, they might well have done for philosophy in their day what St. Thomas did for it in the Middle Ages. Since God does not misinform, they could have won for it a modern reliability which under such higher guidance would have set the whole range of natural truths in perspective. Instead, they both failed.

Modern philosophy is in decline. The willing acceptance of its naturalism and empiricism and subjectivism on the part of the present generation does not render the acceptance wise. It rather indicates, to one who has studied the inanities of modern philosophy in the light of divine revelation, that the present generation may be suffering quite as much from a mental breakdown as from a moral breakdown. Take Kant, for example, who led the way to Hegelianism as well as to the existentialism of Heidegger and Sartre. He disowns logic, the natural expression of the mind. Yet his long-winded argument to prove the futility of logical thinking does itself employ logic. Again, after a heavily-worded analysis of the mind's nature which covers the subject in depth, he jumps to the conclusion that man cannot grasp the nature of anything. "Is he possibly joshing while maintaining a poker face?" is one's first reaction to the selfcontradictions. But then, one comes to realize from the unbroken solmenity of his tone that the man had no sense of humor — and from the absurdity of his principal concept just no sense.

That concept, taken out of a ponderous context, comes down to this: the knowledge of anything exceeds our mental grasp, so that truth for us is not what it is in itself, but what anyone chooses to think it is. It can be different for different persons. Such a philosophy, needless to say, vindicates in religion the use of private interpretation. And Immanuel Kant helped himself to the liberty drastically enough to draw a rebuke from the stricter Lutherans who believed in but followed the same liberty with reserve. On so important a fundamental as original sin he disagreed sharply with St. Paul. To Kant it meant no more than a natural tendency to evil in man from the start, and did not derive from Adam, and was not to be associated with an actual transgression. To Kant every doctrine of faith must be understood symbolically, not literally. To Kant, as might be surmised, Jesus Christ for all the grandeur of His humanity was not God.

Now doesn't he sound for all the world like a whole

Philosophy Itself Needs Guidance

chorus of our new theologians? Only the wording should be turned around: they sound like him. He had their ideas first. What he did in his time a good two centuries ago these updated experts now do: they will accept no doctrine for the objective truth it is, but must submit it to their personal judgment, which has been pre-instructed to find it at best a mere *symbol*. The very term is Kant's. Leo F. Miller hit the target with this remark: "The application of the philosophy of Kant to Catholic doctrine is Modernism."[3]

But Kant must share his dominance over the modernist mind with his even more influential disciple, the philosopher who inspired the Communist Bible, *Das Kapital*. The Kantian subjectively he retains when dealing with ideas. But Hegel treats of them with a difference. He understands them as ever progressing by virtue of a pantheistic life force toward an ultimate perfection. The advance comes through a triple development called the dialectic: any established idea provokes a counter idea and out of the conflict between the two there emerges in due time a third and better idea, which does not rest satisfied but immediately begins the procedure anew. All the world's ideas are thus evolving with the world toward — I don't think Hegel himself ever knew what. Nonetheless, the process theologian has taken the dialectic unquestioningly to heart, making it his own method of explaining divine revelation not as a fixed but as a changing body of truths on their way — again, to what? Let his answer to that be what it may, he admittedly knows doctrine better than the magisterium. He has become a pope to himself.

One scarcely expects the theologian who takes orders from Hegel to like this Thomistic statement: "The premises of Christian theology are revealed truths, accepted on the word of the teacher who reveals them. Its typical method is therefore the appeal to authority, which does not impair its scientific dignity, for while to cite human authority is the poorest form of argument, the appeal to divine authority is the highest and most cogent."[4] And theology so built upon the rock of God's authority, the angelic doctor found with St. Augustine, begets a wisdom from its certitudes that sets all other knowledge in perspective. It brings order out of confusion.

But you don't have to be a theologian to find that out. A layman, a graduate from Oxford with honors, learnt from experience that it was not his profane education but his Catholic religion which drew from the intricacies of life a unity of purpose. "Faith," Hilaire Belloc accordingly writes, "when it is exercised upon those unprovable things which are in tune with things provable, illumines and throws into a right perspective everything we know."[5]

Philosophy does not have within its natural resources the power to do that. It has tried. It has failed. Its history ought to convince any open mind of its fumbling efforts. One system of thought has given place to another, the like of which enjoyed vogue long before the system it now replaces. It in turn will be replaced. "What has been is what will be" and "there is nothing new under the sun" are not idle words but God's words.[6] And if in the light of them the present generation would only forego priding itself on having come of age, as though every previous age had not done the same, it might learn to see through the pretension of evolutionary progress and to realize it is but the revival of a once discredited failure. The next century, if there is one, may well pass the verdict that the twentieth used up its time in hot pursuit of a mirage.

The human mind, created in the likeness of God's, is a superb faculty. However, it once suffered impairment. It has never been the same. It has ever since shown a tendency, even on the natural level, to establish false premises or from the right ones draw false conclusions.

On the supernatural level it must be informed and act on the information. It has that information from Holy Scripture and from the Church with her God-given authority to

Philosophy Itself Needs Guidance

interpret the sacred text against the threat of misunderstandings. Deny the Church that authority, and what follows? Divine revelation, like philosophy, becomes a jumble of contradictions.

Philosophy, to get rid of its confusions, would require no less than does Christianity the services of an infallible guide. Where is such a guide to be found? Who is he? As Cardinal Newman pointed out to his generation, he is the Pope at Rome, the successor of St. Peter in his chair of authority, the custodian of those revealed truths which make clearer the whole range of lesser truths. He is in our day, at the present, a consecrated man of the hour who has already shown the world his spiritual leadership, one who bears an insatiable love in his heart for the human race, the especial friend of children, the intrepid guardian of the Faith, the Christlike Pope John Paul II.

* * *

Notes

1. Paul J. Glenn: *An Introduction to Philosophy*, B. Herder Book Co., St. Louis, London, 1949, pg. 109.
2. *St. Thomas Aquinas*, Ch. VI, People's Library, Fodder & Stoughton Limited, London, 1933.
3. *A History of Philosophy*, Part IV, Ch. IV, Joseph F. Wagner, Inc., New York, B. Herder, London, 1927.
4. St. Thomas Aquinas: *Summa Theologica* 1, 1, 8.
5. "Pedants" from *This, That and the Other*, Methuen & Co., London, 1924.
6. Eccles. 1:9.

4.
The Primacy of Peter

WHOEVER dislikes the institutional Church has Jesus Christ to blame. No other kind did he found. He selected his apostles, two now, another two later, and then gradually the rest of them until the total reached twelve. He conferred upon them his authority, though not equally. One received the primacy, so that the others were expected to exercise thir jurisdiction in unison with Simon Peter's, never in opposition. "I will give to you," the Son of God said to none but Simon Peter, "the keys of the kingdom of heaven, and whatever you bind on earth shall be bound in heaven, and whatever you loose on earth shall be loosed in heaven."[1]

There are those of her children who in the current rebellion against law and order have come to resent the institutional Church. Grown ashamed of her magisterial character, they have found a voice for their sentiments in the denunciations of many a self-anointed theologian. They clamor for change. They want the Mother of Christendom so altered as to destroy, in the name of renewal, her secret of endurance: they would do away with her authority.

The Church will survive their disdain. She has been

through the ordeal before. Already in the second century of her existence a breed of reactionaries were demanding a democratization of her official structure. These were the Gnostics. They all had education. They had their esoteric revelations, so they said, which rendered them immune to the magisterial dictates of the Church. They were not too bashful to admit that their inner enlightenment made of them the elite, the illuminati, the elect. They formed their own magisterium.

Their reasoning followed from their premise of a higher inner enlightenment. If the teaching Church continued to insist on the Virgin Birth against their charismatic denials, on the reality of Christ's human body which they knew to be a mere phantom, on the binding force of the Decalogue when salvation requires nothing but a loving faith: if thus, in one instance after another, the outmoded Church would not yield to the superior intelligence of their up-to-date scholars, Trypho, Carpocrates, Saturnilus and Basilides, then who needs her? No Gnostic, imbued with the desirability of sexual expression, could respect a dictatorship that condemns debauchery.

By what right did the Church rebuke higher critic Marcion of Sinope for rejecting the Old Testament *in toto?* By what right did she condemn his reduction of inspired Scripture to the first two Epistles of Paul and, with the proper deletion of its earlier chapters on the Virgin Birth, the Gospel of Luke? It was his decision to make, not hers. What did her apologist Justin know of true enlightenment? Did the Church really think that his *Dialogue with Trypho* settled the issue? Let her hierarchy, let the Holy See, respect the Gnostic mind. If not, away with them![2]

The rebellion did not last. It died out. But it did establish the pattern to be followed by such periodic uprisings in the Church ever since. These invariably have posed a threat to her gradational form of government under the pope; they may begin with the denial of certain doctrines but eventual-

The Primacy of Peter

ly turn the brunt of their attack on the authority that upholds the doctrines. Thus Joachim of Flora, a twelfth-century abbot, dreamed of an epoch when the primacy of the Holy See and the entire episcopacy would have become extinct. He railed against the hierarchy, exposing its abuses, predicting its collapse. He wrote with conviction, gloating over the prospect, that the papacy must go.

Through an interval of eight centuries now, which has posed many a grave threat to its survival, the papacy has not obliged Abbot Joachim. It has not made good his prophecy. It has not conformed to his dream. His obituary for it does not apply.[3]

The Church, impervious to the long succession of death warrants upon her institutional authority, has gone right on having a pope. Nor in her conviction that he represents Peter does she intend to update him by downgrading his jurisdiction. The documents of her late council ought to prove that. To read "On the Hierarchical Structure of the Church" is to be reminded why she takes seriously the duly elected individual who forms, in the choice phrase of Newman, her Rock of Authority. The idea, to be sure, did not originate with Newman. It was Another who said, not to a committee of disciples, not to a democracy of followers, but to one chosen man: "You are Peter, and on this rock I will build my Church."[4]

Peter received from Christ a jurisdiction unique, personal, complete. He had been given the keys of the kingdom, and the assurance that whatever he should hold lawful or unlawful on earth would be so ratified in heaven. There were no restrictive qualifiers attached to that divine assurance: it was forthright. And the scholars, who have tried to qualify it and even tried to torture its meaning to death, would better have spared themselves the embarrassment of a hollow effort.

His fellow apostles had no trouble recognizing in the preferential treatment accorded to Simon Peter the divine intention to confer on one among them the primacy. Never do they deny him the initiative. When John outraced him to the sepulchre of their risen Lord, he waited at the entrance until Peter caught up, so that the prince of the apostles might enter first. With never a dissent they accept him as their leader, their spokesman. In neither the Gospels nor the *Acts,* which show them together often, do they once question his priority. It is there, on page after page, implicitly respected. Whenever the record proceeds to name a group of apostles, if in that group Peter is included, his name comes first. "The names of the twelve apostles are these: first, Simon, who is called Peter." Thus does evangelist Matthew begin the enumeration. Peter receives mention almost three times more than the next highest among the twelve. He has been found, surely for another reason than his personality alone, the most newsworthy.[5]

St. Paul, in his selective account of the Resurrection, deems it worthy of report that the risen Savior appeared to Cephas first among the apostles. Again using the Aramaic name for Peter, the great convert admits going to Jerusalem to look up Cephas, not the other apostles, although he did in the event meet James. But it was not with James, it was with Cephas that he stayed fifteen days. In the story of the twelve, turn to whatever part of it, one apostle stands out.[6]

The *Acts of the Apostles* in all its earlier section makes Peter the hero — until he departs the Jerusalem area and out of the scope of action. Those first twelve chapters could not do else with the man whom the people revered with an ardor short of idolatry. Let the record speak for itself: "They even carried out the sick into the streets, and laid them on beds and pallets, that as Peter came by at least his shadow might fall on some of them."

The apostle, chosen by the Good Shepherd to feed His flock, dominates the scenes. It is Peter, after the Ascension, who summons a meeting of the hundred and twenty disciples and directs their election of Matthias to the vacancy

The Primacy of Peter

of Judas Iscariot. It is Peter, on Pentecost Sunday, who silences the din to explain to the excited crowd the meaning of the stupendous turn of events. And as Peter is the first of the apostles to preach the Gospel to the Jews, so again it is he who under the supervision of an angel receives into the fold the centurion Cornelius to inaugurate the great incoming of Gentiles.

Peter's exploits run high with drama. The first of the apostles to work a miracle, which by now should not surprise, he has neither gold nor silver to give the expectant cripple as an alms, "but I give you what I have; in the name of Jesus Christ of Nazareth, walk." Whereupon the man lame from birth jumps to his feet and goes walking with Peter and John into the Temple, leaping and praising God as he does. To get results for the paralytic of eight years Peter has merely to say, "Aeneas, Jesus Christ heals you; rise and make your bed." Instantly the invalid, out of it and on his feet, makes that bed. To lifeless Tabitha, laid out for burial, Peter who has been sent for speaks again his miraculous word. She opens her eyes, sees Peter and sits up.

Peter holds the centre. In court with his fellow apostles, after spending the night with them in jail, he speaks for the group. Locked separately into prison another time, he has the whole Church praying for him. His escape, when an angel loosens the chains from his wrists and guides him out, creates a sensation. Only during the interval of his absence from the area, in which the scenes are laid, is he out of the story. When he re-enters its range of action on his return to the Holy City, it is to attend and give his sanction to the Council of Jerusalem. After much debating by the assembly, Peter draws an authoritative conclusion. It decides the issue. His primacy commands respect. He holds the keys of the kingdom.

He therefore holds a higher responsibility than the other apostles. Their authority, subserving his, complements it.

They with Peter have been commisioned to teach the nations and with Peter have been promised the guidance of the Holy Spirit: yet to him alone belongs the supremacy. "I have prayed for you that your faith may not fail" are words of the confidential kind always directed to Peter; "and when you have turned again, strengthen your brethren." To what does the prediction "when you have turned again" refer? Obviously to Peter's repentance after his triple denial. For, after his disgraceful lapse, he resumes his leadership over the apostles and by his repentance strengthens their faith.[7]

So from the start did the other apostles, with their coworkers, understand the Christ-given prerogative of Peter. The Council of Jerusalem affords proof in detail. It is Peter who brings the discussion to order, and after Paul and Barnabas then cite experiences from their missionary tours to support him, James the resident bishop acknowledges the general asent. Nor do the many in assembly doubt whose influence aided their final unity of action around the person of Peter. What they unanimously decided, they admitted, "has seemed good to the Holy Spirit and to us."[8]

The early Church, ever conscious of this heavenly guidance, never doubted the authenticity of her hierarchial structure. She acted as though it could only have come from Christ. The apostles did not hesitate to teach with his authority, an authority that demanded respect for the truth, as Ananias and Sapphira found out from Peter, and Elymas from Paul. Nor did the apostles hesitate, by virtue of their authority, to "lay on hands" in the gradational rites of ordination. They felt it important to keep the Church supplied with deacons, priests, bishops (then called guardians, superintendents, overseers). Stephen with six other candidates on one occasion, Saul and Barnabas on another, submitted to the apostolic imposition of hands because, clearly, they deemed it necessary for the validity of their ministerial roles. To them it was emphatically not an empty gesture.

The Primacy of Peter

And Saul, be it remembered, submitted to the function after his dialogue with the majestic voice out of the radiant sky. He cannot but have believed that Christ willed it.[9]

It was at the Last Supper that Jesus conferred on his apostles the power of the priesthood. He had just instituted the Holy Sacrifice of the Mass to the end of time. But its continuation, as the unbloody renewal of his death on the cross, would require priests. Without delay Jesus met the requirement. "Do this in remembrance of me," were his words which gave the apostles and others after them the power to do what he had done. Three evenings later, on Easter Sunday, the risen Savior added to this sacerdotal power of theirs the power to absolve the penitent. "Receive the Holy Spirit," Jesus first said to the assembled apostles in the Upper Room. And then: "If you forgive the sins of any, they are forgiven. If you retain the sins of any, they are retained."[10]

We do not have from Scripture any mention of our Lord's having taught the apostles the rite for ordaining priests. But that does not nullify its possibility. He could have taught it to them, if not before his death, then after his resurrection during the forty days he repeatedly appeared to them, "speaking of the kingdom of God."[11] Scripture has not come near to reporting all that Jesus did. The omissions, the concluding verse of the final Gospel admits, would fill books. But if the record does not say, neither does it have to say, how the apostles had acquired their practice of imposing hands. Obviously, they either learnt it from their Divine Master, which is likely, or intuitively learnt it from the Holy Spirit, whose enlightenment Jesus had surely told them to expect whenever the emergency arose.

What matters is, they did it. They also baptized and confirmed and celebrated the Eucharist and forgave sins and anointed the sick. What was it that Pope St. Fabian of the third century wrote to the bishops of the East? "Our predecessors," he informed them, "learnt from the apostles that

Jesus at the Last Supper, after he had washed their feet, taught them how to prepare the Holy Oils."[12] Certainly the *Acts of the Apostles* makes it abundantly clear that they, as well as the deacons and priests whom they ordained, went about their sacred functions like men well instructed. Knowing what to believe, they knew what to do. They did not grope. They showed decision of purpose.

Our Lord, when He ascended into heaven, left the world no books from which it might learn his doctrines. He had written none. Nor would the evangelists have their versions of his Gospel ready for some years to come. Meanwhile, with no appreciable delay, there was action. It began on Pentecost Sunday. It wasted no time. By nightfall those listening to Peter alone, and baptized by him, numbered "about three thousand souls." Jesus had left the world his apostles, his disciples, his visible Church.[13]

That Church grew fast, as the apostles set about preaching Christ crucified and Christ risen, administering his sacraments, preserving the purity of the faith from every taint of error. No false mercy was shown to the doctrinal innovator who might corrupt the unwary. "If any one comes to you and does not bring this doctrine, do not receive him into the house or give him any greeting," is what St. John in his charity admonishes. St. Paul, taking the identical stand, speaking for self and co-workers, warns more drastically still: "As we have said before, so now I say again, If any one is preaching to you a gospel contrary to that which you received, let him be accursed." The apostles and their following all shared the strength of an organizational unity of belief.[14]

The apostles had been empowered at the Last Supper to do in his memory what Jesus did there, and again empowered three evenings later in the same Upper Room to forgive sins. Yet they did not understand this double power to be reserved to them alone. It was to be transmitted. They accordingly selected and ordained recruits for the priesthood in place

The Primacy of Peter

after place to ensure the faithful a continuation of the Holy Sacrifice, their reception of the Eucharist, their absolution from sin. The Epistle to the Hebrews devotes its fifth chapter to the sublime vocation. It relates that "every high priest chosen from among men is appointed to act on behalf of men in relation to God." It says of the administrator of the sacraments, the celebrant at the altar: "He can deal gently with the ignorant and wayward, since he himself is beset with weakness. Because of this he is bound to offer sacrifice for his own sins as well as for those of the people. And one does not take the honor upon himself, but he is called by God, just as Aaron was." It is of course the *Acts* that especially features in action the organized Church, from her supreme pontiff through a hierarchy of bishops and priests and deacons down to the newly baptized.

This operational Church, now under attack from a disgruntled faction of her children, will not yield. She dare not, if she would remain true to her Founder. But in reality are they still her children? Should they positively deny any of her defined doctrines, one of which is the Infallibility of the Pope properly understood, they have departed from her embrace and may at best be called her estranged children. What belongs essentially to the Church cannot be done away with: her apostolic treasury of faith, her apostolic sacraments, her apostolic priesthood, her apostolic authority or magisterium of bishops and their primate. To say that Peter enjoyed the primacy over his apostolic fellows suggests that so must his successors enjoy it over their colleagues, for Christ established the governmnt of his Church to last until the end of time. It is permanent. The magisterial structure may not and cannot be reformed.

None the less the attempt at such a reform which would not renew but destroy the Church rages on. Its propagandists are more closely allied to the early Gnostics than they may care to think. They demand, as did their like-minded antecessors, the ordination of women to the priesthood. They betray the same tendency to raise man above law in their defiance of authority. They would deny authority even to God whose commandments they make light of. They deify conscience, undisturbed by the least shade of suspicion that it could be erroneous. They demand an autonomous democratization of humanity over whom they, the elite, feel it their right to exert authority. Thomas Molnar has diagnosed the trouble. "The Church," he writes, "is battered today from within by neo-Gnostics preaching the separation of the Elect (themselves) from the unregenerate (the institutional Church) until such time that, with the aid of secular doctrines, all may be integrated in an earthly Jerusalem."[15]

They are to be pitied. Despising the Church, they resemble the former Jansenists in that they do not disclaim their membership. They refuse to heed the warning from the popes: that the rejection of a single dogma of the Faith *ipso facto* excommunicates. It doesn't seem to bother them. They live in delusion. They cherish a hope. They feel attached to the Church, not as the Church is, but as they intend to make the Church. They accordingly remain within to sabotage the present organization. Pope Paul of blessed memory pleaded in vain with them to stop "crucifying the Church." Who did he think he was? Their campaign went on.[16]

It shall not prevail. It brought tears to Pope Paul VI. It is now resisting the magnetic appeal of Pope John Paul II. It has scandalized the faithful. It has weakened when it has not destroyed the faith of many. It has inflicted anguish far and wide. The effort cannot succeed.

The Divine Founder, who entrusted to his Church his authority, also promised it an endless duration. Not without reason does the evangelist Mark relate that Simon received from Jesus the surname of Peter.[17] To repeat what is worthy of repetition, the name means *rock* and, in its application to Peter, an indissoluble rock. For not even the onslaught of Antichrist, with all the fury of hell broken loose, will be able to bring down the Church standing on that rock. The

The Primacy of Peter

day that Satan's inspired reign of terror expires shall find the Church, however battered, however weakened, the surviving miracle of the ages.

The divine metaphor holds the invincible truth: "You are Peter, and upon this rock I will build my Church, and the powers of death shall not prevail against it."[18]

* * *

Notes

1. Mt. 16:19.
2. Cf. St. Irenaeus: *Against Heresies*. St. Justin: *Dialogue with Trypho*. Rev. Reuben Parsons: *Studies in Church History*, Vol. I, Ch. 2.
3. Edmund G. Gardner: The Catholic Encyclopedia, Vol. VIII, Joachim of Flora.
4. Mt. 16:18.
5. Mt. 10:2.
6. I Cor. 15:5; Gal. 1:18-19.
7. Lk. 22:32.
8. Acts 15:28.
9. Acts 5:1-10; 13:8-11; 6:6; 13:2-3.
10. Lk. 22:20; Jn 20:23.
11. Acts 1:3.
12. *Second Epistle to Bishops of the East*. Cf. *The Roman Catechism in Latin* (Mayence, Muller).
13. Acts 2:41.
14. 2 Jn. 10; Gal. 1:9.
15. *Ecumenism Or New Reformation?* Ch. 3. Funk & Wagnalls, a Division of Reader's Digest Books, Inc., New York, 1968.
16. From an Address during Holy Week in 1968.
17. Mk. 3:16.
18. Mt. 16:18.

5.
The Primacy of Peter Remains

P<small>OPE</small> P<small>AUL</small> in his 1969 address on the feast of St. Catherine of Siena cited her as a model of devotion to the institutional Church. She died to preserve it. To break the threat upon its governing body at the very source, the papacy, the heroic stigmatist offered her life in an expiatory sacrifice which she knew from her visions would atone for and eradicate the wrongs. She saved the papacy.

She did more than suffer, she acted, to restore its integrity. Over an interval of somewhat less than half a century the supreme pontiffs had been residing in Avignon when Catherine implored Pope Gregory XI to move the papacy back to Rome. In a letter to him she wrote: "Be valiant and not fearful; answer God who calls you to come and to fill and to defend the place of the glorious pastor, St. Peter, whose successor you are." He defied the political pressure on him not to go, and went. Upon his death the next Holy Father in the legitimate line of succession remained in Rome under the name of Urban VI.

This led to the Western Schism, for a faction of thirteen cardinals under a change of mind met at Fondi to elect an antipope who took up residence in the old papal quarters at Avignon. The outrageous scandal spread anxiety and confusion through the Church. The faithful, wanting to acknowledge the rightful claimant, could not be sure of him. The young Dominican tertiary from Siena, however, who suffered so much else, suffered no such pangs of uncertainty. The political chicanery did not bewilder her.

Clear-headed, fearless of heart, she denounced at every opportunity the play-it-safe attitude of those in authority who straddled the issue. She told the timeservers, in words of persuasive force, which side to take. She corrected even the redoubtable St. Vincent Ferrer who, like so many others, had in good faith decided in favor of the wrong claimant. Their error was one of fact, not principle, due to a historic complication. They believed as firmly as St. Catherine in the primacy of Peter's successor. But who of the two contestants, and later three, was really he? May not the election of the incumbent at Rome have been invalid? "No!" the Dominican tertiary insisted. She never wavered. She sent off an enormous output of letters (nearly 400 of which are still extant) to kings and cardinals and lesser dignitaries, to high and low, in her arduous campaign to win for Pope Urban VI his rightful recognition.

Most of all, she corresponded with him, encouraging him, admonishing him, reproving in him an unruly harshness that was turning away many of his followers. Distinguishing between his natural flaws of character and his supernatural right to the throne of Peter, she urged him not to abdicate: but he must cool his petulance to a firm and abiding patience. She herself lashed out at his opponents, from an irrepressible impulse of love for the Church. The faction was endangering its unity in attacking the necessary center of that unity, and the saint would have none of it.

Catherine hurried to Rome, at Pope Urban's request, to

The Primacy of Peter Remains

afford him the benefit of her personal visits. She stayed, never again to return home. This greatest woman of her day was fighting her life out, suffering unto death, to break the stubborn schism. It would not be broken in her day. The Council of Constance, which would end the outrage, lay in the future. But Catherine died, within two years of her coming to Rome, certain of the eventuality.

The saint has described her premonition. She said that in one of her apparitions she could feel the weight of a ship on her shoulders, crushing her down as its expiatory victim. It was the Barque of Peter, and she was saving it. At the age of thirty-three, paralyzed, stigmatized, wracked with pain, the heroine died in an agony that was ecstasy. Her last breath was nothing like a gasp. It was a prayer spoken aloud, strong and confident, for the unity of the Church under the supreme guidance of one Shepherd.[1]

If Catherine of Siena is known today as the patron saint of the papacy, and deserves to be, it is because she considered Urban VI the duly elected Bishop of Rome and the genuine successor of its First One. She would not swerve an inch from her stand, fearing no man, however high and mighty, clerical or lay. She saw clearly and demanded others to see: that an election, once valid, does not become void. She would not let herself be harangued by the faction who had sanctioned the choice of Urban and then retracted. History has shown her right. Its direct line of pontiffs from Peter to John Paul II includes Catherine's pope and his three successors during that hectic interim of forty years, while it excludes from the count the three contemporary antipopes.

That St. Peter went to Rome to finish out his days, to die there a martyr, is not likely to be contested nowadays. The contrary assumption, feebly introduced by the Waldenses, and never seriously broached until the sixteenth century, has lost credit. Archaeology, having unearthed the martyr's tomb beneath his basilica on Vatican hill, has dealt it a death blow.

But the assumption never did have an ounce of plausibility. St. Peter's own Epistle to the Christians of Asia Minor, conveying to them greetings from "Babylon", thereby fixes his place of residence in Rome. It is the cryptic name which the Sibylline Books and *Revelation* from St. John and contemporary Jewish writing all used in referring to the licentious capital of the Empire.

Another finding of archaeology, this time in the Roman catacombs, bears strong witness. Their art abounds in portrayals of St. Peter, showing over three hundred of them, featuring scenes from his life, giving him a priority next to that of Jesus and Mary as a favorite subject. St. Paul, though finishing his missionary labors and dying a comartyr at Rome, does not come near. Nor in the catacombs is he ever pictured together with Moses. St. Peter definitely is. One of the drawings actually has Christ handing to him a scroll that carries the inscription: "The Lord confers the Law." The meaning looks out of the design as unmistakably this: the Son of God appoints his Moses of the New Dispensation. Thus does Roman art accord St. Peter a dignity proper to his primacy while treating him with an intimacy it could scarcely feel for a stranger beyond the city walls.

Peter did not take his primacy with him to the tomb. He passed it on to his immediate follower in the Roman See, and from Linus to Cletus, to Clement, to Evaristus, to Alexander and the rest of the continual sequence. Never for a moment did the early Christians think that Jesus, in founding his Church, intended his foundation for it to crumble at the death of Peter. Each one of his successors they regarded no less truly the vicar of Christ, the supreme pontiff. They showered upon the Bishop of Rome an esteem that would in due course bring him the title of *Papa mundi,* Father of the world, the Pope.[2]

St. Irenaeus of the second century enumerated by name the papal successsion from Peter to Eleutherius, all of them Bishops of Rome. His testimony carries impressive creden-

The Primacy of Peter Remains

tials. He had for his teacher St. Polycarp, who had for his the "beloved disciple" John, who had for his the Omniscient. Young Irenaeus received an education of apostolic quality. When therefore, as the first eminent apologist, he upheld in his book *Against Heresies* the primacy of the Roman See it must be supposed he was expressing the apostolic mind.

Peter and the other apostles saw to it that their Christ-given powers would survive them in a priesthood and an episcopate which they understood from their Master would reach to the end of time. Their actions in the *Acts* prove it. Other records verify it. The historian Eusebius, who attended the first ecumencial council in 321, boasted that all the bishops in attendance could trace their lineage back to the apostles. The records of certification, he said, were available to any scholar who cared to examine them.

He himself saw fit in his *Ecclesiastical History* to identify name by name the episcopal pedigree in some of the major patriarchal sees, tracing that of Antioch from his contemporary Cyril back to Peter, its first bishop; that of Alexandria back to Mark the Evangelist, whom Peter taught and consecrated; that of Jerusalem back to James the Less, meaning James the Younger. But no other lineage of bishops, the historian well knew, could rival in majesty and importance that of Rome. He accordingly listed its pontiffs in an unbroken sequence from Peter, the Rock, dating the reign of each, documenting the evidence.[3]

A year after Eusebius had completed his great masterwork of ten volumes, earning from it the soubriquet *Father of Church History,* he had the honor of delivering the opening address at the Council of Nicaea. He welcomed the assembly, thanked Emperor Constantine for having provided transportation for the many attending bishops, and in the next breath admitted that as Bishop of Caesaria he would not and dare not preside over the meetings. That distinction belongs only, he went on, to "the head of all the bishops of the Catholic Church, the Bishop of Rome, our Holy Father Sylvester. Though not here in person," the speaker explained, "he has sent his delegates, Bishop Hosius of Cordova in Spain, and the Roman priests, Vitus and Vincent. You will find that when the official acts of the council come to be signed, the first signatures will not be those of the bishops of the great Eastern cities, Alexander of Alexandria, or Macarius of Jerusalem, or Eustanthius of Antioch."[4]

Nor, in the event, were they. The three papal delegates signed the documents first. Two of them, not even bishops, were nonetheless Pope Sylvester's representatives. And that sufficed. The aging pontiff, absent, because of ill health, received from the council a full recognition of his primacy.

Bishop Eusebius of Caesaria has the reason why. His readers will run across it recurrently in both his *History* and his *Life of Constantine*. His audience at Nicaea heard it from his lips: the Roman Pontiff owes his supremacy not to the fact that his see lies in the imperial capital but to the fact that he is the successor of Peter whom Christ raised to the supremacy over the other apostles.

Pope St. Clement, third in line from Peter, would never have dared to settle a dispute between the laity and the clergy of Corinth, which in his Epistle to the Corinthians he did, had he not believed in his inherited supremacy of power. The Corinthians apparently believed in it, too. They did not denounce his right to correct them; they heeded him. Nor did St John at Ephesus, not far from Corinth, protest the action. As the lone survivor of the original twelve he cannot have found it an infringement on his own high authority; as an interested neighbor of the Corinthians he cannot have thought it interference from a foreign see; if he had, a man of his fluency and zeal for purity of doctrine would have said so. He said nothing. He accepted it.

Less than fifteen years after Pope Clement had written

The Primacy of Peter Remains

his Epistle to the Corinthians, St. Ignatius as Bishop of Antioch wrote one to the Romans. It was unlike any of his letters to the other churches. It showed the utmost and a unique deference to the Roman Church, declaring its priority, acknowledging its "presidency" over Christians everywhere on earth. If ever a see might reasonably challenge Rome its "presidency", to use the Ignatian term, it would have to be Antioch, since its line of bishops have also descended from Peter. Yet, from then to now, not one of them has raised the counterclaim. That Peter took his supremacy with him to Rome and upon his death transmitted it to his successor there, was the universal belief of Christendom all through its early centuries.

An anonymous but much quoted poem against Marcion, who would not be reconciled to the Holy See, eulogizes "the very chair in which Peter sat" when Peter named Linus its next occupant. As a symbol of papal authority it became a most sacred piece of furniture in the Church. Tertullian, of the second and third centuries, saluted it from Carthage with the fervor of deep veneration. St. Cyprian, the Bishop of Carthage, and of a sufficient prestige to obtain a place in the traditional canon of the Mass, argued the supremacy of the Roman See because it possessed the Chair of Peter. St. Peter Chrysologus, in a letter to Eutyches, implored the Monophysite to heed the Roman Pontiff because "blessed Peter who presides in his chair proffers the truth of faith to those who seek it." History knows of no such celebrated chair at Antioch, or elsewhere than Rome.

If the actual chair is no longer in use and has not been for centuries, the authority it represents remains to the pope. And that is what matters. There does of course stand at St. Peter's a large bronze throne which encases a smaller one of wood commonly considered the apostle's own cathedra. The famous archaeologist de Rossi so believes. But should he be proved wrong, what of it? What the antique symbolizes would still hold good: namely, the continuous transmission of authority from the first to the present Roman Pontiff. The liturgy for the feast of St. Peter's Chair makes that, and nothing more, the theme of the day.

The use of the symbol for the things symbolized enlivens the idioms of daily speech. At an American political convention it is the chair that recognizes the senator from Indiana and invites him to the rostrum. At a university a professor is said to occupy the chair of philosophy, who is known to teach his classes standing up. To say, as Jesus did, that "the scribes and Pharisees sit on Moses' seat" is only the figurative way of saying that they have inherited from Moses the custodianship of the Law. And yet there is the charlatan who in the lecture hall asks, that since St. Peter's seat of authority may no longer exist, does his authority?

That is not the way Cardinal Newman put his questions. He takes the figures of speech which the Founder of the Church used, and understands them for what they are. He accepts the tremendous truth they convey. He asks: "Who has now the keys of the kingdom of heaven as St. Peter had then? Who is it who binds and looses on earth, that our Lord may bind and loose in heaven? Who, I say, if a successor to St. Peter there must be, who is that successor in his sovereign authority over the Church? It is he who sits in St. Peter's chair: it is the Bishop of Rome." Those questions with their answer, let it be recalled for the sake of a future reference, preceded by years the First Vatican Council.[5]

The plain fact is, belief in the prerogative of the Roman Bishop started with St. Peter and continued into the pontificate of his chosen successor, St. Linus.

The sovereignty of the Roman See, early known as the Holy See, received the unanimous recognition of the Eastern and Western Fathers of the Church. When St. Athanasius who would not compromise the Divinity of Christ was

The Primacy of Peter Remains

thereupon driven out of Alexandria by the domineering Arians, the exiled prelate referred the case to the Holy See. Pope St. Sylvester in response threw the weight of his great authority against the heresy to suppress it, in vindication of its denouncer, in condemnation of its perpetrator. And to this day, despite a present and unresolved schism, the Graeco-Slav Liturgy still includes a prayer of gratitude to him which S. Herbert Scott has translated as follows: "Father Sylvester, . . . thou didst appear as a pillar of fire, snatching the faithful from the Egyptian error and continually leading them with unerring teaching to divine light."

St. John Chrysostom, in his turn deposed as the Patriarch of Constantinople, made the same appeal to the Holy See. St. Cyril, in his fight for Mary's divine maternity against the powerful Nestorius, depended upon Pope St. Celestine whom he declared "the foremost Bishop in all the world." St. Jerome, in addressing Pope St. Damasus, said that "I speak with the successor of the Fisherman." St. Basil, when dissension broke out among the churches of Asia Minor, besought the same Pope Damasus to intervene; he knew his request was not out of order; he quoted the example of the previous Pope St. Dionysius whose final verdict had then quieted a similar dispute.

It is St. Augustine who receives credit for the axiom: "Rome has spoken, the question is settled." If in his collected works that quotation in full is not to be found, its second half surely is. In the pulpit, alluding to his dispute with Pelagius and to his submitting the case to the Apostolic See, he announced the final verdict from Pope Innocent with the comment: "The question is settled." But then, foreseeing the obstinacy of the heresy that would abolish the doctrine of original sin from the creed, he added his famous articulate sigh of regret: "Would that the error were also ended!" This great Doctor of Grace, who in a letter to his countrymen asserted the supremacy of the Roman See and in treatises defended the sovereignty of its

Pontiff, has at St. Peter's Basilica an appropriate statue to his memory. The statue is one of four bronze figures that stand beneath the Chair of Peter like pillars, upholding it in its gilt frame of a throne.[6]

The other three supporting statues represent St. Ambrose, St. John Chrysostom and St. Athanasius. The four, two of the Latin and two of the Grecian rite, richly merit their commemoration at St. Peter's. Eloquent expositors of the primacy of the Holy See, they acted accordingly when they petitioned it to settle their disputes with the heretical upstarts in their respective dioceses. They did what wise bishops everywhere have done in age after age. "We should never end," admits historian Olivier, "if we were to cite all the appeals to Rome from the East as well as from the West."[7]

The dissenters who talk as though Vatican I invented papal supremacy, if they honestly believe what they say, cannot have read either the Fathers of the Church or the documents of previous councils. Did not Nicaea rely upon the sanction of Pope Sylvester? Did not Sardica, a followup of Nicaea, decree that any prelate whom the authorities of a province depose retains the unalterable right to appeal to the higher tribunal of the Holy See? Did not the Ecumenical Council at Constantinople in 381, by then an imperial capital, nevertheless received ratification from the Roman Bishop? The affirmative answer to all three questions lies in the official records.

Questions of the kind proceed as fluently as one can think of them. Did not Nestorius of Constantinople who denied the divine maternity of Mary, and Cyril of Alexandria who defended it, both appeal to Pope Celestine for a settlement? Did not the resultant Ecumenical Council of Ephesus applaud his settlement to the honor and glory of the Mother of God? Did not the Ecumenical Council of Chalcedon greet the message from Pope Leo with a standing ovation and the unanimous cry, "Peter has spoken through

The Primacy of Peter Remains

Leo?" Did not the Sixth Ecumenical Council at Constantinople, when a letter from Pope Agatho was read to it, adopt the same thunderous refrain, "Peter has spoken through Agatho?" Did not the Ecumenical Council of Florence, after defining as a dogma the Primacy of the Roman See, name its pontiff the vicar of Christ?

The questions are many, far too many to be all listed here, but the answer remains the same invariable *Yes*. To find out for oneself, one has only to go to the proper library and consult the conciliar texts from Nicaea to Vatican I inclusively, as arranged by Philip Labbe, S.J. But one may as well be forewarned that it will take not a little time. They fill eighteen volumes.

A nineteenth volume, the easily available *Documents of Vatican II*, will be found all in favor of the decrees from former councils. In the third chapter the enquirer, reading about the apostolic origin of the episcopacy, will further read: "But the college or body of bishops has no authority unless it is understood together with the Roman Pontiff, the successor of Peter at its head." The Dogmatic Constitution on the Church does not weaken the teaching of Vatican I about the papacy. It vigorously reaffirms: "In virtue of his office, that is as Vicar of Christ and pastor of the whole Church, the Roman Pontiff has full, supreme and universal power over the Church."

The martyred archbishop of Canterbury, St. Thomas à Becket, was as sure of that as a normal schoolboy is sure of his ABC's. In a liturgical reading for his feastday on December the 29th, he speaks to us from across the centuries of an ageless truth: "The Roman Church remains the head of all the churches and the source of Catholic teaching. Of this there can be no doubt. Everyone knows that the keys of the kingdom of heaven were given to Peter."[8]

The popes have none of them seen fit to renounce their prerogative. They didn't dare. It was not theirs to deny but to use. They held it, they well understood, from the Divine

Founder of the institutional Church. They must profess it.

Pope Leo the Great did, with a grandeur worthy of his title. At a synod, which he called together for the purpose, he condemned a local council of Eastern dignitaries for having exonerated Eutyches of heresy. He then urged the Emperor at Constantinople to summon the bishops of Christendom to Chalcedon for a genuine ecumenical council in order to set right the error that would deny to Christ his human nature. The Emperor Marcian complied. The letter to the imperial court, in which Pope Leo I asked for the council, stated his credentials: "Peter was prince of our Lord's apostles. Peter's see was Rome. Peter's successor I am."[9]

Pope John said the same of himself. On October 4, 1962, a week before he would open the council he had convoked, he visited the Holy House of Loreto. He knelt there to pray to the Virgin Mary who became the Mother of God in this sacred dwelling. In preparation for the history-making event he prayed aloud, acknowledging his especial need of her heavenly aid. He appreciated his responsibility. He knew who he was. The benign pontiff, on arrival at the shrine, had announced: "On the vigil of the Second Vatican Council the humble successor of Peter is here."[10]

In like manner did Pope Paul VI announce his appearance before a general assembly of the World Council of Churches in Geneva, Switzerland, on June 10, 1969. He used the same name of identity. He had come into the meeting hall on a mission of goodwill, responding indeed to an invitation of equal goodwill. He certainly did not want to offend the sensibilities of his benevolent hosts. Nor did he. They knew as well as he, that dialogue which rejoices over the agreements must not in any genuine ecumenism hide the differences that separate. His audience of divines were not shocked. They seemed to expect to hear from their guest his self-introduction: "We are here among you. Our name is Peter."

The Primacy of Peter Remains

The Holy Father, to emphasize his being another Peter, spoke in the pontifical plural. He explained: "Scripture tells what meaning Christ has willed to attribute to this name, what duties he lays on us." And one of those duties, Pope Paul did not fear to say, was that he must not deny or compromise his inherited right to use the keys of the kingdom. The audience understood, listening with respect. "Permit us," he then said, "to recall other titles which the Lord gave to Peter in order to signify other charisms. Peter is the fisher of men. Peter is the shepherd."[11]

No less surely, while at the same time feeling his unworthiness, Pope Paul's successor at his investiture in the Sistine Chapel reminded his audience of bishops and their aides that the primacy of Peter was now his. His homily, simple and of an easy-going style, yet made a concession to formality by adopting the pontifical plural in every reference to himself. It was, from the unassuming homilist, a token of respect for his high office. On a filial note dear to his predecessors, Pope John Paul I concluded: "May she, who with maternal care guided us as a seminarian, a priest, a bishop, continue to enlighten and direct our steps so that, with our eyes and mind fixed on her Son Jesus, we may now as Peter's successor proclaim to the world in Peter's voice and with his joyous firmness our profession of faith: 'You are the Christ, the Son of the living God.'"

At his first public appearance later on, the applauding crowd down in St. Peter's Square applauded vigorously when John Paul I leaned over the balcony railing to show them and his millions of TV viewers a smile. It became, in the popular mind, a certificate of his personality — a likeably outgoing personality which likes people. It served notice, which we could not then know, that his brief reign of thirty-three days was forming an easy transition from sedate Paul VI to mirthful John Paul II. By a design of Providence "the September Pope" in a month's time had prepared the world for the next and 265th successor of

St. Peter who has already been called "the people's Pope."

Never in all history has a public figure appeared before such enormously large crowds in so many countries, and been so enthusiastically received, as Pope John Paul II. He has literally gone out into the world to preach the divinely revealed truths which he maintains the Catholic Church has always taught and will always continue to teach. He compromised none of them to win his popularity. He won it while affirming them.

Papal infallibility, the doctrine that safeguards the whole of the creed, Pope John Paul has never passed up an opportunity to affirm. To doubt so reassuring a dogma, he wrote to the German hierarchy, "means a cutting of the roots from which the Church derives her certainty about the truth she attests and proclaims." Shifting to another metaphor, he added that once you remove its foundation, you have undermined the certitude of faith and invite the collapse of its unity into interminable contradictions. The Holy Father wrote his letter to the German bishops in support of their censure of Professor Hans Küng. The Apostolic See dare not yield its authority from Christ to a dissenting theologian who would assume it for himself.[12]

To his followers in the Apostolic See, as much as to Peter, did the Son of God entrust the keys of the kingdom of heaven, conferring upon them all the authority on earth to bind or to loose. St. Catherine of Siena knew it. Pope John at Loreto and Pope Paul at Geneva announced firmly, if superfluously, that they knew it. Neither did Pope John Paul I nor Pope John Paul II surprise their audiences when the former within the confines of the Sistine Chapel declared that he knew it, and the latter by action as well as word proclaimed to the countries of the world that he no less assuredly knows it.[13] What in fact did he say to an overflow crowd in the cathedral of Saints Peter and Paul in Philadelphia, on October 3, 1979? He said: "Today, by the grace of God, I come here as Successor of Peter." As for St. Matthew who recorded this conferment of power from Christ to his vicars unto the end of time, how could *he* not know it?

Evangelist John, not to be outdone, records from the lips of Jesus another phase of the same commission in a most beautiful parable. He tells of the triple mandate from the Good Shepherd to Peter and his followers in the papacy. To emphasize its importance, it will here be spelled out in capital letters and in the English translation which Ronald Knox found worthiest of its tender sublimity. FEED MY LAMBS. FEED MY SHEARLINGS. FEED MY SHEEP.[14]

* * *

Notes

1. Tommaseo: *Le Lettere di S. Catarina da Siena.* Cf. Ludwig Pastor: *The History of the Popes,* Vol. I, Ch. 1-Ch. 2.
2. Rev. W. Davivier, S.J.: *Christian Apologetics,* Vol. II, Part VI, Ch. V. (Translated from French by Rev. Joseph C. Sasia, S.J.), Joseph F. Wagner, Inc., New York, 1924.
3. Eusebius: *History* IV, 22.
4. Mansi: *Amplisima Collectio Conciliorum* II.
5. Sermon 15, "The Pope and the Revolution" from *Sermons on Various Occasions.* Longmans, Green and Co., London, 1921.
6. Sermon 131. Letter 43.
7. The 69th Conference of Father Olivier.
8. Epist. 74: P L 190, 533-536.
9. S. Leo ad Marc: Epist. 78.
10. Pope John's Italian address at Loreto on October 4, 1962, printed in *L'Osservatore Romano.* Cf. *Marian Era,* Vol. 4, "Lessons of Loreto," for English translation. Franciscan Herald Press, Chicago, Illinois.
11. Pope Paul at Geneva, an Event covered by all the important dailies.
12. Letter of Pope John Paul II to the German Episcopal Conference, May 15, 1980. Cf. *The Pope Speaks,* Vol. 25, No. 3, 1980, pp. 239-246. Our Sunday Visitor, Inc., Huntington, Indiana.

13. Pope John Paul II silenced an applauding audience in the Philippines, on February 18, 1981, with a gesture and the greeting: "My visit to you as the successor of Peter is a visit of love." Whereupon the applause started up again more enthusiastically than before.
14. Jn. 21:15-17.

6.
The Pope Has Always Saved the Faith

For the faithful who find the confusion within the Church since the late council a discouragement, Pope John Paul II has a reassuring answer. He published it, an eight-page letter, for all the world to read. It need not shock us, he points out, that in the long history of the Church dissident theologians have dared to contradict her doctrines. It happened before, time and again. Yet, through the troublesome periods, Christ remained with his Church to turn the storm eventually into a calm — as once he did on Lake Gennesareth to restore confidence to the frightened apostles. And it was always through his vicar on earth that Christ acted, the letter goes on to relate in a fine defense of papal infallibility.[1]

A survey of any discordant period in the Church's twenty drawnout centuries of effort would suffice for the purpose. But the interval between the Ecumenical Councils of Nicaea and Chalcedon is especially rich and abudant in proofs of the creed's historic dependence on the Holy See. We shall find it a period of confusion — much like our own — with a spate of heresies differing from one another and even contradicting one another in their common attack on the defined dogmas. Suppose, for a start, we focus attention on a key figure in the turmoil.

His name for most of his life was held in esteem. After the Council of Nicaea, when the condemned Arians gave new life to their heresy by reinterpreting it under a different terminology, the Bishop of Laodicea was not taken in. He saw through the subterfuge, which more than seventy-five percent of the hierarchy either could not or did not want to see through. He, with St. Athanasius, recognized in Semi-Arianism the same old heresy simply watered down. For this, the Holy See commended the Syrian prelate, Apollinaris of Laodicea.

Apollinaris, who preached the divinity of Christ in his diocese, expected no less of his priests. The priests who spoke against it, having fallen under the Arian blight, or perhaps from a fear of being out of style, drew from him a censure. St. Paul had advised his fellow bishop Timothy to reprove doctrinal error in season and out, even when doing so required courage. Appollinaris had need of extraordinary courage to administer his rebukes.

The Emperor, a good man deceived into believing the Semi-Arian compromise the true doctrine, did not hesitate to exert pressure on the more outspoken among the unyielding minority of bishops. The great Athanasius had already been banished from his see. No one knew who might be next to go into exile. But Apollinaris did not care. He knew he was right. It was his supreme joy and he wanted the whole human race to share his joy that we have, for a brother, God in all his infinite grandeur.

Then something comic as well as pathetic happened. This mitred dignitary, who had pulled hard for the divinity of Christ against Arianism, suddenly lost his footing to topple over backwards into a counter heresy. It is not a rare spectacle in history: that the champion of a doctrine, grown

The Pope Has Always Saved the Faith

proud of his efforts in defiance of authority, blows up his pet doctrine so out of proportion as to belittle another related doctrine. Thus, in predestining souls to hell without their option to avoid damnation, Calvin was understanding God's infinite knowledge to the detriment of his all-merciful justice. There has to be a perfect balance among the revealed truths to ensure their co-ordination. And that is what every heresy attacks.

So long as Apollinaris accepted the Incarnation as taught at Nicaea under the sanction of Pope St. Sylvester, the man remained an edification, for he spared himself no effort to promulgate its sublimity. But once he got the idea of enhancing our Savior's divinity by weakening his equally genuine humanity, and against the warning of Pope St. Damasus insisted on the idea, he fell into the disgrace he had so eloquently deplored in Arius. He made his name in history as a heretic of his own.

Apollinaris might today be known as the seventh canonized saint by that name, did he but persevere in his once perfect faith. He did not. His faith lost its integrity. He became so wrapped up in the conviction that Jesus is God that he blinded himself to the full truth: he reduced the Incarnate Son of God to half a man. That Jesus had a genuine human body from the Virgin Mary the new heretic admitted, but he denied to this human body a human soul.

Here was a heresy that jeopardized, differently than Arianism, but no less certainly, the interrelated doctrine of Redemption. Jesus in his sacrifice on the cross could offer his Father infinite satisfaction for sinful mankind because he was coequally God and in so doing would be adequately representing the human race because he was fully a man, possessed of a human body and a human soul, the latter half of which compound Apollinaris disallowed. Some of the pleaders with him, like St. Basil, narrowed the argument down to a particular which they felt must soften his obstinacy. They put it this way: Adam's misuse of free will, by which he and his posterity fell out of God's favor, could only be rectified by the free-will sacrifice of the new Adam, who could not of course perform a free-will act without an intelligent soul. The appeal went for naught. Apollinaris would not relent.

He turned (if not a deaf ear) a deaf mind even to Pope Damasus, a former admirer, who for that reason pleaded with him through an interval of nearly ten years to recant. In the end, unable to dissuade the bishop, the supreme pontiff deposed him from his high office. This was in 377. Four years later, at the ecumenical Council of Constantinople, the president led the solemn condemnation of one who migh have ranked in history with St. Athanasius but forfeited the honor. Three subsequent councils with the approval of the Holy See repeated the anathema.[2] The Church could not tolerate such a diminishing of her Founder's adorable humanity.

It is regrettable that a bishop, who fought so valiantly against Arianism when it had already contaminated most of the episcopate, then argued himself into an opposite heresy. But it is understandable. The human mind, dealing with the mysteries of divine revelation, cannot by its own natural facility determine their intricacies. It must rely on the infallible guidance which Christ has entrusted for that precise purpose to his vicar on earth, the successor of St. Peter in the Apostolic See. The college of bishops does indeed form the magisterium of the Church and hold authority over the Church *with* their primate, the Pope. But, as both Vatican Councils decree and history indicates, those of the hierarchy who exercise their authority in opposition to the supreme pontiff nullify it.[3]

That is what the many bishops who went Arian had forgotten and now what their antagonist from Laodicea must have forgotten in his defiance of Pope Damasus.

One of the bishops who had gone Arian went further to deny, along with the divinity of Christ, the divinity of

The Pope Has Always Saved the Faith 79

the Holy Spirit. His name, Macedonius. His see, Constantinople no less. From his Arian premise he inferred logically that, if the Son is a creature, how can the Holy Spirit be more? Macedonius reduced the Holy Spirit practically to an angel in the service of Father and Son, holding that the Son had been created by the Father and in turn created the Holy Spirit. For disclaiming the triple coequality and triunity of God he drew an anathema from the council of Constantinople — with Apollinaris. This second ecumenical council did more than sanction the Nicene Creed; it enlarged the formulary of faith with a special salutation to God the Holy Spirit. Pope Damasus ratified the canon of condemnations which the assembled bishops of the East had presented to him.[4]

Heresy begets heresy, and without deference to the Holy See there is no end to the bizarre process. Thus, in the next century Nestorius (another insubordinate patriarch of Constantinople) attacked the divinity of Christ from a new angle. He divided the Incarnate Son of God into two persons, a divine and a human, and when his fellow bishop from Alexandria objected and Pope Celestine insisted with St. Cyril that there was only one Jesus, a divine person, the story of yet another heresy got under way. It proceeded and ended according to form: the heresiarch would not recant, thinking that he knew better than Christ's vicar on earth, and as a result provoked the condemnation of an ecumenical council — this one at Ephesus.

But it was not the Pope Celestine who ratified its anathema, for the saint had died before the seventh and final sesssion brought the council to an end. It was his successor in the primacy, Pope Sixtus III. And that points up the fact that the power of Peter to define doctrine and condemn its misinterpretation is passed on from one occupant in his chair to the next. Isn't that what the assembled bishops were told to their faces? They were beyond a doubt, and by none other than legate Philip from the Roman See.[5]

The council was hearing nothing new from him. Whenever in the West and in the East a fighter of heresy ran into difficulties that threatened a deadlock, be his name Irenaeus or Athanasius or whatever, he knew where to apply for help, where to send for arbitration. He appealed to Rome.

It was what St. Flavian, the Patriarch of Constantinople, did when a priest named Eutyches paid no attention to his censure for attacking the Incarnation yet a different way. This Monophysite, who went further than Apollinaris to deny the complete human nature of Christ, like Apollinaris started out a champion of orthodoxy. At the Council of Ephesus he lent his articulate support to St. Cyril in the condemnation of Nestorius, wherein he again resembled Apollinaris who had aided St. Athanasius against Arius. But in proclaiming Christ one Divine Person and not two seperate beings, he made so much of the divinity of person as to say the divinity absorbed the humanity of our Savior entirely. With Apollinaris, the God-Man consisted of God and half a man. With Eutyches, there was in the hypostatic union no man at all: no human soul and an unreal, illusory body.

So runs the tediuos story of doctrinal errors. This heresy contradicts that one, and in the process may spawn a complexity of variations. It may even copy from another heresy long since dead. The weird notion that Jesus took from his mother the mere phantom of a body did not originate with Eutyches. The Gnostics, the first organized heretics in the history of the Church, had the idea centuries before.

Somewhere in the course of his respectable life in a large monastery, Eutyches lost his sense of logic. Certainly the Savior could not suffer in his divine nature, which the old monk had him do. He could only suffer in his human nature, which the old monk said did not exist. If Christ had no human body to endure the torture of crucifixion and no human soul to will it, no human soul with a mind to experience the anxieties of his agony in the garden or to ex-

The Pope Has Always Saved the Faith 81

perience the dread of being forsaken on the cross, then how were we redeemed? Not being one of us, having nothing of our humanity, as the heretic claimed, how could Jesus have represented the human race?

Moreover, when in the garden Jesus prayed to his Father to prevent his forthcoming Passion if at all possible and then added, "Not my will, but thine, be done," he had to be referring to his human will. The reason is plain. His divine will did not need to submit. It is consubstantial with the Father's. It cannot be different from the Father's.

Years earlier when this revelant text from Scripture was presented to Apollinaris, who admitted the human body but denied the human soul of Christ, he hedged from his original stand. He began now to compromise, saying that Christ had an animal but still not a rational soul. It was a wasted attempt. The modification did not essentially change the heresy. A human body, no matter whose, has more than the inferior soul of a kangaroo.

But to Eutyches, whose heresy exceeded the other's, the text meant nothing. This aged superior of more than three hundred monks would not budge from his obstinacy. He defied not only Patriarch Flavian, his own bishop, but Eusebius of Dorylaeum as well, and finally the primate of bishops, Pope Leo the Great.

The ecumenical Council of Chalcedon condemned him. Patriarch Flavian, who had reported the recalcitrant to Rome, was not present. He had previously died of injuries inflicted on him in exile by the Monophysites. And who had ordered his exile? The emperor at the time, now also deceased, whose successor in deference to Pope Leo convoked the council.

It was a sensational turn of events. At the council every mention of the martyred saint drew applause. More than that, the very letter which Pope Leo sent to Flavian in support of his action was read aloud to an exultant audience. No sooner had the Roman legate finished his reading, in which Eutyches and the other desecrators of the Incarnation were denounced, in which indeed the hypostatic union was given its final and classical definition, than the crowd rose to their feet with a medley of outcries: "This is the belief of our Fathers, this is the belief of the Apostles." "This we believe, this all orthodox Christians believe." "Anathema to him who does not believe."

If human saints in heaven ever listen to what is being said on earth, as certainly the angels do, then the martyr Flavian must have rejoiced while listening to his letter from the supreme pontiff read out to that assembly of delegates there at St. Euphemia's in Chalcedon. St. Athanasius had written well of the hypostatic union, and St. Cyril after him. But neither could match Pope Leo, in this letter known as *The Tome,* for finish of phrase. Pope Leo himself cherished its finesse. Otherwise he would not have used entire paragraphs from it in later homilies. It had to be an entranced audience which heard from his lips on a Christmas morning in the fifth century the following excerpt which you will find with ever so slight a change of wording in the famous tome:

"The Son of God who was *in the beginning with God, through whom all things were made, and without whom nothing was made,* became man to free him from eternal death. He stooped down to take up our lowliness without loss to his own glory. He remained what he was; he took up what he was not. He wanted to join the very nature of a servant to that nature in which he is equal to God the Father. He wanted to unite both natures in an alliance so wonderful that the glory of the greater would not annihilate the lesser, nor the taking up of the lower diminish the greatness of the higher.

"What belongs to each nature is preserved intact and meets the other in one person: lowliness is taken up by greatness, weakness by power, mortality by eternity. To pay the debt of our human condition, a nature incapable of suf-

The Pope Has Always Saved the Faith

fering is united to a nature capable of suffering, and true God and true man are forged into the unity that is the Lord. This was done to make possible that kind of remedy that fitted our human need: one and the same Mediator between God and men, able to die because of one nature, able to rise again because of the other."[6]

The phrase "one and the same Mediator" is a direct thrust at Nestorius who would divide our Redeemer into separate persons, as other phrases in the papal brief strike hard at at Arius for denying his divinity and at Apollinaris for lessening his humanity and at Eutyches for refusing it altogether. Profoundly stirred, the Fathers at the council in formulating their consensus of belief copied from Pope St. Leo his sharp distinctions in the balancing of an intricate and supreme truth of the creed. And in that ancient church of St. Euphemia the downgraders of triumphalism could not have sat comfortable in their chairs, if any such were present, as the assembly broke into its proclamation at full voice:

"We declare that we confess one and the same Lord Jesus Christ, who is perfect and complete in his Godhead, and perfect and complete in his manhood, truly God and truly man, consubstantial with the Father as to his Godhead, consubstantial with us as to his manhood, in all things like unto us, sin alone excepted."

On and on the words came, saying over and over what had been said, and saying it for the continuous joy of hearing it again.

"We confess one and the same Jesus Christ, the only-begotten Son of God, in two natures, unconfounded, indivisible, immutable, inseparable; the difference of the natures being in no wise taken away by the union; on the contrary, the property of each is preserved, and concurs in one person and one hypostasis; so that he is not parted or divided into two persons, but one and the same Son of God, God the Word, our Lord Jesus Christ."[7]

Aglow with admiration over her turning back the many such threats upon her deposit of faith throughout her centuries, one of her converts, in a burst of triumphalism of his own, envisions the Church as "a chariot behind madly rushing horses, seeming to stoop this way and to sway that, yet in every attitude having the grace of statuary and the accuracy of arithmetic. . . . She swerved to left and right, so exacly as to avoid enormous obstacles. She left on one hand the huge bulk of Arianism, buttressed by all the worldly powers to make Christianity too worldly. The next instant she was swerving to avoid an orientalism which would have made it too unworldly.

"The orthodox Church never took the tame course or accepted the conventions; the orthodox Church was never respectable. It would have been easier to have accepted the earthly power of the Arians. It would have been easy, in the Calvinistic seventeenth century, to fall into the bottomless pit of predestination. It is easy to be a madman; it is easy to be a heretic. It is always easy to let the age have its head; the difficult thing is to keep one's own. It is always easy to be a modernist; as it is easy to be a snob. To have fallen into any of those traps of error and exaggeration which fashion after fashion and sect after sect set along the historic path of Christendom — that would indeed have been simple. It is always simple to fall; there is an infinity of angles at which one falls, only one at which one stands. To have fallen into any of the fads from Gnosticism to Christian Science would indeed have been obvious and tame. But to have avoided them all has been one whirling adventure; and in my vision the heavenly chariot flies thundering through the ages, the dull heresies sprawling and prostrate, the wild truth reeling but erect."

And who, do you think, has always driven that chariot? Who, would you say, still drives it? I wish you God's grace in choosing your answer. For it would be bad history on your part to select any but this one, the only correct answer: the Pope of Rome.

* * *

Notes

1. Letter to the German Episcopal Conference, May 15, 1980. Cf. *The Pope Speaks,* Vol. 25, No. 3, 1980.
2. Denzinger 85, 216, 223, 271, 710.
3. Denzinger 1824, Vatican Council I. The Documents of Vatican II, *Lumen Gentium* 18, 22.
4. Denzinger 85, 86. Cf. *Church History*: Poulet-Raemers, Vol. 1 (B. Herder Book Co., St. Louis, London 1945) pp. 171-172.
5. Denzinger 112.
6. Sermo I *in Nativitate Domini,* 2.3: PL 54, 191-192.
7. Denzinger 148. Cf. *Church History*: Poulet-Raemers, Vol 1, pp. 246-247. Also: *The Catholic Encyclopedia,* Vol. III, Council of Chalcedon.
8. G.K. Chesterton: *Orthodoxy,* Dodd, Mead & Company, 1908, New York, London, Ch. 6.

7.
Arius - the "New Theologian" of His Day

THE priest who started the century-long turmoil in the Church, as described in the foregoing chapter, received but a passing notice when his vile importance deserves a complete treatment. It shall receive that now. It is of the utmost practicability to us, since Arius set or at least confirmed the precedent of double-talking many into believing his denial of Christ's divinity to be a new insight into it. Isn't that what the modernist theologian is also doing? If through a duplicity of speech Semi-Arianism, when not Arianism, misled more than three-fourth of the hierarchy of that era, has not Modernism by means of the same technique done the same to a woeful percentage of clergy and laity alike?

Yet, let it be repeated for the comfort it brings, the modernist theologian has no more misled in our day than Arius did in his day the Roman Pontiffs. The Holy See has been and remains adamant in defense of true doctrine. Arianism did not intimidate Pope St. Sylvester and Semi-Arianism did not intimidate Pope St. Julius I into silence. Nor has the present onslaught against the Faith discouraged an outspoken condemnation in current encyclicals.

Arius was not long a priest in the Egyptian diocese of Alexandria when he began preaching his denial of Christ's divinity. He was not easily silenced. He was not silenced at all — until his death. His bishop tried at first to dissuade him gently; too gently, many think; but St. Alexander, the patriarch of Alexandria, had hopes of softening the obdurate. It was a grievous miscalculation. "The mischief which ensued from his misplaced meekness was considerable," writes Newman. And well known is St. Jerome's lament that, because as a spark in Alexandria he was not put out, Arius became a conflagration that laid waste the world.[1]

The slick dialectician who would reduce the Second Person of the Trinity to sheer creaturehood continued to talk out suavely, fluently, and with a duplicity in praise of Christ our Lord that placated the unwary while ever careful not to concede his divinity. If the Son is a subordinate to the Father, Arius would argue, remember that he remains the first of subordinates through whom the Father created all the others. If he is not coeternal with God, at least he of all creatures came the nearest to being so, and enjoys the status of a demigod who may even be called God since he preceded the ages of time. It was so much double talk, which confused many.

It did not confuse Patriarch Alexander. Even while he was still dealing patiently with Arius, he clearly saw the heresy for what it was. He pleaded with his difficult priest. He warned the faithful. In a pastoral to his churches throughout Egypt and Libya he reproached the Arians for teaching that "God was not always a Father" since "the Word of God has not always existed, but was made out of nothing."[2]

His patience worn out from years of fruitless leniency,

Arius - the "New Theologian" of His Day

the metropolitan now took action. He invoked a synod of his suffragan bisops to review the Arian argument and to pass judgment. It was clear to them what in conscience they must do and to the presiding prelate, after their vote of condemnation, what he must do. Inviting his wayward priest once again to reconsider, but still to no avail, Patriarch Alexander of Alexandria then excommunicated him.

Arius defied the synod of bishops, ridiculing their censure, and fled beyond the range of their jurisdiction into Palestine. The exile did not pine away in silent loneliness. He was not lonely, nor silent. The tall, soft-spoken dialectician, whom St. Epiphanius describes as "downcast in visage, with manners like a wily serpent," set to work arguing his fallacy anew in his new environment.[3] He aimed through his subtleties to convey the impression that to agree with him was to belong to the culturally elite. This anything but bashful man, while having little success with the general run of the laity, did gain the support of high society and of the military and, sadder to relate, of certain influential members of the hierarchy. Eusebius of the imperial Nicomedian See (not to be confused with his namesake of Caesarea) even granted the denier of God the Son a home at his episcopal residence.

As the guest of so influential a bishop, Arius now felt secure enough to begin writing his *Thalia,* an admixture of prose and light verse, intended to promote the advancing heresy. The handbook, read aloud at banquets and other merry gatherings, caught the fancy of the revelers. They were the socialites of the day, who somehow did not find obnoxious the boast that "I, the famous among men, the much-suffering for God's glory, and taught of God — I have gained wisdom and knowledge." But it may not be said of Arius, as it may of the Montanist, that being taught of God meant to him having a private line of communication with the Holy Spirit. Convinced that only the Father is God, he could no more believe in the divinity of the

Third than in the divinity of the Second Person of the Trinity.

Despite the gravity of an error that would demolish the Triunity of God if it could, the Nicomedian patriarch pretended not to understand why Arius had been condemned. He ascribed the action to the ignorance of the judges. He could only believe, or so he said, that Alexander and his suffragan bishops were incapable of following the subleties of a superior mind. Eusebius who had before favored Arianism more or less secretly, now with the other Eusebius of Caesarea openly espoused a modified form of it. This would prolong the life of the heresy, rendering it more palatable to the many who could not see through the tricky shiftiness of Semi-Arianism. Arius himself made the most of the opportunity.

Less than twenty years before, following the emperor's victory at Milvian Bridge and the consequent Edict of Milan, the Church had emerged from the suppression of centuries into what promised to be an era of unmolested peace. Lactantius caught the sentiments of the faithful in his appeal to them: "Let us observe the victory of the Lord with songs of praise, and honor him with prayer day and night, so that the peace which we have received may be preserved to us." It looked as if it would be. It was not. Arius had seen to that. He stirred up a turmoil in the Church, to produce a worse kind of anxiety than ever the old persecutions had done.[4]

This doctrinal threat to the peace of his empire, which was growing rampant, alarmed Constantine. He urged the two pivotal bishops, Eusebius of Nicomedia who sided with Arius and Alexander of Alexandria who took the orthodox stand against Arius, to come to an agreement. Both refused. Bishop Hosius of Cordova had accepted the role of go-between in the hope of resolving the differences in favor of sound doctrine. It was a foolhardy attempt. Possibly advised by the same Hosius, Constantine now called together an

Arius - the "New Theologian" of His Day

ecumenical council. Pope Sylvester would not attend it because of age, but over its proceedings his legate would preside.

So it came about in mid-year of 325, that upward of three hundred bishops assembled in the imperial summer palace at Nicaea to form the First Ecumenical Council. The emperor himself was there, delivered an introductory address in Latin, then sat by to allow Bishop Hosius as the papal legate to preside over the theological discussions. Patriarch Alexander, who had brought with him from Alexandria a helpful young deacon named Athanasius, went to the rostrum to insist on the divine coequality of the eternal Son with his eternal Father. Granted a hearing, Arius still disagreed. He aroused a predominant reaction of dismay. He did not, of course, lack outspoken defenders. But they were few, however tenacious, and it was easy to see at an early stage of the proceedings that the condemned priest was going to be overwhelmingly condemned anew.

For the present, a creed must be drawn up and so formulated as to defeat any insidious attempt at misunderstanding. Could a key word be found to that purpose? Yes, a voice in the hall was even now announcing one. Though the minutes of the council have been lost, we know from a reliable source that it was Bishop Hosius of Cordova who proposed that precisely right word. Athanasius, the deacon who was there from Alexandria, would in his future writing give unstinted credit to the presiding chairman, the representative of the Holy See, for introducing to the assembly the all-important term *consubstantial*. The idea promptly went into the Nicene Creed in the definitive phrase *one in substance with the Father*.[5]

The Nicene Creed met the approval of all but five, and then two, of the attending bishops. These two alone refused to sign the formulary of faith. Suprisingly, or perhaps expectedly in view of his devious character, Eusebius of Nicomedia was not one of the two. He signed. So did Eusebius of Caesarea sign. In due order the many signed. But the first to put their signatures to the document were the president and his assistants direct from Rome, Victor and Vincentius. The assistants, though only priests, signed immediately after Bishop Hosius of Cordova and before all the other prelates. The trio enjoyed priority as emissaries of Pope Sylvester.

The council condemned Arianism, anathematized Arius with the two dissenting bishops, and closed in a burst of applause. It was applause for the divinity of Jesus Christ, vehement and prolonged. It sounded as though the happy delegates didn't want their applause ever to stop. When it did stop, Emperor Constantine thanked them for having reached their decision, promised for the sake of unity in the empire to respect that decision, and forthwith made good his promise by ordering Arius into exile. And not only Arius. He included in the banishment Eusebius of Nicomedia because this troublesome bishop, who had indeed affixed his signature to the Nicene Creed, withheld it from the supplementary *anathema*. With Arius, he left Nicaea in disgrace.

By contrast, Patriarch Alexander went back to Alexandria a rejoicing old man. Possibly too lenient toward the ugly heresy at first, once he decided to act he fought it vigorously from then on. He could die in peace now. And five months later, breathing his *Nunc Dimittis,* he did.

Alexandria soon had a new patriarch, whom Alexander had recommended for the see, his deacon-secretary at the council, his protege who would outdo the venerable prelate in the defense of truth. I like to believe and do believe he was God's response to the crying need of the hour. *Athanasius contra mundum* suggests the heroic tenacity of his courage; he would withstand the world rather than budge an inch. Arius, once out of exile, was going to learn that to his chagrin.

Eusebius came out of exile first. He had engineered his

Arius - the "New Theologian" of His Day

release. In a letter to the emperor he pleaded that Semi-Arianism had not been properly understood at the council and that really the Semi-Arians were not unwilling to profess the consubstantiality of God the Son with God the Father and would in their way adopt the Nicene Creed. It was sheer pretence, as their later equivocations would show. But it worked. The emperor, with no mind for dialectic niceties, wavered. Then at the urging of his sister Constantia, who favored the expelled bishop, he yielded. He recalled Eusebius from exile. Back in Nicomedia, where Constantine still held court before his move to Constantinople, the master of ambiguities again had easy access to the sovereign and a good chance to exert his influence.

Within a year's time he had talked the emperor into recalling Arius from exile, too. Constantine received Arius at court, listened to his ambiguous profession of faith and was satisfied with it, and then sent off a stiff mandate to Patriarch Athanasius to admit the excommunicated priest to full communion in the cathedral at Alexandria. Standing beneath the labarum after his decisive battle at Milvian Bridge, Constantine had resolved to serve the Holy, Catholic and Apostolic Church. At the Edict of Milan he ensured it freedom from persecution. At the Council of Nicaea, which he had arranged, he knew and kept his place as a passive observer. But of late, under the new influence in his life, he had become an ecclesiastical meddler, overreaching his authority, usurping the role of supreme pontiff.

Athanasius refused the mandate. Rather than reinstate an excommunicated priest, who had never retracted his heresy, he would prefer whatever penalty the emperor might impose — be it even death by torture. The great champion of Christ's divinity was not misled, as were so many others, by a double talk that tried to hide without withdrawing the denial. For Arius with a solemn face would admit that Christ Jesus is very God and then add "because he was made such." This evasive causality might come upon the unwary ear as a high-sounding choice of words without malice. It did not deceive Athanasius who could catch in it the hidden contradiction: "Accord to Christ the title of God, if you will, so long as you remember he had to be created to become the Son and therefore did not share the Father's unbeginning eternity." The shiftiness, which would allow in one breath that Christ is truly God and insinuate in another that he is not quite God, was intended to suggest a discriminating mind of genuine insights. It suggested to Athanasius nothing better than a shameless quibbler.

Athanasius sent his refusal to Constantine in a letter explaining why he would not restore Arius to good standing at Alexandria. Simply, the heretic had not repented his heresy. If with the Semi-Arians he was now using orthodox terms, this made him the more dangerous, for he only used them in order to twist a false meaning out of them. But aside from that, by what right did a civil ruler dictate to a primate in a matter of doctrine? Let it be said in his praise, the emperor humbly accepted the rebuke. He withdrew his mandate. Arius did not obtain reinstatement in his native diocese of Alexandria.

If the emperor was disposed to let well enough alone, Eusebius in the imperial city was not. He arranged a synod of mostly Arian bishops at Caesarea to have them pass sentence on Athanasius for an alleged crime. It was a gravely serious one: namely, that Athanasius had killed a certain Bishop Arsenius of Meletia and that, not content with just a murder, amputated a hand from the corpse to take to his cathedral for magical purposes. The insanity of the accusation against the absent "murderer" came to light when into the synod, by a quirk of circumstance, walked none other than Bishop Arsenius with both hands still firmly attached to his living body. Naturally, the emperor could not be expected to take action against a crime so dramatically proven not to have happened: and the Alexandrians for the time being retained their beloved archbishop.

Arius - the "New Theologian" of His Day

The bizarre accusation, which the Arians might have known would be refuted, rather indicates their present self-security in the empire. They could dare to be reckless because they felt they had the doctrinally confused emperor at a disadvantage. It was a correct judgment. They did have. An aggressive party with an enormous inclusion of Semi-Arians and the benefit of a co-operative army, they posed a threat to the peace of the empire if not humored. But we must not be too severe on Constantine, a layman, when a rapidly increasing number of bishop set him the bad example of either accepting or silently tolerating Arianism.

How did it happen? How did Arius, once but a spark in Alexandria, produce a conflagration? He first attracted around him a clique of theologians from the priesthood and the episcopate to help him spread the error. "This mere handful of divines," Newman did not hesitate to say, "unscrupulously pressing forward into the highest ecclesiastical stations, set about them to change the conditions of the churches thus put into their power."[6]

Arius himself, bearing the *anathema* of the council, the clique did not get restored to favor. But through their influence on the wavering emperor, which Eusebius at Nicomedia was in a perfect position to exercise, they did manipulate other unfit priests into bishoprics after the imperial army had ousted the orthodox prelates. Moreover, the saintly old stalwarts of the hierarchy who had so admirably acclaimed the divinity of the Son of God at Nicaea had one by one gone to their eternal reward only too often to be replaced by undesirables who in their confusion of mind lacked certitude of faith.

Thus did the aggressive Arians and Semi-Arians gain control of diocese after diocese.

Meanwhile, as the faithful old bishops from the Council of Nicaea had been dying off, Arius enjoyed an ever sturdier health that promised him many more years on earth. It was not to be. The scoundrel's influence would continue to dominate — only a few years longer. Then, maybe by a stroke of Providence, the arch heretic met a drastic and unexpected death.

* * *

Notes

1. Cardinal Newman: *The Arians of the Fourth Century,* Ch. 3, Sect. I. Longmans, Green & Co., London, 1895.
2. Ibid., Ch. 2, Sect. 5.
3. St. Epiphanius in his treatise on heresies, *Panarion,* 69, 3.
4. Lactantius: *De mortibus persecut.* P.L. VII, 52.
5. Denzinger 54.
6. *The Arians of the Fourth Century,* Ch. 2, Sect. 2.

8.
Arius in His Haughtiest Hour Drops Dead

It was a mysterious death. No thug had attacked the theologian to lay him low. No sadist had slit open his body. No weapon in any human hand did the deed. It just seemed to happen.

Might it have been the direct vengeance of God? The historian Socrates was inclined to think so. Emperor Constantine, from his sudden turnabout of policy, must be accredited with having thought so. Cardinal Newman, who even quoted Gibbon as not ruling out the likelihood, unreservedly thought so. But not to be swayed by their verdict, suppose we finish our review of the turbulent career that ended so tragically, and judge for ourselves.[1]

Successful as Arius was in winning followers who dominated the emperor, the excommunicated and unrepentant priest could not get himself restored to good standing and readmitted to his own diocese of Alexandria. St. Athanasius stood in the way — he and the laity who admired and loved and idolized the man. The emperor wanted no uprising from them.

In view of which, the saying, *Athanasius against the world,* must be interpreted to mean, not that he had no backing, but that the clergy of the East let him stand alone against the well organized Arians. If in the East at an early stage of the conflict a few other militant prelates had aided him, as St. Hilary and St. Eusebius of Vercellae were doing in the West, the Catholic Church might have been spared an ordeal that required another ecumenical council in 381 to terminate. As it was, the needed few did not rise to the occasion. They were not heard from. They were not forthcoming. St. Athanasius at the start had no zealous allies to rally around him, as heretic Arius had. Eventually, St. Basil and St. Gregory Nazianzen and St. Gregory Nyssa and others would distinguish themselves in the fight to preserve pure and undiminished the Nicene formulae, but that lay in the future. For too long a time St. Athanasius had not one bishop of the Orient to share with him his heroic isolation.

But why in the East was the majority of orthodox bishops dwindling to a minority? Perhaps the lapsed had lost their confidence from exposure to an incessant barrage of Arian equivocations that would so talk around the precision of the Nicene formulae as to make a compromise sound plausible. Anyhow, with the Arians taking the initiative while in the East all the orthodox bishops but one were dozing, it lessens the blame upon Emperor Constantine that at last he ordered Athanasius out of Alexandria into exile in Gaul. The saint, who had been ordered out once before and then allowed to stay, would have to go this time. The injunction carried with it the threat that, if the primate did not leave, the army would force him out. And that was only the half of it. The other half demanded again the return of Arius to Alexandria as an exonerated priest.

It was a sorry mess, a farce, a travesty. For here we have a Catholic-hearted sovereign only doing what a synod of ecclesiastics at Tyre had clamored for: the banishing of the

Arius in His Haughtiest Hour Drops Dead

Church's most zealous patriarch from his patriarchate because he dared to talk up for the abused rights of his Savior and God. Arians everywhere rejoiced. With Athanasius out of the way, this bulwark of a man, what could possibly stop Arius from re-entering the diocese of his early priesthood to function there again? In that, however, they miscalculated.

The Catholic populace of Alexandria seethed with indignation. They loved and revered their deposed archbishop as ardently as they despised their renegade priest. They were dead set against allowing the calumniator of their Lord an entrance to the cathedral or any of their churches to officiate as a priest. Let him renounce his blasphemy that Jesus is not true God, and if he doesn't, let him beware trying to force his way into their sanctuaries. For the people meant to stand guard. They were furious.

To appreciate their heated resentment of Arius we must remember what the Arians did whenever and wherever they had gained control. St. Athanasius and St. Basil have related in detail what they did. So has Socrates who writes: "Those who acknowledged the doctrine of consubstantiality were not only expelled from the churches but also from the cities. And although expulsion at first satisfied the Arians, they soon proceeded to the worse extremity of inducing compulsory communion with them. . . . They resorted to all kinds of scourgings, a variety of tortures, and confiscation of property. Many were punished with exile, some died under torture, and others were put to death while being driven from their country." Nor does Newman miss the opportunity to point out that the Arians "were the first among Christians to employ force in the cause of religion."[2]

Did the atrocities perturb the conscience of Arius in whose name they were committed? Apparently not. His suavity never deserted him.

Alexandria in the future would suffer the atrocities, too, but as of now the city was free of them. And the natives were determined that it stay free of them. They carried out their determination, blocking every attempt of Arius to gain access to their sanctuaries. Possibly because of their dogged hostility the emperor, who wanted peace in the empire at any cost, would not permit the Arians to force their choice of a bishop on the patriarchate. The Alexandrian see remained without an officiating bishop until St. Athanasius would return to it in triumph.

Constantine, fearing the possibility of bloodshed at Alexandria, sent word to the unwanted to leave the city at once and come to his court for questioning. There Arius swore under oath that he accepted without reservation the Nicene Creed. Without reservation? Had he forgotten his contortion of the key phrase "one in substance with the Father" into meaning "like in substance to the Father"? The witness to his oath may have suspected him of perjury. For the emperor said to the man's face that if he had sworn honestly and his words bore no double meaning, it would be to his credit: if not, God would avenge the lie. It was an ominous statement.[3]

The Arians, knowing that Constantine would not allow Arius to go back to Alexandria, did not take their frustration passively. Under the guidance of Eusebius at Nicomedia they tried another expedient. They cajoled the emperor into exerting pressure on the old patriarch of Constantinople to grant Arius communion in his cathedral, which would no less dramatically serve their purpose. A victory for them in the metropolis, perhaps better than at Alexandria, would show the world who had control of the Catholic Church. But again they miscalculated. They wanted to think the patriarch a pushover after their experience with Athanasius, and so indeed did think him, mistaking his quiet manner for a craven timidity.

The venerable metropolitan received the mandate to open his cathedral to Arius with a shock. It meant lifting from the unrepentant priest the *anathema,* and restoring him to duty. It was an outrage. It defied the Council of Nicaea. It in-

Arius in His Haughtiest Hour Drops Dead

sulted the Blessed Trinity. He would not obey the immoral mandate. He, who did not have the Athanasian competence to force a fight with the Arians, would not back away from it when they brought it to him. He would rather die. Only, it was not he who would die in this bitter contest of wills. Arius would.

Curiously enough, Arius met his first and his final opposition from bishops of the same name: Alexander of Alexandria and Alexander of Constantinople. Both are canonized saints. Neither had the daring of Athanasius, being of a milder temperament. None the less, when the showdown of a challenge forced them to get involved, they put up a resistance which the audacious heretic could not break.

Patriarch Alexander of Constantinople promptly wrote to the emperor, imploring him in God's name to cancel the injunction to readmit Arius to the sanctuary, for under existing circumstances it would not be carried out. The emperor sent back his refusal, setting the date for the unholy invasion of Constantinople's cathedral. Having but eight days left, the distraught patriarch from an urge of hope within him knew what to do. He started a campaign of prayer in the cathedral. Day after day he and his parishioners prayed together there, day after day they fasted in their homes, in their appeal to a higher court. On the day before the dreaded date, at three in the afternoon the patriarch threw himself prostrate on the sanctuary floor to offer his Eucharistic Lord a final petition. The attendants around saintly old Alexander heard his words distinctly.

This in brief and in essence was the petition: "Jesus my Savior and my God, if Arius communicates here tomorrow, first take your servant out of the world, I implore. But if you care for your Church, as I know you do, take Arius away."[4]

On that same Saturday, in the evening, Arius with a noisy following came marching through the streets of Constantinople, all of them defiantly merry in anticipation of his forced entrance to the cathedral sanctuary tomorrow, the Lord's day. They held a rally at Constantine Square, where of a sudden Arius felt ill, excused himself and went off alone. The others, suspecting nothing serious, took for granted he would soon return. He did not.

They found his body lying dead, its underbelly split open and the entrails scattered about. The body lay unattended on the ground floor of a building. The building became a metropolitan curiosity, Socrates relates. Passersby would point to it and lower their voices to speak awesomely of the death. The laity by and large saw in so dreadful a death under such circumstances the avenging wrath of Providence. Let it be remembered from Newman that they, in the face of Arianism, "were the obstinate champions of Catholic truth, and the bishops were not."[5]

The next day in the crowded cathedral, instead of an Arian takeover, the patriarch was thanking God for having prevented it. Not a word of contumely against Arius did the congregation hear from their venerable bishop; there was no gloating; there was rather an undertone of awe in his thanksgiving.

The emperor, who had less than a year to live, reacted in his own way to the mysterious death. During the interval left to him, he reflected on the meaning of it and came to understand that Athanasius must be restored to Alexandria. He decided upon recalling the maltreated saint from exile, making his decision known, but died before writing out the rescript. Emperor Constantine II ratified his father's behest: and the foremost hero in the struggle to preserve to the Faith the coequality and coeternity of God's only Son received from Alexandria a tumultuous welcome back.

Arianism, which corrupted most of the hierarchy while the laity and a minority of bishops resisted it, threatened the integrity of the Faith during three fourths of a century. It did not die with Arius when his body burst open and the entrails fell out. Its unabated fury raged on into the reign

Arius in His Haughtiest Hour Drops Dead

of Julian the Apostate, who in withdrawing state support from it weakened it until the Council of Constantinople in 381 could stifle it.

The enormity of the harm which an arrogant priest thus originated cannot but suggest to the thoughtful this question: does not Holy Scripture record of another traitor to Christ Jesus that "he burst open in the middle and all his bowels gushed out"?[6] The vengeance of God required no knife in either case. Not without reason, from a long accumulation of evidence, has Arius been called the Judas Iscariot of his day.

Yet, not impossibly, the stricken may have used his dying breath to acknowledge from a contrite heart the Divinity of our all-merciful Savior. The forgiven thief on Mount Calvary had had none too good a record at death, either.

* * *

Notes

1. Socrates: Hist. Eccle., Bk. 1, Ch. 38. J. H. Newman: *Essays on Miracles*, Essay 2, Ch. 5, Sect. 6. Longmans, Green and Co., London, 1892.
2. Newman: *The Arians of the Fourth Century*, Sect. 1, Ch. 3. Longmans, Green and Co., London, 1895.
3. Ibid., Sect. 2, Ch. 3.
4. St. Athanasius: *De morte Arius*. The author got his firsthand information from Macarius, a presbyter at Constantinople, quoting from him the prayer of Patriarch Alexander.
5. Socrates: Hist. eccle., Bk. 1, Ch. 38. Also, Cardinal Newman: *Essays on Miracles*, Essay 2, Ch. 5, Sect. 6. Also, *Arians of the Fourth Century*, Appendix, Note 5. Newman, while berating the majority of bishops for their cowardly silence, if not lack of faith, did not fail the courageous few. He had his honor roll of them: Athanasius, Hilary, the Latin Eusebius, Phoebadius, Basil the Great, Gregory of Nazianzen, Gregory of Nyssa, and in his last days, Alexander of Constantinople.
6. Acts 1:18.

9.
Truth Again in Crisis

JUST as a widespread falsification of the Nicene Creed divided the Church after the first ecumenical council, so have the modernists misapplied the documents of Vatican II to cause a like confusion today. The similarities, down to the barest detail, are noticeable — and promising. The Holy See then, backing up St. Athanasius and later stalwarts of his kind, finally broke the Arian strangle hold. And over the present crisis, let the faithful have no fear, the Holy See with its firm demand for pure doctrine will no less surely prevail.

When the current dissent within the Church had reached full tide, James Hitchcock decided it had gone too far. So he wrote a book which he wished to heaven "did not have to be written." This admitted progressive, who yet would not change a single dogma of the credenda, minced no words in *The Decline and Fall of Radical Catholicism*. From liberal publications he documented his evidence of a breakaway from true doctrine. He concluded the exposé with an appendix enumerating "twenty-six heretical notions" among the dissenters.[1]

Against all such heretical tendencies Pope Paul spoke out

that same year. He deplored the polarization in the Church, but knew where the blame should go. "We must not think," he warned a general audience on October 6, 1971, "about changes, evolutions or transformations in the Church on matters of faith. The Creed must stand intact. About that, the Church is tenaciously conservative."

At St. Peter's the week before, September 29, he had spoken on the same subject with still greater force. As reported by Farley Clinton in *The Wanderer,* "the Pope attacked an individual. It was an outcry against Satan worthy of the feast of St. Michael. The Pope had never seemed so angry."

He had reason to be. The best of reasons! A Catholic priest, sworn to uphold the defined doctrines, had gone on Italian TV to question their permanence: to propose a shift of attitude toward them. Whatever dogmas conflicted with the modernist temper must be reinterpreted. They must be made amenable. They would now have to be understood in a different sense than the sense in which they had been formulated and until the present have been held. This, the speaker had the effrontery to add, simply meant applying a new and vital insight into the very truths he would destroy.

He proposed an easy way to assure results. The Church had only to forego her right to dogmatize, give up her institutional authority, and let the People of God alone. Oh, have no fear, they would not be left without guidance: the guiding authority would remain. Spouting his irrelevancies into his TV microphone, the new dogmatist made it clear that from now on the dictates would come from a better enlightened magisterium — the self-chosen popes like himself.

Pope Paul, not the first spiritual leader of gentle temper who has on occasion lost it, belongs to a select group. The prophet Moses flew into a rage at seeing his people dance in unholy merriment around a brazen idol. His anger, an expression of his outraged ardor for the only true God, "burned

Truth Again in Crisis

hot." He threw down the stone tablets with a force that broke them. He ground the calf to powder. This meekest of men was fit for a stroke.[2]

A greater than Moses, of meek and humble heart, did not stand by to watch in passive silence the desecration of his Father's house into a den of robbers. "Making a whip of cords, he drove them all, with the sheep and oxen, out of the temple. And he poured out the coins of the money-changers and overturned their tables."[3] To the perverse of will he did not come to bring peace. He said it himself, in an answer to his own question. "Do you think that I have come to give peace? No, I tell you, rather division." Not once did the gentle Savior hesitate to take sides with right against wrong, with truth against error: and if the errant should refuse and continue to refuse his correction, he did not alter his doctrine to win their approval. He accepted the estrangement.[4]

He certainly would not alter his doctrine to appease a hard core of disbelievers in his own town of Nazareth. They therefore "led him to the brow of a hill on which their city was built, that they might throw him down headlong." He escaped miraculously. But this did not change their minds. They would not relent. Nor did he.[5]

The dialoging that went on between Christ and the Pharisees did not soften their obduracy. Accused of having a devil, Jesus informed them to the contrary of his intimacy with the Eternal Father, "of whom you say that he is your God. But you have not known Him. I know him. And if I said, I do not know him, I should be a liar like you." The condemnation stung them to fury. They took up stones to throw at him — yet could not. He wasn't there of a sudden. Jesus had again escaped.[6]

Only days before he would die, pleading with them, explaining to them, Christ gave His professional hecklers a last opportunity in the Temple to change their minds. They did not. They would not. To the end they were asking him insidious questions, not desiring the truth, trying by every artifice of deceit to catch him up in his answers. In a burst of indignation, Jesus hurled at them eight consecutive denunciations, calling them "hypocrites!" "you blind fools!" "you serpents, you brood of vipers!" He concluded the tirade with a devastating question: "How are you to escape being sentenced to hell?" The rift was complete, irremediable, final.[7]

God does not coerce the human will. The Pharisees were free to resist their Messiah, but in turn he must not yield to them. He could not. To have denied his teachings to appease error would have meant a self-repudiation. "I am the way and the truth" is what Christ said of himself. In not coming to terms with the Pharisees, he did what his nature demanded. He could not tolerate unity at such a cost. It would have been a lie, a disunified unity, no unity at all, a false pretence. He would go to his crucifixion, which he did, rather than sacrifice his doctrine to their fallacies.[8]

Jesus lived for the truth. His words to Pilate say it best: "For this was I born, and for this I have come into the world, to bear witness to the truth." Jesus died for the truth. Nor (except for Judas) did his apostles fail their commission from him. After their Lord had ascended into heaven, they continued to insist on the purity of his doctrine. "There will be false teachers among you," Peter cautions the faithful, "who will secretly bring in destructive heresies, even denying the Master. . . . They will exploit you with false words."[9]

Such exploitation, from which the Church now suffers, she suffered from the start. Ours is not the first age that needed to be told: "Jesus Christ is the same yesterday and today and for ever. Do not be led away by diverse and strange teachings." St. Paul's warning against the ordained imposter of his day who "preaches another Jesus than the one we preached" has not outworn its relevancy. It applies just as pointedly to the contemporary progressives who sup-

Truth Again in Crisis

pose that Christ is not at all the same but is evolving with the world toward perfection. That the falsifier of doctrine enjoys the privilege of Holy Orders need not surprise while it disturbs. Not a few of the ordained, of the episcopacy itself, have drawn an anathema. Their kind, St. Paul says right out, "are false apostles, deceitful workmen, disguising themselves as apostles of Christ. And no wonder, for even Satan disguises himself as an angel of light."[10]

"No greaer joy can I have," writes the apostle of love, "than this, to hear that my children follow the truth." He merited his Master's name for him, son of thunder, by his vigorous defense of the Faith. He never backed away from a challenge. St. Irenaeus, who heard St. John preach, reports his denunciation of Cerinthus for teaching that Jesus was the Son — not of God — but of Joseph. The apostle attacked all the other Gnostics of the day for denying or making light of the Divinity of their Savior. There was no false sentiment about his charity. He could and did advise: "If any one comes to you and does not bring this doctrine, do not receive him into the house or give him any greeting; for he who greets him shares his wicked work."[11]

The apostolic letters bristle with such directives. "I appeal to you, brethren," writes St. Paul, "to take note of those who create dissensions and difficulties, in opposition to the doctrine which you have been taught; avoid them." "Avoid such godless chatter," the same pen warns against erroneous dialogue, "for it will lead people into more and more ungodliness, and their talk will eat its way like gangrene." Then two of the godless chatterers are mentioned by name, "Hymenaeus and Philetus, who have swerved from the truth." Jacques Maritain wrote in similar vein, for which he was taken sharply to task by certain shouters for a fraudulent ecumenism, when he pleaded with his co-religionists to "beware those brotherly dialogues in which everyone is in raptures while listening to the heresies, blasphemies, stuff and nonsense of the other. They are not brotherly at all."[12]

How could they be? To endanger another's faith in divine revelation, defined in the dogmas of the Church, is to threaten the person's most precious endowment. The injustice, under a pretence of charity, abuses charity. It violates the soul of the threatened: a violence we have been divinely advised to fear more than assaults upon the body. "Speaking the truth in love" defines the kind of dialogue which St. Paul recommends.[13]

False dialogue led to the Fall. Satan brainwashed Eve when she glibly talked things over with the arch liar. She relished his proposition, then ran off to babble it to Adam who quickly agreed to it. That began their trouble: an estrangement from their all-lovable Creator and even a disharmony between themselves. The couple had never quarrelled before; they were doing it now, each trying to shift the blame. Dialogue in lies does not aid unity.

The modern mania to be free of dogma, and to talk others free of it, offends the dignity of man. It has about as much to do with charity as teaching a child not to be restricted to the set answer that twice two is four but to feel uninhibitedly free to think it five or eleven or anything else than the truth. The relativist who thinks it the highest form of charity to liberate the human mind from all fixed norms of faith ought to learn from St. Paul that charity "takes delight in the truth" (according to one translation) and "rejoices with the truth" (according to another) or "rejoices in the right" (according to the third) but in whatever version cannot be happy without the truth — without being in the right. And that in context means objective truth, the solid and definitive and eternal truth of divine revelation. The Pauline Epistles along with Scripture in general have been written to inculcate no other kind. In the light of which, and by a necessity of logic, philosopher Maritain finds it "impossible for the Christian to be a relativist."[14]

The relativists, who consider themselves of the Church while determined to remake her dogmas, apparently do not realize the incompatibility. They cannot succeed in their ambition. They have only succeeded in creating a rift between their following and the traditionists who refuse to yield the certitudes of faith to the whims of such theological upstarts who in resentment say that the term "upstarts" rather applies to the conservatives of doctrine. They are dead wrong. The Creed being the center of dispute, its innovators and not its adherents must be called the wilful party of reactionaries.

That "the truth is in crisis" Pope Paul knew. They are his very words. He spoke them to a general audience on May 20, 1970, when flouting the pleaders for situation ethics, the secular humanists who have forgotten God's priority in their cult of man. The Holy Father used the opportunity to call attention to the so-called God-is-dead believers whose irrationality has blinded them to the truth. He disposed of them with the squelcher: "They have dared to think that their blindness was the death of God."

If his immediate successor in the Chair of Peter did not follow Pope Paul's tireless fight against error, it was not that Pope John Paul I differed in attitude, but that his brief reign of thirty-three days did not afford him the time. As for Pope John Paul II, he has already notified the world that he stands firmly behind the entire *Credo of the People of God*. He has given the world a catechetical survey in the world's languages on TV, addressing live audiences of record-breaking dimensions, in Italy, the Dominican Republic, Mexico, Poland, Ireland, the United States, France, Brazil, Germany, and elsewhere. In this, he is simply outdoing the example set by Pope Paul. Nor will the apostolic traveler be satisfied, one gathers from his remarks, until he has landed on and kissed the soil of the remaining countries and in a face to face meeting begins preaching to their people of our common human dignity through Jesus Christ.

His 1979 address to the Latin American hierarchy made this the theme: "Your principal duty is to be Teachers of the Truth, the Truth that comes from God. He cautioned the bishops "to be watchful of the purity of doctrine." Quoting Pope Paul, he reminded them that "unity of truth is always urgent for us." He further reminded them that they have inherited from Christ and the apostles the responsibility to bear witness to the Faith: to correct and, if not heeded, then to denounce the wolves in sheep's clothing who ravage their flocks.

The apostles, except for the traitor, did not allay opposition to their preaching by joining it. They continued to preach the Creed. They would not give it up. They welcomed a cruel martyrdom, including John who miraculously escaped it, rather than fail their Divine Exemplar who in his prayer for unity implored his Father in heaven "to sanctify them in the truth." They fulfilled the prayer. These men of conviction preferred death to a surrender that would have made peace with the world and have brought them the anguish of Judas Iscariot.[15]

To maintain silence when in a position to rebuke a public assault upon the truths of faith is not charity. It is a cold-blooded diffidence that either is afraid to act or couldn't care less. To compromise a doctrine so as to make others feel at ease — deceptively at ease — this is doing them no favor. It would deny them the benefits of belief. It offends charity as much as it offends truth.

When the divisions among Christians, and between Christians and potential Christians, will give way to perfect unity — who can say? As of now, the most discouraging drawback to the prospect is the dissension within the Catholic Church, which has become a scandal to the ecumenical movement. The dissidents who have created the cleavage used to blame Pope Paul and now blame Pope John Paul for it, in order to make themselves look good. They look bad. In their rejection of a divinely appointed teaching authority they threaten the only genuine stabilizer of religious unity on earth.

Truth Again in Crisis

They thought that Pope Paul had no right to issue his noble defense of human life against the immoral abuses that would defeat it. But now Pope John Paul, with equal zest, proclaims the sanity of *Humanae Vitae*. They thought it unbecoming of Pope Paul, the keeper of heaven's keys, to acknowledge heaven as mankind's only true paradise in opposition to the humanist fantasy of an earthly one. But now Pope John Paul goes about reaffirming the same dogma to many more and much larger audiences, so that the protesters might as well have kept their mouths shut.

They nevertheless go right on ignoring the admonitions from both pontiffs: to honor the integrity of doctrine and not to reinterpret to death every article of the credenda which has fallen into discredit with Modernism. The Modernists pretend originality. In reality they have but rehashed old errors long since condemned. They have surely copied the early Gnostics who formed an elite faction to get away from the "unenlightened" and then put the blame on these for the split.

Disharmony has a long history. It preceded mankind. Satan started it — not Michael. Heaven was enjoying perfect harmony when Satan disrupted it, dividing the angelic world. The infernal instigator of discord has been behind all the mischief of evil against good, of error against truth, ever since. Of that, Scripture has used up plenty of ink to keep us informed.

We had better face it: the division between right and wrong does for a certainty reach into eternity. "Come, O blessed of my Father" and "Depart from me, you cursed, into the eternal fire" are an invitation and a rejection that spell out clearly a rift. And ne'er the twain shall meet. Hell will always remain hell. Heaven will always remain heaven.[16]

The damned suffer an inferno of dissensions, having lost the capacity or the desire to love, every individual of them hating all the others while being hated by all the others. The blessed in heaven know the ecstasy of an endless harmony in being loved and loving back. There will be no interchanging of places. "Between us and you," meaning the saved and the lost, "a great chasm has been fixed in order that . . . none may cross from there to us." The separation will have become final. No one gets out of hell. No one, once in, is evicted from heaven. Either way, it's forever.[17]

* * *

Notes

1. Herder and Herder, New York, 1971.
2. Ex. 32:15-20.
3. Jn. 2:15.
4. Lk. 12:51.
5. Lk. 4:29.
6. Jn. 8:48-59.
7. Mt. 23:13-36.
8. Jn. 14:6.
9. Jn. 18:37; 2 Pet. 2:1-3.
10. Heb. 13:8-9; 2 Cor. 11:4, 13-14.
11. 3 Jn. 4; 2 Jn. 10-11. St. Irenaeus: *Against Heresies* 1, c.XXvi. III. c.XV.
12. Rom. 16:17; 2 Tim. 2:16-18. Maritain: *The Peasant of the Garonne,* Ch. 5, Holt, Rinehart and Winston, New York, 1968.
13. Eph. 4:15.
14. I Cor. 13:6. *The Peasant of the Garonne,* Ch. 5.
15. Jn. 17:17.
16. Mt. 25:34, 41.
17. Lk. 16:26.

10.
The New "Dogma" of Process

POPE PAUL, as we have seen, warned the faithful in 1971 not to be misled into believing that the dogmas of the Church are subject to change. It was a necessary warning. For process theology was gaining momentum at the time, and is still going strong. Its practitioners, assuming as a first principle that everything is evolving, disallow the fixed truth and then have the inconsistency to give their first principle the status of a dogma. Some even think it new. It is not. It dates back to Heraclitus.

They called him "the dark philosopher." He wallowed in the obscurities of a heavy verbiage that did not so much express as it kept his tortuous arguments locked in confusion. "According to the ancient writers," states the Greek-Roman Classical Dictionary, "neither critics nor philosophers were able to explain his productions."[1] Heraclitus left them groping for his meaning. By contrast, his countryman Aristotle who wrote profoundly wrote to be understood.[2]

And yet, behind the murky reasonings of Heraclitus, lies a clear-cut basic principle. This he does not obstruct. He wants it known. He sets it forth plainly. It is the rationale of his confused philosophy: *all life evolves.*

To him the Life Force (his notion of God) has no terminal. It continues in an unending process of formation. Whatever it forms it constantly changes. Nothing is. Everything is only becoming. There are no fixed absolutes. Heraclitus the Obscure, the first of the evolutionists, the precursor of Hegel, might fittingly be known by another title, the father of process theology.

Process theology adopts the same basic principle. It disallows the fixed truth. It considers nothing permanent but mutability, which it honors as a dogma. Even God, not exempt from the dictate of the dogma, must undergo change. Father James Empereur of Berkeley had for an interviewer some years ago the ready answer why: "Because to be perfect means in process thought to become more what you are."[3] But the blessed in heaven know, and so does the teaching Church on earth, that God enjoyed an infinitude of perfection from eternity; that he never had to become more himself; that he always was and will always remain completely himself.

Scripture so obviously vindicates the teaching Church that the process theologian must do violence to the sacred text to get his way. Nowhere in the Old and New Testaments does the Supreme Being evolve. It takes an incredibly flexible mind to interpret "I am who am" into meaning "I am who become." "From the beginning I am the same," which Isaiah quotes the Lord God as saying of himself, does not promise the evolutionary exegete an easy time of it. And when he reads of the Second Person of the Trinity, that "Jesus Christ is the same yesterday and today and for ever" he ought to give up.[4]

But he doesn't. As far as he is concerned, St. Paul might as well not have warned against the error of preaching "another Jesus than the one we preached."[5] The progressive type of theologian rather believes with Teilhard de Chardin

The New "Dogma" of Process

that the eternal Son of God has not remained the same Jesus, but is evolving with the cosmos toward a continual betterment. Caught in the web of process thinking, his mind ought not to admit the self-evident truth that 2 + 2 was 4 a thousand years ago and stays 4 today and will forever come out 4. The correct answer does not evolve to a higher figure.

Process theology would have its followers believe that the dogmas of the Catholic Church evolve out of their former meanings into new ones because their interpretation depends on the human mind which under the influence of a passing culture changes from age to age. Thus Father Raymond Brown does not hesitate to say: "It is a fact of history that we have re-examined and re-understood doctrines."[6] But who are his "we"? Certainly not the faithful who prefer to heed the warning of Vatican Council I than the pronouncement of a theologian who seems quite indifferent to the warning. "If anyone shall say," goes the warning, "that as science progresses a meaning may at some time be attributed to the Church's dogmas different from that which the Church has understood and understands, let him be anathema."[7]

And that suggests another condemnation of like import. Worded by Pope Pius X, it was spoken by a number of process theologians who either have forgotten or have chosen to ignore it. When being ordained to the priesthood, they took the oath against Modernism which includes this clear-cut promise: "Fourthly, I sincerely accept the doctrinal teaching which has come down from the apostles through the faithful fathers in the same sense and meaning to our own day; and so I positively reject the heretical misrepresentation that dogmas evolve and change from one meaning to another, different from the one which the Church previously held."[8]

Obviously, what the Church has held in the past remains open to a better understanding as time goes on. The believer comes by, or is given, deeper insights. In that sense a dogma develops, grows in meaning. But the meaning does not change into what it was not. It unfolds like a bud into full flower. It was implicitly all there from the start, to be more sharply defined, more precisely explained, more solidly appreciated. It remains in essence what it was.

But the process theologian does not seek deeper insights into this or that dogma. He wants it essentially changed. He would destroy it. Taking care not openly to deny it, he still argues it away. His interpretation empties it of its meaning. Under the guise of giving it a new significance to bring it up-to-date and thereby do it a favor, he annihilates it.

Here is how one modernist interpretation treats the Resurrection. The event is freely admitted, though not as a physical fact, rather as an eschatological fact, if you please. The admission, seen through the fog of such double talk, is seen nonetheless to be a denial after all. For in this devious reunderstanding of the dogma, the Resurrection does not mean that the slain body of our Savior rose alive from the tomb. It only means that his faith in God has survived his death to become the living inheritance of his disciples. The whole hazy idea runs counter to the angel's forthright announcement to the holy women: "He is not here, for He has risen as He said."[9]

Cardinal Danielou calls the bluff of these quibblers. He writes: "The word *Resurrection* does not have two senses. Either it signifies that the body of Christ lay no longer in the tomb, but he was alive by the power of God and therefore able to be unmistakably identified as he always had been by witnesses — or it signifies nothing."[10]

The mania to remake doctrine, under the pretense of giving it relevancy, threatens the entire creed. No dogma, however sacred, is likely to escape. In his treatment of the Holy Eucharist, Father Edward Schillebeeckx argues that the consecrated bread at Mass remains bread because the idea of its becoming the Body of Christ and retaining in the transubstantiation only its color and taste and weight and shape "has lost significance in our times."[11] Why so? How does the traditional doctrine, admittedly suitable to the past, now of a sudden lose significance? It is the same adorable mystery of faith as ever it was. How could its credibility in the first century, or the thirteenth, have grown impossible to the twentieth? "You might as well say," argues back Chesterton, "that a certain philosophy can be believed on Mondays, but cannot be believed on Tuesdays. You might as well say of a view of the cosmos that it was suitable to half-past three, but not suitable to half- past four."[12]

The misinterpretation, like most of the New Theology, is not new. Dr. Schillebeeckx has but given us a rehash of an old error even to the point of allowing that, while the consecrated bread does not change into Christ, it may be said to change in the sense that it has now become a *sign* of his presence. To the Catholic Church, "this is my body" means precisely that. She prefers to take the Lord's word as it is than to accept the insinuation that he didn't know his own mind and really meant to say "this signifies my body."

Nor will the Church agree to the proposition of Father John Kersten, that "Jesus is present in the bread and wine as the giver in the gift."[13] The bread and wine no longer exist after the consecration, the Church unreservedly teaches, so that there can be no simultaneous co-existence. There is, exclusively, the Real Presence. What looks or tastes like bread and wine, but is not bread and wine, has become Jesus Christ. "If anyone shall say that, in the most holy Sacrament of the Eucharist, the substance of the bread and wine remain conjointly with the Body and Blood of our Lord Jesus Christ, and shall deny that wonderful and unique conversion of the whole substance of the bread into the Body, and of the whole substance of the wine into the Blood — the species alone of the bread and wine remaining — which conversion indeed the Catholic Church calls transubstantiation: let him be anathema." The Council of Trent, in so declaring, could not have made the meaning of the sublime mystery clearer.[14]

Neither could Pope Paul in his encyclical *Mysterium Fidei*.[15] He spells out the meaning of transubstantiation, defending the word, insisting upon it, glorying in it. The word must be kept. Those progressives who would discard it as out of date and hopelessly unintelligible to the modern mind like to say their quarrel is not with the dogma but with that particular term. Are they sincere? Is it really an unintelligible term to the contemporary mind? Children, trained in any honest catechism of Catholic doctrine, understand what it means. The faithful at large do.

Calvin of four centuries ago surely did. Of all the earlier disbelievers in the Real Presence, was there a single one who did not? These dissenters took from the term the understanding that at Mass the reality of bread and wine is transubstantiated (or, if you will, transformed) into the Body and Blood of Jesus Christ. They understood perfectly — and simply would not agree. It was the dogma, which the term so well explains, that bothered them. And so Pope Paul, whom the dogma does not bother but rejoices, applauds the term. He does it not only in the encyclical but again in his *Credo of the People of God*. "This mysterious change," he writes of the miracle of consecration, "is very appropriately called by the Church *transubstantiation*."[16]

Pope Paul in his recount of the revealed truths was speaking for all the faithful. Why else did he call it their creed? And he issued it to close out the Holy Year which he had established between midyear of 1967 and that of 1968 in the hope of abating the growing menace of infidelity. The menace did not abate, however. Frank Sheed wrote a telltale book at the time, in which he unhappily had to admit: "There is hardly a doctrine or practice of the Church that I have not heard attacked by a priest."[17]

Think of it. Men ordained to preach the unalterable truths and then as cultists of change itching and attempting to undo them, what a mockery! Mr. Sheed was not exaggerating. It happened and is still happening, as who doesn't know? Dog-

The New "Dogma" of Process

ma after dogma in the credenda has suffered from the attack of priests who are proud to be called process theologians. Characteristically, their idol had this to say barely two years before his death: "Christianity will only recoup its power to influence the world when it . . . sets itself to the task of rethinking the doctrine of original sin in terms of progress rather than of a Fall." So wrote, again a priest, Pierre Teilhard de Chardin in 1953.[18]

Three years previously, Pope Pius XII who had seen what was happening put his finger on the primary cause. He touched upon it deftly in his *Humani Generis*: "The fictitious tenets of evolution, which repudiate all that is absolute, firm and immutable, have paved the way for the new erroneous philosophy." They have, beyond doubt. One doesn't need to probe far into process theology to sense that. *The Stuff of the Universe* openly concludes that "a whole series of reshapings of certain representations or attitudes which seem to us definitely fixed by Catholic dogma has become necessary if we sincerely wish to Christify Evolution." Who would sincerely wish to do that, as if Christianity must subserve the fantasy of a mere theory? Who would write such a conglomeration of wishful thinking as *The Stuff of the Universe*? Teilhard would. He did.[19]

Evolution, which has given the incentive to process theology, meanwhile remains an unproved theory. Harvard's respected anatomist, Thomas Dwight, may have worn an amused smile when he said: "We have now the remarkable spectacle that just when many scientific men are agreed that there is no part of the Darwinian system that is of any great influence, and that, as a whole, the theory is not only unproved but impossible, the ignorant, half-educated masses have acquired the idea that it is to be accepted as a fundamental fact." The process theologian unquestioningly accepts it. What is worse, religion teachers by a large count follow his directives to the detriment of their pupils who are being starved of the great, fixed, eternal truths.

The harm that the false but fashionable dogma of an ongoing revelation has done to catechetics is a disaster crying to heaven for vengeance. As for heaven, take a look at what Father Leon McKenzie wants done to that supernatural realm of the blessed: "The task of the religious educator is to demythologize heaven." To his way of thinking, heaven has not yet come into being. And when it does it "will be this world at its final stage of fullness." He made the statement in *Process Catechetics*. But others of his kind have said no less. Peter de Rosa reports of a group of them, with whom he consulted, that they understand the paradisal state in *Genesis* to be "a projection, not a piece of history." Meaning what? That "there will be a state like this in the future." [20]

Process theology simply will not abide by the definitions of council or pope, the *de fide* decrees. It must alter them to fit the advancing times. And in doing so, it thrives on long-winded vapidities which can be made to sound important. Certainly the Dutch Catechism requires more than ten pages of lofty language to explain original sin, but never gets to the point. That is, to the correct point. Adam escapes blame beautifully: "Original Sin is the sin of mankind as a whole." And do you know why? Our view of the world is not what it was. It used to be static. "But now our picture of the world has changed. We can see further into the distant past. It helps us to see that the world is involved in an upward movement, in a process of growth." [21]

What vague nonsense! But at least the flow of words has a cadence to adorn the shallow content. And that is more than may be said of this rigmarole from a good nun who instructs teen-agers and adults in Iowa. "I believe in Jesus," she writes in the *Religion Teachers' Journal*, "a man placed in first-century history and caught up in the web of structure and the pressure of his culture." Do her pupils ever hear from Sister that the Incarnate Son of God willed His lowliness and, far from being an impotent slave of circum-

The New "Dogma" of Process

stance, did not lack the power to break out of the web or escape the pressure? Undaunted, Sister Arlene sticks to her theme: "I believe he evolved through Process to the completion of the Perfect Man, who would be the exemplar of human freedom." As if that were not enough, there is more coming. "And I finally believe he affirmed by his life and death the possibility of mankind's owning in some distant future the full realization of Christogenesis."[22]

If that is the sort of Heraclitean obfuscation which Sister Arlene teaches as well as writes about, I wonder what her pupils make of it. I know what Jacques Maritain made of it, as he studied it in Teilhard. He reviewed the convoluted explanation of an evolving cosmogenesis under the influence of the cosmic Christ toward the Omega point, with the noosphere becoming of course Christosphere, and having reviewed it the wise old layman found it "theology-fiction" and tagged the whole of it "the Great Fable." The truth is not in it.[23]

That the Church's faithful on earth are already members of the Mystical Body of Christ, and that infidels are invited into the membership, reduces to hot air "the possibility of mankind's owning in some distant future the full realization of Christogenesis." That at death heaven awaits any human soul in sanctifying grace, after whatever delay in purgatory, if any, and that on the last day the body of that soul will rise up in glorified form to rejoin it, and with the soul share forever in the Divine Life, in the unimaginable joys of the Blessed Trinity: here we have a certitude of belief to diminish to an insipidity the Teilhardian fable. And the very world which the fabulist considered pantheistic and therefore indestructible is in reality on its way to destruction, only to be renewed by its transcendent Creator to a greater splendor.[24]

Why should process theology presume to improve on the creed? How dare its more extravagant meddlers in doctrine say that God himself changes for the better and may alter a former decree to a new meaning and an up-to-date relevancy? Away with this so-called *continuing* revelation! Away with the whole false mess of reinterpretations! Incomparably superior to the most ambitious of them, transcending them all with a grandeur that is Truth Eternal, are the divine articles of faith as they stand, taught by the Church, unchanged in essence and unchangeable.

* * *

Notes

1. Charles Anthon: *Roman-Greek Classical Dictionary.* Harper & Brothers, New York, 1851.
2. Aristotle criticizes Heraclitus in his *Metaphysics,* 4th book.
3. Interview with Father James Empereur in the *National Catholic Reporter,* Feb. 1, 1974.
4. Ex. 3:14; Is. 43:13 Confraternity; Heb. 13:8.
5. 2 Cor. 11:4.
6. *The Virginal Conception and Resurrection of Jesus.* The Paulist Press.
7. Denzinger 1818.
8. Denzinger 2145.
9. Mt. 28:6.
10. *La Resurrection* from which Cardinal Wright quotes in his article, "Did Christ Rise or Not?" *Friar* Magazine, April, 1973.
11. *The Eucharist.*
12. *Orthodoxy,* Ch. 5.
13. John C. Kersten, S.V.D.: *Bible Catechism.*
14. Denzinger 884.
15. *Mysterium Fidei,* published a few days before the final session of Vatican II.
16. *Credo of the People of God,* proclaimed on June 30, 1968, to close out the Year of Faith.
17. *Is It the Same Church?* Pflaum Press, Dayton, Ohio, 1968.
18. Cf. Donald Gray: *The One and Many.*
19. *L'Activation de L'Energie.* Paris, Editions de Seuil, 1963.
20. Peter de Rosa: *Christ and Original Sin.*
21. *A New Catechism.* Authorized Edition of the Dutch Catechism. Herder & Herder, New York, 1967.

22. "My Statement of Belief in Jesus" by Sister Arlene Einwalter in the *Religion Teachers' Journal,* April, 1973.
23. Jacques Maritain: *The Peasant of the Garonne.* Holt, Reinhart and Winston, New York, 1968.
24. 2 Pet. 3:10-13; Is. 34:4; 65:17; 66:22.

11.
Taking Orders from Hegel

A STRAIGHT thinker has again shown his devotion to truth by an alarming statement. Yet, should it alarm? To believe you are a genuine member of the Catholic Church while accepting her dogmas, not as they are, but as you want them to be, this is plain self-deception. Christopher Derrick was simply telling the logically inescapable truth when he wrote: "There has been a widespread loss of faith among the Catholic intelligentsia; many of those concerned are unwilling to face the fact of their loss and therefore desire most urgently (and at any cost in intellectual absurdity) that Roman Catholicism should somehow transmogrify itself into something in which they still do believe."[1]

They would seem to have fallen prey to the philosophic principle now in fashion: that reality is subject to the mind, and that there can be no truth aside from what the mind thinks it is. Kant worked the principle to death. Or no, one only wishes he had. It remains vigorously alive. For Hegel, his disciple, has enhanced its nonsense, giving it a new dimension.

No philosopher exerts so dominant an influence over the modernistic world as Georg Wilhelm Friederich Hegel. His admirer Lenin admits that, without an understanding of his flair for contradiction, *Das Kapital* would make no sense. The difference is, Hegel saw in his dialectic a spiritual process which Marx reduced to a continuous tension between purely material forces. At the same time Hegel did not mean to imply by his spiritual process a personal, transcendent God. Far from it! Like Heraclitus of old, he believed in a pantheistic soul that inheres in the world and along with the world struggles constantly toward some vague sort of betterment.

Hegel presupposes, as a first principle of his system, that a clash of opposites begets progress. First comes the affirmation of an idea, then its equally valid denial by another idea, to be followed by a compromise between the two which establishes a new idea. But the new idea does not remain fixed, having an ongoing fluidity. What it does is start the process all over again by producing a contradiction of itself and coexisting uneasily with that contradiction until the tension ends up once more with a third, another new idea *pro tempore.* Thesis, antithesis, synthesis: there you have the Hegelian method of, not achieving the truth, but finding and holding it for a while — before it evolves into something else.

That Marxism has adopted the Hegelian dialectic runs true to form. But who in advance would have expected the so-called higher critic of biblical scholarship and the resultant process theologian to submit to it? Yet so they do. A look at the two of them at work, who are often the same person, will reveal their Hegelian dependence. These slaves to the dialectic do not fit philosophy or theology to the demands of God's revelation to man, as did St. Augustine and St. Thomas Aquinas. They do the reverse. They even subject

Taking Orders from Hegel

their omnipotent and self-sufficient Creator from eternity to the evolution of progress.

It was a Lutheran, Ferdinand Christian Baur, who founded the biblical school of higher criticism at the Uuniversity of Tübingen in the early nineteenth century. To say it another way: he introduced the Hegelian dialectic to exegesis.[2] Let it be recalled that Hegel saw in all historical developments three stages. First, a stand on some principle is firmly taken; then others take the opposite stand; and the conflict results in a third stand, neither one nor the other, but a hybrid of the two when not something altogether different from them. Applying this procedure known as historicism to the *Acts of the Apostles,* Dr. Baur established his thesis upon the Jewish converts of St. Peter who were of a legalistic mind, and his antithesis upon the Gentile converts of St. Paul who were just as vigorously hostile to the law, and his synthesis upon the fusion of the two parties into the Catholicism of the second century.

The fact that the council at Jerusalem ended in perfect agreement to refute such balderdash did not bother the founder of higher criticism. He declared *ex cathedra,* that is, from his professor's chair, that St. Luke's account of the council must be spurious for the simple reason that Paul of the *Acts* was not the genuine St. Paul who wrote *Galatians, Corinthians, Romans,* and no other Epistles than these three.[3] It was an easy way out, setting the precedent for future liberal biblicists in a tight squeeze. Whatever would defeat their argument, by wind from the mouth is blown away.

The modernist theologian, whose methods identify him with the higher criticism, goes about examining doctrine through the same Hegelian process. He nullifies it. What Baur did, he does. To the article of faith that Christ rose from the tomb he agrees. But he affirms it with the tricky reservation that Christ did not rise bodily from the tomb. He then in a perfect synthesis concludes that Christ did in truth rise from the tomb, but symbolically, not bodily. And that is quibbling. He has insidiously denied the doctrine as the Church understands it and insists upon its being understood.

Carol Jackson Robinson shows how this modern trickery is worked upon the unsuspecting minds of Catholic school children. She relates it with calm humor: "Yes, students should be taught the doctrines of the bishops' guidelines. But let these doctrines coexist in the classroom with the new results of theological speculation which contradict them. Then what? . . . We have these two contradictory claimants and we must decide between them. How?"[4]

That's easy. Historicism will solve the dilemma with its pat formula. Something new must be found and in the name of progress will be found to take the place of the two outmoded contraries. Against so relentless a process no dogma can stand immune. For evolution through a continuity of change advances the world and with the world every principle of theology to an ultimate perfection. Just give it time. Revelation far from being static, goes on and on and on.

It does not apparently disturb the process theologian that the current philosophy on which he bases his faith is essentially a rehash of discarded philosophies and therefore not the outcome of an unbroken progress. Its pantheism, its evolutionism, its Manichaean equation of good and evil with God are of antiquity. Even its most original element, a flair for contradiction, owes not a little to Kant and perhaps still more to twelfth-century Averroes who maintained that what is true in theology may be irreconcilably false in philosophy. Anyhow, Hegel's penchant for balancing every affirmative with a contradiction led him to his silly postulate that the same thing can be and not be at the same time. Tell that to a pedestrian on the street, suggests Chesterton, but be prepared for his snicker of incredulity. Of this normal man without the higher learning, G. K. says with mock solemnity: "The moron refuses to admit that Hegel can both exist and

Taking Orders from Hegel

not exist; or that it can be possible to understand Hegel if there is no Hegel to understand."[5]

Chesterton's man on the street has plenty of learned company. Coleridge and De Quincey, prominent in English Literature, thought Hegel self-contradictory, affected and nugatory insofar as he could be understood.[6] Sydney Smith, known for his acute mind, said of Hegel more than of Kant that his obfuscation defies understanding.[7] Professor James Frederick Ferrier raises and answers his own indignant question: "Who has ever uttered one intelligent word about Hegel? Not one of his countrymen, not any foreigner, seldom even himself."[8] Somerset Maugham, of all the philosophers he read, found only Hegel a bore. "I found him terribly long-winded and I could never reconcile myself to the jugglery with which it seemed to me he proved whatever he had a mind to."[9] But that is a mild denunciation compared with the next. "The lowest stage of degradation was reached by Hegel," writes Schopenhauer. He "turned philosophy into an instrument of obscurantism . . . and drew over her a veil of the emptiest verbiage and the most senseless hodgepodge ever heard out of Bedlam."[10] So on the debunking goes.

Allegedly Hegel himself said on his deathbed: "Only one man ever understood me, and he didn't."[11] Was he that man? Certainly the contradiction that he both did and did not understand his own philosophy, if it were he, would be entirely in character. The negation of a previous affirmative typifies his kind of thinking.

The most important condemnation of Hegelianism, in the interest of faith and morals, came from Pope Pius IX. In the *Syllabus of Errors,* eighty of them in all, the first proposition to be listed is the briefest summary of the philosophy that nurtures Modernism. The Holy Father translates its obscurities into intelligible speech to give us a clear idea what it is he condemns. Would that Loisy and Tyrrell had heeded Pope Pius IX to prevent the excommunication of the former and the near excommunication of the latter by Pope Pius X.

Here is what Hegel taught and Pope Pius IX in 1864 condemned: "There exists no supreme all-wise, all-provident God, distinct from the world; and God is the same as the nature of things and therefore liable to change; and God comes into being in man and in the universe, and all things are God and they have the same substance of God; and God is one and the same as the world, and therefore also spirit is one and the same with matter, necessity with liberty, the true with the false, the good with the evil, and the just with the unjust."[12]

In that papal condensation, as Paul H. Hallett with his accuracy of insight points out, we have a more lucid statement than Hegel himself ever gave us of his confused pantheism and of his jumbling together as co-equals any pair of contradictories as far apart as virtue is from vice.[13] What a twisted mind! To maintain as a serious premise that the true is identical with the false, good with evil, the just with the unjust, because all of them alike are God and have the same substance as God: surely this perverse reasoning must bring a shudder to the most incorrigible process theologian. It would have shocked the great minds of Grecian philosophy. The *non-sequitur* that evil, being God, has as much right as good to exist in the ongoing dialectic, would have drawn from Socrates a blast of his best irony and from Aristotle a devastating rebuttal, if either had heard of such nonsense in their day. As for Plato, he would beyond doubt have agreed with the classic argument in *The City of God,* which proves evil no more than a lack of what ought to be, without any right to exist at all. Did Plato possibly give St. Augustine the idea?

Georg Wilhelm Friedrich Hegel knows how to produce upon the mind somewhat the effect of a telephone call when the operator at her switchboard has absentmindedly plugged the wrong holes and an onrush of discordant voices answers back. "Somewhat the effect," I say, for through the jumbled

Taking Orders from Hegel

lingo the trained reader learns to pick up what he can of the pattern of thought, however perverse, and to detect not an absent-minded but a determined effort. It is not to be dismissed as of no consequence. The reason stands clear: while the idea of evolutionary progress under the impetus of a pantheistic life force dates back to Heraclitus, with the obfuscation, Hegel has added to that the novelty of his triple dialectic to become the modern rage. He dominates contemporary thinking outside the religious spheres of influence, and into these he has seriously intruded.

A philosophy to teach the great certitudes must of necessity accept the guidance of divine revelation. There is no other way. The unguided titans of Greek philosophy went far in their search for the ultimate truth. Their effort was honest. It was noble. It was not enough. The supreme answers from God which give repose to the questing spirit, except for those deducible from the natural order, Socrates and Plato and Aristotle missed.

We have simply to compare the works of Plato with those of Augustine or the works of Aristotle with those of Aquinas to see what an enrichment resulted from the decision of the two doctors of theology to adopt the best from the pagans in order to Christianize it, purify it of errors, fill in the omissions, so that the intake would befit its Catholic context. Why were we born? Where do we go from here? Why must we die? What happens to the soul after death? Is the grave the body's final destination? These are questions for which divine revelation alone has the complete answers. Hundreds of similar questions remain: and if the answers are not known, the attempt to find them on the part of profane philosophy becomes little more than a guessing game in which one participant contradicts another.

Knowing this, Cardinal Newman did not keep the knowledge to himself. Grateful to his Protestant upbringing for the many revealed truths he had received from it, but at the same time regretful that the denominations had broken away from the Mother Church who preserves the creed intact, he went into the pulpit to speak his mind. "It will be found," the homilist tells his mixed congregation, "that either the Catholic Religion is verily and indeed the coming in of the unseen world into this, or there is nothing positive, nothing dogmatic, nothing real in any of our notions as to whence we come and whither we are going."[14]

Another statement, no less positive than pertinent, deserves to be quoted. "How I wept," the yet unconverted Augustine addresses the God of his yearnings, "when I heard your hymns and canticles, being deeply moved by the sweet singing of your Church. Those voices flowed into my ears, truth filtered into my heart, and from my heart surged waves of devotion."[15]

Do you know what put the ecstatic joy in his tears? The sudden conviction that the body of doctrines expressed in the liturgical chant were true, had to be true, had to be eternally true, because the Church in her infallible authority from Christ taught them to be true. Without that guarantee, the doctrines would not have been believed by one who understood from his schooling in philosophy the vagaries of human reasoning on its own resources. Read the convert's perfectly clear admission: "I would not believe the Gospel unless moved thereto by the authority of the Church."[16]

The Bishop of Hippo knew that it was not Athanasius who won the battle for the divinity of Christ against Arius, but Athanasius with the backing of the Holy See. He knew that it was neither Eusebius of Dorylaeum nor Flavian of Constantinople who won the battle for the humanity of Christ against Eutyches, but these two members of the hierarchy with the backing of the Holy See. Did not the doctor of grace, when locked in combat with Pelagius over the doctrine of original sin, refer the case to the Holy See? He knew that in the chair of Peter sat the only Infallible Authority on earth to settle the issue.

The grand harmony of doctrines, which the creed is and

which God's infallible vicar on earth protects, brought satisfaction at last to the restless thinker who has immortalized his profound contentment in *The Confessions*. His conversion to the Faith, he was quick to admit, gave meaning to the otherwise insolvable complexities of life. How often have we not read of a like acknowledgement from other converts! The process theologian, on the contrary, even when he claims to be of the Faith, obviously derives no such comfort from its fixed certitudes: he has committed himself to the impossibility of altering them to fit a false philosophy. He seems to have a grudge against them.

By contrast, he bears no apparent grudge against Darwinian evolution which vindicates his working principle that everything changes. To him it is not an unproved hypothesis, nor even an unprovable daydream in his own brain. To this odd sort of theologian who does not believe in objective truth, evolutionism has become — yes, an established dogma. He has faith in it, an undoubting faith which Arnold Lunn describes in a witty paraphrase of St. Paul. "Faith, it would seem, is the substance of fossils hoped for, the evidence of links unseen."

* * *

Notes

1. *C. S. Lewis and the Church of Rome*, Introduction, Ignatius Press, San Francisco, 1981.
2. Cf. Baur's essay in the *Tübingen Zeitschrift* for 1831.
3. *Paulus, der Apostel Jesu Christi, sein Leben und Wirken, und seine Lehre*, (1845).
4. "The Credibility of Father Brown," *The Wanderer*, Nov. 8, 1973.
5. *St. Thomas Aquinas*, Chapter 6, People's Library, Hodder & Stoughton Limited, London, 1933.
6. John Sterling: *The Secret of Hegel*, Vol. 1, Preface.
7. Ferrier: *Moral Philosophy*, Longmans, Green & Co., London, 1850.

8. John Sterling: *The Secret of Hegel*, Vol. 1, Preface.
9. *The Summing Up*, Chapter LXIII, Doubleday, Doran & Company, Inc., Garden City, N.Y., 1945.
10. Wallace: "The Logic of Hegel," *Dublin Review*, July, 1894.
11. *Encyclopaedia Britannica*, Vol. II, "Hegel, Georg Wilhelm Frederick."
12. Denzinger 1701.
13. "Syllabus of Errors Revisited" by Paul H. Hallett in *The National Catholic Register*, April 30, 1978.
14. "Mysteries of Nature and of Grace" from *Discourses to Mixed Congregations*, Longmans, Green & Co., London, 1893.
15. *The Confessions of St. Augustine* as quoted by Pope Pius X in his apostolic constitution *Divino afflatu*, 1911, AAS 3 633-634.
16. Contra Epis. Manich. Fund., n. 6.

12.
A Fairy Tale for Adults

THE theologian who rides evolutionism with the confidence of a boy on his hobby horse suggests still another happy-go-lucky rider:

"There was a young lady of Niger
Who smiled as she rode on a tiger;
They returned from the ride
With the lady inside,
And the smile on the face of the tiger."

A similar reversal awaits the process theologian who professes the Catholic creed. He must hold on to its traditional dogmas while at the same time admitting that nothing remains static. He gets around the difficulty with a self-complacency that might well put a smile on his face. He keeps the dogmas, as he says, but only reinterprets them out of their old meaning to give them a sense they did not have before. No longer reasoning within the limits of sound doctrine, he does his speculating from within the confines of something quite different. Evolutionism has swallowed him alive.

In its confinement he breathes and thinks and has his being. He would accordingly like to believe that a whole generation of better advanced apes graduated into men and women. But there stands in his way the dreadful thought that, if Adam's body did evolve from a lower animal, it is the only human body that did, for the Church dogmatically teaches that all the rest of the human race sprang from him as a common ancestor. Mind, the Church does not in the least intimate that the first human body evolved from a beast; that is not her concern; but she does allow the unproved proposition to be investigated. What she does insist on, and with dogmatic force, is that every human soul is directly created by God and that every human body after Adam's came from Adam.[1]

Including Eve's body? Yes, including hers. "The formation of the first woman from the first man," as recorded in *Genesis*, must be interpreted in "the literal and historic sense." So did the Pontifical Biblical Commission under Pope Pius X rule in its answer to the third of eight questions sent in for a solution.[2]

But that does not deter the process theologian from broaching the question: "May not Adam in the singular, as *Genesis* records him, be construed into meaning a widespread group of Adams? The Church replies with a stern prohibition. "No Catholic can hold," writes her supreme magisterium, Pope Pius XII, "that Adam is merely a symbol for a number of first parents." Polygenesis, in *Humani Generis* as well as in the decrees of Carthage, Orange and Trent, stands condemned.

Oddly enough, the process theologian who dares to question the dogmas of the Church never questions the theory of evolution. To him it is more than a theory. It is with him the one immovable truth in a world of constant change. It offers his trend of reasoning the motive power to proceed at all. Nor does he seem ever to have feared that he labors under a grand illusion. Rather than be embarrassed,

A Fairy Tale for Adults

he is likely to turn a deaf ear to this quip from Harvard's eminent anatomist, Thomas Dwight: "We have now the remarkable spectacle that just when many scientific men are agreed that there is no part of the Darwinian system that is of any great influence, and that, as a whole, the theory is not only unproved but impossible, the ignorant, half-educated masses have acquired the idea that it is to be accepted as a fundamental fact."

Whether the human body evolved from a lower animal or not, science does not honestly know. Its fashionable textbooks pretend they know, but in the pretense must admit the embarrassment of some missing links. Anthony Standen, a holder of degrees from Oxford and the Massachusetts Institute of Technology, ridicules the gullibility of those who speak of only one missing link in the chain. He thinks that more of the chain is missing than what is there, if "there is a chain at all."[3]

It is astonishing, not that hundreds of prominent scientists have declared evolution simply unprovable, but that the official textbooks either do not know of these protests or, knowing, are determined not to let their readers know. But the deprived readers can easily enough find out by an independent reading in private. They might well start with the works of the great ornithologist, Douglas Dewar, who decries the educational conspiracy to "warp" the mind of youth as "monstrous." And they might best start with *Is Evolution Proved?* since this book, being an exchange of letters between Dewar and a confirmed evolutionist, gives both sides of the controversy in depth. H. S. Shelton, in the course of the correspondence, presents all the arguments of Darwin, Thomas Huxley, Spencer and the like: but he is answered, letter for letter, by a scientist who once himself accepted those arguments and now, from a wealth of experience, demolishes them one by one. Incidentally, Sir Arnold Lunn served the two as their moderator and editor.[4]

Douglas Dewar, F.Z.S., devotes all of four books to his

refutation of the evolutionary theory. The most elaborate of them he entitles *The Transformist Illusion*.[5] In it the author leaves no stone unturned. But it is in his *Man a Special Creation* that he writes out his clearest of statements for the layman who would like to know as briefly as possible why the Darwinian theory breaks down: "There appears to exist no mechanism whereby a new type of organism can arise from an existing one. This explains why all breeds of dogs, pigeons, etc., despite their great diversity are still dogs, pigeons, etc."[6]

Dr. W. R. Thompson, a geologist of international repute, has pointed out that for want of real proof the evolutionists resorted to fraud. He cites the Piltdown Man, the original human jawbone of which was stealthily replaced by the jawbone of an ape. He next refers to an equally detestable hoax, the now discredited Java Man, the perpetrators of which had so pummeled away at its skull, the skull of a gibbon, as to make it look half human and half anthropoid. Nor of course did the perpetrations stop with these two. Others followed, no less bizarre, to force from Dr. Thompson the admission that "the success of Darwinism was accompanied by a decline in scientific integrity."

And where of all places will you find the admission? In the introduction which Dr. Thompson wrote for a re-edition of Darwin's own *Origin of Species*.[7] Some years later in one of the books he himself authored the worthy geologist says what "nature shows, indeed, is not an evolutionary flux but a world that is stable within narrow limits." That man descended from the brute, he saw no evidence to believe. Take his word rather than mine: "When we survey the animal kingdom as a whole, the data do not really support the idea of the gradual transformation of animal mentality into human intelligence."[8]

Not only does science discourage but the Church forbids the belief that the mentality of a lower animal could ever evolve into human intelligence. God directly creates in every

A Fairy Tale for Adults

human body an immortal human soul *out of nothing*. A Catholic who believes that at least Adam's body evolved from a lower animal's dare not conclude that Adam's mind also emerged from the beast — along with Adam's body. The Church takes *Genesis* literally in ascribing to Adam a mind immediately capable of forming a decision of such gravity as to condemn the human race to the dire consequences of his sin. Adam was no moron, as some biblicists would like to think he must have been.

The frauds, with their mad effort to vindicate the Darwinian thesis that man descended from the ape, bespeak an utter desperation. Paul Lemoine, Maurice Vernet, Louis Vialleton, prominent among the scientists of their country and the world, reject that thesis and ridicule the deceptions to promote it. Louis Bounoure, the national director of Scientific Research in France, and once an avowed evolutionist, now shares the conviction of his colleague, Jean Rostand, who does not pull the punch of his words: "Evolutionism is a fairy tale for adults. This theory has helped nothing in the progress of science. It is useless."[9]

With the esteemed member of the Academie Francaise, geologist William Dawson of Canada agrees: "It is one of the strangest phenomena of humanity; it is utterly destitute of proof."[10] Sir James Gray, professor emeritus of Zoology at Cambridge University, says of evolution: "No amount of argument, or clever epigram, can disguise the inherent improbability."[11] The American Robert Millikan and the English Peter Medawar, both of whom won the Nobel prize, speak to the same effect. The latter in his critique, *The Art of the Soluble,* expresses surprise that Teilhard de Chardin could have been so incredibly naive toward the glaring weaknesses of a mere theory which he mistook for the unassailable truth.[12]

Sir Ambrose Fleming, a renowned physicist and inventor of the thermionic valve, obviously concurs with his countryman: he founded in England the Evolution Protest Movement. In Sweden, H. Nilsson, the distinguished professor of Genetics at Lund Univerity, while not a member of that group, thinks as does the group. So does Albert Fleischmann, G.R., professor of Zoology and Comparative Anatomy in the University of Erlangen, who in a 1931 publication said outright: "I reject evolution."[13] Then there is Reincke, one of botany's ranking experts, who after much thought has come to the conclusion: "The only statement consistent with her dignity that Science can make, is to say that she knows nothing about the origin of man."[14]

Many reputable scientists who favor evolution are not so sure of it as are, by a quirk of irony, dyed-in-the-wool process theologians. "If one takes his stand upon the exclusive ground of the facts," writes Yves Delage, "it must be acknowledged that the formation of one species from another species has not been demonstrated at all."[15] A second advocate of evolution, but only as a working hypothesis, bears a name equally well known to the academic world, George Gaylord Simpson. "It is necessary," he admits, "to keep other possibilities in mind, and especially to keep before us evidence adduced in support of other theories."[16]

And here follows a stunner. All that Thomas Huxley wrote to convince his generation of Darwinism, his grandson now declares invalid. Sir Julian Huxley, a hopeful evolutionist still, yet has the courage to say that the arguments of his grandfather based on orthogenesis and Lamarckism are at present usless. "They are out; they are no longer consistent with facts. Indeed, in the light of modern discoveries they no longer deserve to be called scientific theories, but can be seen as speculations without due basis of reality, or old superstitions disguised in modern dress." What finally nullified them, grandson Huxley adds, was the new understanding of heredity.[17]

It was of course Gregor Johann Mendel, a Catholic priest from Austria, who discovered the now accepted laws of heredity. With Darwinism all the rage at the time, however,

A Fairy Tale for Adults

his painstaking work went unrecognized for thirty-five years. Then at the turn of the century three geneticists who had conducted separate experimentations found theirs dovetailing with his, and they eagerly publicized the coincidence. According to Darwin, let it be recalled, young organisms might so much differ from their parents that the strongest of them could in the course of centuries spring into new species. Later he modified his theory to adopt Lamarckism. But Mendel's laws, once they became well known, altered the whole general concept of inheritance to disprove Darwin and Lamarck. As a recent book compiled by twenty scholarly scientists asserts, in full accord with Julian Huxley: "It is now known that genes do not change except by mutation, which rarely occurs."[18]

"Thus," the same book concludes, "Darwin did not succeed in accounting for the origin of new characteristics, which he believed provided the substance of evolution." Then why should this defeated evolutionism retain its prestige in the official textbooks? Arnold Lunn cites a teacher of science who in a statement may have let the cat out of the bag. "At a meeting of the British Association in 1929," writes Lunn, "Professor D. M. S. Watson remarked that the reason for 'the universal acceptance of evolution' was that 'the only alternative *Special Creation* was clearly untenable.' "[19] Clearly untenable? Why so? And isn't it strange, to say the least, that Watson in claiming its universal acceptance did not know of the hundreds of great thinkers and the hundreds of great scientists who do not accept evolution? Could the professor have been scared out of a good look at the evidence by the tyranny of fashion?

Certainly Professor Sedgwick of Cambridge University was not. Father Desmond Murray quotes him in *Species Revalued* as finding Darwin's concoction "a dish of rank materialism cleverly cooked and served up, merely to make us independent of the Creator." In total agreement with which, Dr. William Tinkle, a specialist in genetics, developed into a treatise his suspicion that disbelief in direct creation does not come from a study of the facts but from the modern prejudice against the supernatural.[20]

Make of it what you will, the New Theology also betrays an aversion to the supernatural. It cultivates that aversion. Its pre-occupation is with this world to the neglect of eternity. It apparently feels a compulsion to rationalize away all mystery in the transcendent truths of the Faith. It must "demythologize."

But to return to Dr. Tinkle, whose name is listed in *American Men of Science,* he joined a distinguished group of scholars who share with him, surely not an aversion to, but a strong faith in the supernatural. Founded in 1963, the Creation Research Society by 1971 already boasted an American membership of over 350 scholars, everyone of whom holds a post-graduate degree in some branch of science. What these biologists and geneticists and ornithologists and botanists and paleontologists, and so forth, all believe in common is that life from the start existed in a wide variety of forms and that Almighty God directly created the basic kinds.[21]

Dr. Henry M. Morris, president of the Society, has made the self-evident statement: "Discussion of origins is not, strictly, *science.*" How could it be? No scientists from the universities were there to see life begin or to watch the various forms spring into being. "Therefore," comes the conclusion, "the problem of origins is simply incapable of solution by scientific means."[22] *The Fossil Record,* an invaluable 1967 publication in London, does not solve it. The charts in this study of some 2,500 groups of animals and plants by 120 specialists reveal not a trace of common ancestry. They rather disprove the claims of evolutionary descent, showing that each kind of animal or plant has had a history distinct from and unrelated to all the other kinds.[23] Then there remains the testimony of Dr. G. A. Kerkut of Southampton University who probed into the seven basic assumptions of the evolutionary theory only to find they

A Fairy Tale for Adults

have not been and cannot be verified. Those of his students who think otherwise the professor upbraids for being gullible "opinion-swallowers."[24]

The editors of *Science and Creation*, a handbook for teachers, tell in the preface why it was given to the public. The key statement in their preface reads as follows: "The creationist is convinced that the actual facts of science are far better explained by creation than evolution."[25]

Now, to be sure, there are those who believe in both creation and a divinely directed evolution. They believe that God created, if not just one form, then a few basic forms of life and left them alone with the power he instilled in them to produce in due process of time the other numerous forms: but Father Patrick O'Connell, no mean paleontologist, rejects out of hand evolution as such. Especially does he point out to the Catholic who argues in favor of man's evolution from the brute the inherent weakness of such an argument, since every genuine Catholic must believe Adam to be the father of the whole human race, and since the often misrepresented encyclical *Humani Generis* forbids the Catholic to teach the descent of the first human body from a lower animal *as a fact*.[26] Father O'Connell, who has written voluminously on the subject and has documented his evidence, would feel at ease with the statement of Dr. Morris: "The most reasonable explanation for the actual facts of biology, as they are known scientifically, is that of biblical creationism."[27]

To go back for the moment to the preface in that handbook for teachers, it puts forth the plea that in the spirit of fair play "*both* creation and evolution should be taught, if *either* is to be taught, in the schools." But does the unbiblical evolutionist, now in control of education, care to hear of an alternative to his fond theory? Isn't he satisfied to maintain a closed mind? Once in England, the Evolution Protest Movement challenged the Rationalist Press Association to face the arguments of Douglas Dewar in written debate. The challenge was turned down. The R.P.A., it would seem, was not interested in the other side.[28]

Pope Pius XII had reason to point an accusing finger to those who, to foster atheism, "support the monistic and pantheistic notion that the whole world is subject to continual evolution." He named them. "Communists eagerly seize upon this theory," he said, "in the hope of depriving souls of every idea of God."[29]

And so they do. The genuine Marxists admitted as much from the first. In a letter to his friend Karl Marx, which bears the date of December 12, 1859, Friedrich Engels writes: "Incidentally, I am just reading Darwin and find him excellent. One side of theology" (which insists on an eternal, personal, omnipotent Creator, independent of and transcendent over nature) "had not been smashed yet. This has happened now."[30] After Marx had found the time to read *The Origin of Species by Means of Natural Selection*, he replied to Engels: "This is the book which contains the basis in natural science for our view." He went further, expressing his enthusiasm in another way. To the author he presented a complimentary copy of his own *Das Kapital* with the inscription: "To Mr. Charles Darwin on the part of his sincere admirer Karl Marx, London, 16 June, 1873."[31]

It is a discredit to the scientific world that Mendel's laborious discovery of the now unquestioned laws of heredity should have been for so long a time so completely overshadowed by the inferior and, even Julian Huxley admits, invalid *Origin of Species*. Did the hitherto devout Protestant help along his own popularity while the non-evolutionist languished in obscurity? Father Patrick O'Connell thinks he did. "Darwin's *Origin of Species*," he says, "might have died a natural death as soon as it was published except for two things which he did to attract attention; the first was to announce that he had ceased to believe in God; the second, the publication of his second book entitled *The Descent of Man*."[32]

A Fairy Tale for Adults

Here at last was what the atheists and agnostics of the world had been looking for: a convenient scientist and fellow infidel to assure them that man evolved from a lower animal and that indeed the very first forms of life came of themselves, out of nothing, by spontaneous generation. There was no need for outside motivation from a transcendent Creator. He did not exist. Nature did it all, and did it on its own.

"*Schola Stultorum,*" Belloc thunders at the teachers of such nonsense, "that new herd of fools peculiar to our day" who "give emptiness creative power."[33] But Dr. W. R. Thompson, the great scientist already quoted, conveys the impression of being rather sad than angry in his remark that from that time on belief in the supernatural began its modern decline.[34] It continues to decline much to the satisfaction of the atheist, which is to be expected. After all, evolution gives him some sort of trumped-up reason for so complicated and highly designed a universe without God.

What one would not expect is that the process theologian, who says he is Christian, registers neither anger nor sorrow over the degrading success of evolutionism. It does not appear to bother him at all. Fond of discovering what he calls the myths in Scripture, such as our First Parents, and prone to disallow the actuality of its recorded facts, such as our Lord's bodily resurrection, he yet finds nothing to quarrel with in Darwin. He takes in silence the embarrassments of the Neanderthal Man, the Peking Man, the Java Man, the Piltdown Man, whose fradulent portraits disgrace the pages of handy textbooks. What scientist Paul Lemoine has said of evolution — namely, that "in reality despite appearances, no one believes in it any longer" — does not in the least disconcert the theologian of progress.[35] He has his mind made up. Evolution remains to him sacrosanct.

Thus we have theologian Leslie Dewart of Toronto University writing the commendatory foreword to a book which argues that Catholicism has no choice but to evolve into

Communism. Title of the book? *From Anathema to Dialogue.* Name of the author? Roger Garaudy, the French Communist philosopher, who in the book praises Teilhard for his dismissal of original sin and quotes Teilhard to the effect that the eventual merging of the Christian God of the Above with the Marxist God of the Ahead "is the only God whom we shall in the future be able to adore in spirit and truth."[36]

Not much less shockingly does Leslie Dewart write in one of his own books: "The evolution of man has brought about a change in the very nature of 'religious' belief." Evolution dominates all. Using traditional terms, this pro cessor forces into them meanings to justify his preconceived premise. He thinks that "faith originates when man suddenly discovers himself to be already existing, to be part of an ongoing world which is already in process."[37] In another of his books the ongoing gibberish rolls glibly along: "Revealed religion does not descend from above." That would be too supernatural a concept. You must keep your feet on terra firma and your head out of the clouds to realize: "Religion is the conceptual, cultural form of the experience of reality as such."[38]

And this experienced reality is in constant flux, no process theologian will ever let you forget, so that each doctrine of the Creed has to be understood according to the advanced mind of the age. In other words, says Leslie Dewart in unison with his colleagues, the Church must submit to history — by which they mean historicism. Only the dogma of evolution escapes the process. That admits of no reinterpretation.

Now do you see how that monster Evolution has swallowed up the process theologian? Never mind that the monster may be no more real than a fable. The enclosed victim disallows the possibility and reasons out his theology within confines of his own desire, let them be ever so imaginary. He is quite self-satisfied. He gets his work done, not realizing his plight.

A Fairy Tale for Adults

He needs guidance from the Holy See.

* * *

Notes

1. *Humani Generis*: Pope Pius XII, 1950, paragraphs, 37, 38.
2. Date of issuance, June 30, 1909. Cf. Denzinger 2123.
3. *Science Is a Sacred Cow* (paperback), E. P. Dutton & Co., Inc.
4. *Is Evolution Proved? An Argument between Douglas Dewar and H. S. Shelton*, Hollis and Carter, London, 1947.
5. Dehoff Publications, 1957.
6. Cf. Rev. Patrick O'Connell: *Science of Today and the Problems of Genesis*, Christian Book Club of America, Hawthorne, Ca., 1969, pp. 51-53.
7. Everyman's Library, 1956; Dent, 1963.
8. *Philosophy Problems in Biology*, St. John's University Press, 1966.
9. *Le Monde et La Vie*, October, 1963.
10. *Fatima International*, August 14, 1973.
11. *Nature*, February 6, 1954.
12. Methuen & Co., Ltd., 1967, p. 71ff.
13. *Fatima International*, June 6, 1974.
14. Arnold Lunn: *Within That City*, Sheed & Ward, N. Y., 1938, p. 64.
15. *Ibid.*, p. 76.
16. Evan Shute: *Flaws in the Theory of Evolution*, Craig Press, Nutley, N. J., 4th printing, 1969, p. 3.
17. Julian Huxley: *Evolution in Action*, p. 48.
18. *Biology: a Search for Order in Complexity*, Zondervan Publishing House, Grand Rapids, Mich., 2nd printing, 1971; p. 402; editors: John N. Moore & Harold Slusher.
19. *Within That City*, p. 78.
20. *Heredity: a Study in Science and the Bible*, St. Thomas Press, Houston, Texas, 1967.
21. Creation Research Society, 2717 Cranbrook Road, Ann Arbor, Mich., 48104.
22. Preface to *Biology: a Search for Order in Complexity*.
23. *The Fossil Record*, The Geological Society, London, 1967.
24. *Implications of Evolution*, Pergamon Press, 1965.
25. *Science and Creation*, Creation-Science Research Center, San Diego, Ca. 92116, 1971.

26. *The Origin and Early History of Man* (paperback), John English & Company, Ireland, 1968. Available at St. Paul Auxiliaries, Box 13072, Houston, Texas.
27. Preface to *Biology: a Search for Order in Complexity.*
28. Arnold Lunn: *Within That City,* p. 77.
29. *Humani Generis,* 1950, par. 5; edited by A. C. Cotter, S. J. Weston College Press, 1951.
30. Karl Marx - Friedrich Engels: *Briefwecksel,* Vol. 2 (1854-60), p. 548. An Exchange of Letters.
31. "Satan's Pincer's Attack" in *Fatima International,* April 16, 1974.
32. *The Origin and Early History of Man,* Chapter 3, p. 47.
33. *The Cruise of the Nona,* Houghton Mifflin Company, Boston and New York, 1925, p. 161.
34. Preface to a re-edition of Darwin's *Origin of Species,* Everyman's Library, 1925; Dent. 1963.
35. Dewar so quotes Lemoine in *The Transformist Illusion,* 1957. Cf. "Evolution: a Dissolving Fantasy" by Fr. Albert J. Herbert, S. M.: *The Wanderer,* February 24, 1972.
36. *From Anathema to Dialogue,* Herder & Herder, N. Y., 1966, p. 54. See also: Msgr. Leo S. Schumacher: *The Truth about Teilhard* (paperback), Twin Circle Publishing Company, N. Y., 1968; Dietrich von Hildebrand: *Trojan Horse in the City of God,* appendix, pp. 227-253, Franciscan Herald Press, Chicago, Ill., 1967; Roger Garaudy: *Le Pere Teilhard, le concile et les marxistes,* Europe, No. 431-32, 1965.
37. *Religion, Language and Truth,* p. 17.
38. *The Foundations of Belief,* p. 470.

As for the title, it is a quotation from the great French scientist, Jean Rostand who called evolutionism precisely that. Similarly Ed Blick, the American nuclear expert, dismisses evolutionism as "a scientific fairy tale."

13.
Angels in the Universe

EDITH MYERS back in 1968 wrote a critique under the provocative title of "Funny Catechisms." It did seem perversely humorous to her (and I hope to her readers) that these textbooks, advertised as studies in Christian doctrine, contained little or no straight doctrine. For example, high school students with the *Bible Catechism* in their hands were duly informed why we humans are here on earth. "As co-workers with God," they would read, "we are supposed to take part in the great process of evolution." I suppose that this is supposed to mean that we are all to get behind God and help push the world onward toward perfection. The reader is further enlightened: "To sin means to refuse to be part of all this."

Edith Myers, seeing for herself that the unproved hypothesis of evolution only too often dictated what went in and what stayed out of these manuals, had a hard time to find any angels in them; and when she did, she had a harder time to recognize them as genuine. Obviously, even the good ones are a dreadful embarrassment to that type of evolutionist who is equally an earth-bound humanist. First of all, created on the instant and already at that instant fully evolved, they do not fit into the evolutionary scheme of things. No need of processing there! Moreover, to explain them ever so briefly would still have to include some reference to the heaven they enjoy and want us to enjoy with them eternally. And that simply would not do, it contradicts the fond belief that our world is even now in the process of becoming a heaven of its own, a heaven on earth. So away with the supernatural! Away with that other world of the angels! Let them keep their heaven to themselves! "Paradise at the end of man's evolution" shall be our destiny, whatever Father Robert Francoeur understands by that, for Edith Myers in her critique does not say. After all, her task is not to explain the vapidities which are not hers, but to present them, which she does — not without a touch of mischief.

Her irony reaches its summit when she reports from this or that teacher's manual: how the demythologists choose to get around the difficulty of unwanted spirits from heaven in the Catholic catechism. Let the teacher, they urge, ignore the intruders insofar as possible. "In telling the story of the annunciation," for instance, let the teacher take care "not to stress the role of the angel." Naturally it would not be a story of the annunciation without the angel who did the announcing: but, in relaying it to pupils, make out as if he were not there and said nothing.

How do you like that for backing off from the truth? How do you like that for showing Archangel Gabriel the cold shoulder, the contemptuous and fatuous snub? At that, it is not the worst snub of its kind. For the advice "not to stress" does grant the teacher a reluctant permission to speak of the angel in an uninterested and uninteresting tone of voice.

The distinction of supplying us with the classic sample of all such catechetical evasions belongs to *Joy* magazine in its December 14, 1969 issue. In the Christmas story for children, telling them of the closed inn and what happened outside Bethlehem, it has this to offer: "Jesus was born in the quiet cave. Mary and Joseph told no one. But someone,

Angels in the Universe

though, told some shepherds to come to see Jesus." Think of that. St. Luke's "angel of the Lord" is reduced to an undistinguishable *someone*. And to be sure, the heavenly choir suddenly there in the sky with him to sing down into the world the first Christmas carol — to be sure, not to overdo the supernatural, this triumphant display of angels and their *Gloria* just had to be omitted from the account.

Paraphrasing and quoting from the defective material while restraining her comment, Edith Myers got off a masterpiece of irony in low key. This was back in 1968. "Funny Catechisms" which appeared in *The Priest* magazine in June of that year now has its sequel from the same gifted pen. The follow-up article, under the title of "Demythologized Catechetics," is to be found in the October 1981 issue of the *Homiletic & Pastoral Review*. During the long interval between the articles the Holy See had been urging a purification of the tainted texts. To what avail? Most of the guilty ones in error then, still are. Their falsifications Edith Myers points out in detail.

Have a look at some of the absurdities. This, for a start: "The Mass is a dinner at which Revolutionaries gather in the presence of their Leader to celebrate what has been accomplished and to commit themselves to the completion of what has begun." And this: "Science has exploded the myth of some other part in the universe where one might go to find that other place called *paradise*." And this, of Jesus: "He brought God out of the distant heaven, out of the uncertain future of an afterlife, and put him in men's hearts." No, it is not a misprint. "The uncertain future of an afterlife" is what the catechist means to say. After more and more and more of like shockers, Edith Myers has abundant reason to blame demythologized catechetics for the fact that the young "are leaving the Church — not because they reject its teachings but because they *know nothing about* its teachings."

The mass of evidence shows that the predominant error in the texts under review is their evolutionary fixation that, "if God's world is on the way to or in the process of its own perfection," then who needs to look elsewhere for heaven? Hence, indeed, the desperate attempt to treat the inhabitants of eternity as irrelevant to the needs of this world. Typical of which, one catechist of some renown pussyfoots around a dogma of the Faith in a hope against hope that it may be an open question after all. Here follow his words, none too neatly expressed: "Perhaps Scripture simply presupposes angels and devils as part of the biblical milieu, rather than directly affirming their actual existence as part of God's Revelation." Immediately following so desperate a proposal comes another: "Nor does the existence of angels and devils seem to be part of the strictly dogmatic teachings of the Church."

Apparently the priest who authored the *Christ Among Us* catechetical series never learnt that the Fourth Lateran Council, the Second Council of Lyons, the Council of Florence, the Council of Trent all had said what the First Vatican Council confirmed in these words: "God by his infinite power created from the beginning of time both the spiritual and the corporeal creature, namely, the angelic and the mundane, and afterwards the human, a kind of intermediate creature composed of body and soul." And as to whether Satan exists or not, while Father Anthony Wilhelm thinks it may remain an open question, the Council of Braga under Pope John III sharply disagrees. It warns in its 7th denunciation: "If anyone says that the devil was not first a good angel made by God, . . . let him be anathema."

Father Wilhelm, who has since defected from the priesthood, could have consulted Pope Paul's *Credo of the People of God* to see that the official Church still believes in angels, good and bad. When offering Mass in those years of his catechetical career, did this liberal theologian think that the Liturgy in its repeated acknowledgment of the angels was but playing a game? That he knew nothing of the General Catechetical Directory, sanctioned by Pope Paul, and then

Angels in the Universe

issued by Cardinal Wright as far back as April 11, 1971, would be hard to believe. That he could not have cared less for its insistence on Catholic dogma in a Catholic catechism, one would prefer not to believe.

The late John Cardinal Wright, in diagnosing the organized mania to eliminate angels from the human mind, went to the root of the madness. He saw through the symptom. "The denial of the angels," he wrote in *L'Osservatore Romano*, "has become a sign of rejection of the whole spiritual order, a symptom of doubt about the life of the world to come." There, in that article of July 6, 1972, you have the insanity exposed for what it is: a modernistic dogma that this world on earth is man's be-all and end-all. So that settles it. Don't allow the angels to remind you of a better world. Ignore them. Deny them. Make out as if *they are not*.

But they are. And not only do the angels of heaven exist, which the Bible says they do; they move unseen through our visible world, which the Bible also and often says they do. What a refreshment it is, after reading catechetical manuals without angels, to see them on the wing in the great tomes of traditional scholarship. Our jets cannot compare.

Edmund Fuller, who does not customarily indulge in flippancy, nevertheless did, for once, in his review of *A Dictionary of Angels*.[1] It was uncharacteristic of him. It was even an understandable deviation from the judicious tenor of his style. But it occurred.

What provoked the gibe was St. Augustine's proposal in his *Eighty-Three Questions* that "every visible thing is put under the charge of an angel."[2]

The reviewer saw fit to say of the quoted theologian, by way of exposing his hypothesis as an absurdity, that he "had some bad counsel in his day." But is it so bad to have heeded the high-minded reasonings of such an outstanding Father of the Church as St. Ambrose? Did not Pope Gregory I and most of the Fathers, both of the East and the West, draw the same conclusion? And before them, did not the ancient exegetes of the Torah?

St. Thomas cites the hypothesis in his *Summa Theologica* in order to agree with it. "St. Gregory says," says the angelic doctor, "that in this visible world nothing occurs without the agency of invisible creatures."[3] Origen himself did not outwrite Aquinas in their mutual contention that Scripture convincingly implies, if it does not openly state, the delegated power of the angels to run the universe: to carry out for God the laws of nature and, in whatever emergency he so wills, to interrupt those laws. One might think from the journalistic snub that St. Augustine kept no respectable company in his view of the universe.

St. Jerome, it is true, was not of that company. He preferred to think inanimate creation perfectly able, by its inherent power from the Omnipotent, to operate on its own.[4] Why must it have help from the angels? But that begs the real question. To be sure, Providence could have endowed nature with the self-ability to function without extraneous aid; the point is, did he? An emphatic *No, he did not* lies implicitly in the assertion of St. Augustine: "The angels manage natural things, as the natural order requires, according to the will of him to whom all is subject."[5]

Johannes Kepler, as far as the planets are concerned, agrees. Whether the great astronomer believed with the great theologian in the liability of inanimate material to lapse or err, he did not say. But he did feel, as he studied the unfailing harmony in the complicated traffic of the spheres, that they were propelled by spiritual intelligences. They are, he concluded, "pushed around by angels." Coming from the founder of physical astronomy who evaluated the laws of planetary motion, that carries weight.[6]

Kepler knew as well as St. Jerome that God could have created the sun and stars and all lesser forms of sheer matter without the need of intermediaries to conduct their activities. But did he? He certainly does not will babies into the world,

Angels in the Universe

ready-made, which the Almighty could do. He lets their parents produce them. Does he likewise let angels operate his universe?

Even a former atheist, an eminent nuclear physicist, thinks he might. Dr. Boris P. Dotsenko, now a converted Christian, would find neither Kepler's nor Augustine's statement at all preposterous. He made one of his own which, if not directly assertive of an angelic engineering of the universe, allows it. This former ingrained communist, the head of nuclear research in Kiev Uuniversity, learned his lesson from the laboratory. He learned it from the scientific law of entropy, which awakened him to the fallacy of materialism, so that he could no longer with conviction deny the spiritual world. He defected to the West, from the Soviet espionage service no less.

In Canada early in 1973 he issued his statement to the press. According to the law of entropy, he insists, "all the material world should have turned into a cloud of chaotic dust a long, long time ago," since the particles that form its many bodies "have a tendency to run wild." Why do they not? "I thought about this," Dr. Dotsenko concludes, "and it dawned upon me that the world is being held in existence by a non-material power that is capable of overruling the destructive entropy."[7]

The great Aristotle, who in his philosophy reasoned out the necessity for an infinitely transcendent and eternal Creator of whatever exists, also favored the idea of a creature superior to man: and that in Catholic theology would be the angel. His argument makes sense. The human mind, while it has learnt much about the material world, cannot hope to grasp all that remains to be known. The struggle of science to add to its discoveries by having time and again to discard its theories for better ones indicates thereby its liability to error and even its inaccessibility to the innermost secrets of nature. Astronomy does not come near to having and has no assurance of ever having the complete count of the stars.

Therefore, the argument continues, if God created the vast universe to show off his wisdom and power and grandeur, and since man lacks the necessary intelligence for a comprehensive appreciation, why should there not be a higher than human creature who did have the necessary intelligence? Nor did the great sage of Greece give this higher than human creature merely the role of appreciating. He put the bodiless spirit to work, running the universe for the Creator.

Curiosity raises a question here. How would Mr. Fuller, who acknowledges the angels as God's ministers of grace, go about disproving the possibility of their being the providential agents behind the operation of nature's laws as well? Surely not from the Bible. Of the Creator the inspired text says that he "makes his angels winds and his servants flames of fire." Scripture often uses the figure of speech known as metonymy, which in this case identifies God's spiritual agents with the physical effects they produce.[8]

Their power over nature has an impressive record. An angel kept a shipwrecked St. Paul from drowning by not letting the turbulent waters sink the boat.[9] An angel prevented the fire from so much as touching the three youths in the raging furnace.[10] An angel restrained the lions in the den from harming Daniel.[11] The angel, who would roll back the boulder from Christ's sepulchre, announced his flight to earth by having it quake.[12] There seemed to be nothing of physics, or of chemistry, or of anatomy, that the angels of Scripture did not know. An angel by just touching Jacob's thigh threw it out of joint.[13] One angel after another, sometimes more than one, even "a company of destroying angels," could bend the laws of nature to their purpose of wreaking God's vengeance on the guilty.[14] Thus of a sudden in Israel, from the northernmost city of Dan to the southern extremity of Canaan, seventy thousand died of pestilence and when the Lord "said to the angel who was working destruction among the people, 'It is enough, stay your hand,' " the angel did. And the pestilence was gone.[15]

Angels in the Universe

It is not in the least a doctrine of faith that the angels have been given the physical governance of the universe. However, in the words of Paul Hallett, "it is a legitimate and a fascinating hypothesis."[16] Nor does it run counter to science which has no way of either proving or disproving it; which for that matter remains equally in the dark as to how the invisible soul acts on the human body. But that his mind and will do motivate a man's deeds, who may doubt? Paul Claudel of the French Academy believed in "the action of the angels on material things," comparing their action to the influence of a melody's *sentiment* upon the composer and then upon the playing instruments and finally upon the dancers who move to its rhythm.[17] Cardinal Wright with his sharp appreciation of a fellow dignitary writes that "Newman finds the angels unseen everywhere in nature, lurking and in operation within and throughout all the physical universe on its every level."[18]

That is true. The vicar of St. Mary's at Oxford did not confine the power of the angels over nature to the functions and traffic of the stars. Kepler may have been satisfied with so restrictive a belief. Dr. Newman in his pulpit was not. As much as Ambrose, Augustine, Gregory the Great, Origen and too many others to be given mention, he not only had the angels in control of astronomy but added to their dominion any minutest particle of the material world.

We see men, he says, "move, speak and act, and we know that all we see takes place in consequence of their will, because they have a spirit within them, though we do not see it. But why do rivers flow? Why does rain fall? Why does the sun warm us? And the wind, why does it blow?" The fluency of the argument pauses momentarily to explain against any possible misunderstanding, that the self-sufficient Creator requires no agents to carry out his magnificent designs in the universe. But, the argument resumes, what is the fact? "Now here Scripture interposes, and seems to tell us, that all this wonderful harmony is the work of angels."[19]

The theme moves fluently on. Now wouldn't it be embarrassing to a scientific materialst "when examining a flower, or a herb, or a pebble, or a ray of light, which he treats as something so beneath him in the scale of existence," if he "suddenly discovered that he was in the presence of some powerful being who was hidden behind the visible things he was inspecting?"[20] Well, that was the supposition the speaker in the pulpit presented to his audience. And they could not but know from the whole tenor of his sermon that such a discovery, while it must exceed his fondest expectations, could not come upon him as a surprise. As Cardinal Wright has said, with the eyes of faith Newman habitually saw through the apparent into the angelic world.

Thirty years later in his *Apologia* Father Newman quotes the same sermon, *The Powers of Nature,* in order to explain anew that he still considered those influencing powers to be the angels. He was not dreaming. A multiplicity of vivid suggestions from the Bible, if not direct statements, had put and fastened the idea in his head. The author of the *Apologia* then ventures the opinion that all this implicit supposition of Holy Writ might well graduate in due time to an explicit dogma from the Church. He tells why: "The visible world still remains without its divine interpretation." Pantheism, as an explanation of its supernal wonderfulness, is not the answer. It is rank heresy.

"I viewed them," the religious autobiographer sums up his belief in the angels, "not only as the ministers employed by the Creator in the Jewish and Christian dispensations as we find on the face of Scripture, but as carrying out, as Scripture also implies, the Economy of the Visible World."[21] With his favorite Fathers of the Church he was convinced that, behind the phenomena of the natural world, such as motion, light, sentient life, inanimate matter, abides the hidden domain of superior creatures who cause the phenomena. An English poet of the same conviction sets it to verse:

The angels keep their ancient places;

Angels in the Universe

Turn but a stone and start a wing![22]

Nothing better reveals the angels' power over matter than their ability to assemble for their own use a human body, bringing together its component parts after finding the particles wherever they can, and then in that bodily shape appearing to whomever God has chosen for the honor. The angel Gabriel looked like a man to the prophet Daniel, however resplendent, and with adaptable ease spoke as man to man in the latter's native language.[23] St. Teresa of Avila saw as well as felt an embodied seraph pierce her heart with a lance. She went deeper into ecstasy from this mystical wound of love, much as St. Francis had done under similar circumstances on Mount Alverna. The wound did not heal. It remains discernible in her incorrupt heart, after four centuries, to certify the event. That wounded heart, kept on display in a glass case, has been seen by thousands of tourists to the Carmelite convent in Avila.

The angels in all their known apparitions are never at a loss what to do in our world. Its materiality does not mystify them. They feel at home with it. They behave as if they are its masters. If they should need a lance, as Teresa's particular angel did, they will suddenly have one in hand. If they desire for their purpose a staff in hand, as did the angel who conversed with Gideon under the oak tree, it somehow materializes.[24] And in whatever environment they come they understand their way about: it holds no secrets from them. The angel who awakened Catherine Labouré from her sleep on the night of July 18, 1830, knew just where her convent was in Paris and just what alcove to approach in that novitiate dormitory of the convent.

The novice did not have to direct him. He directed her. The radiant guide in the disguise of a young boy led the saint into the chapel on a lower floor, knowing exactly where it was, and into the sanctuary toward an empty chair — when presently it wasn't empty. For the two hours that Sister Catherine knelt at that chair, resting her arms on the lap of heaven's queen, listening to her maternal instructions and replying and never feeling uncomfortable on her knees for the joy of being there, the angel stood by. He did not interrupt. He let the two women talk it out in the presence of the Blessed Sacrament, minding his business, which was to wait until they had done. Then he escorted the novice back out of the chapel and up the stairs to the dormitory and to her curtain-enclosed cot. He understood the errand he had been sent to perform and with courtesy but without fuss did it — and vanished.

We speak of this world as ours. But as his creation it is God's, and his angels roam it. Not that their sphere of activity is illimitable; only God enjoys ubiquity; but within their widespread range of endeavor they can rely on a resource of energy, of knowledge and an agility which baffles the imagination. The weakest angel could outfight an army, the least intelligent outwit a university, the slowest outspeed the velocity of light which travels a mere 186,000 miles a second. It is a feature of their astonishing endowment that, in attending to their interests on earth, these spirits of heaven do not abandon their eternal preoccupation. Raphael made that clear to his earthly charge when they walked together and talked together all the while the angel was enjoying the Beatific Vision.[25] Another has told us, too. "Their angels," is what Jesus said of the children's dedicated guardians, "always behold the face of my Father who is in heaven."[26]

Where heaven is the angels are, who do not on that account neglect their ministrations to the material world. A school of theologians is therefore inclined to think that the invisible domain of the blessed may underlie and overlie and enclose the visible universe, of which the earth since the Annunciation is no insignificant planet. They could be right. We do not know from divine revelation. That heaven *is,* not *where* it is, constitutes the article of faith. Newman, cherishing that article of faith, yet favored the same location for both worlds. In his veritable panegyric on *the invisible world*

Angels in the Universe

he says, "It is among us and around us."[27] In another of his earlier sermons he asserts: "Heaven at present is out of sight, but in due time, as snow melts and discovers what it lay upon, so will this visible creation fade away before the greater splendors which are behind it, and on which it depends."[28]

The material world, as we now know it, is of truth to undergo a dreadful disappearance. We have the truth from an unimpeachable source: "There will be signs in sun and moon and stars, and upon the earth distress of nations in perplexity at the roaring of the sea and the waves, men fainting with fear and with foreboding of what is coming on the world; for the powers of the heavens will be shaken."[29] Having heard that prediction in person from his Lord, St. Peter relates in further detail: "The day of the Lord will come like a thief, and then the heavens will pass away with a loud noise, and the elements will be dissolved with fire, and the earth and the works that are upon it will be burned up."[30] The most obdurate atheist should find the prophecy none too difficult to accept when he cannot but know of the hidden reserves of nuclear bombs and weapons that could prove quite capable of carrying it out insofar as it involves the earth. "The earth shall be utterly despoiled, for the Lord has spoken this word." announces the prophet Isaiah, and in a consequent passage, "the heavens shall vanish like smoke."[31]

It will be the depravity of mankind under the domination of Antichrist that is to provoke such vengeance on the world. Nor need we hesitate to believe, since Scripture has abundantly prepared us for the belief, that the angels as servants of God's justice will take part in the action to stir the elements to a fury beyond the puny destruction which vice-ridden humanity will have let loose upon itself. Two of God's angels certainly demolished Sodom. We have their word for it, and no angel of heaven has ever been caught in a lie because he never tells one. "We are about to destroy this place," they forewarn Lot, "because the outcry against its people has become great before the Lord, and the Lord has sent us to destroy it."[32] The two of them did. The rain of brimstone and fire upon the city may have erupted from a volcano, as the commentators commonly think, but it was the angels who agitated the eruption.

The day of reckoning, when "the Son of Man comes in his glory, and all the angels with him," will terminate the long reign of evil on earth.[33] Satan will have done his worst, but now a look of command from the triumphant Christ will force him to the confines of hell, which never again can he leave. It will be his additional frustration to see the world he seduced only destroyed to be renewed. It will be transformed to an immortal grandeur, of which its present beauties are but a suggestion.

The very voices that have predicted the world's end predict the renewal. The prophet Isaiah, having seen the heavens disappear like smoke, then quotes the Lord as saying: "The new heavens and the new earth which I will make shall remain before me."[34] The prince of the apostles, having foretold the world's destruction by fire, then remembers from Jesus the most reassuring of words and writes that "according to his promise we wait for new heavens and a new earth in which righteousness dwells."[35] Conveniently the apostle John puts the double prophecy into a single sentence. Of his vision, in which the firmament vanishes with the earth, he reports: "Then I saw a new heaven and a new earth; for the first heaven and the first earth had passed away."[36]

In this transformation of the demolished into a lasting and more glorious cosmos, Thomas Aquinas has reasoned that the angels will again be active.[37] It is not animism, which as a heresy the saint abhors. No, these blessed spirits are not at all the indwelling souls of the inanimate objects of their influence. They are distinctly themselves, the highest of creatures, with the commission from Providence to operate his universe. As such, with evil now eternally confined to hell, they will find no hindrance in working to retain an unbroken harmony in the new creation and to maintain from the slightest touch of deterioration its superior magnificence. The angelic doctor, to support the idea of its greater splendor than that of the present world, quotes Isaiah: "Moreover the light of the moon will be as the light of the sun, and the light of the sun will be sevenfold."[38]

The English pen that has written so well along the same lines to enrich theology with its treatment of the spiritual universe deserves a final quoting. But there arises a dilemma between two equally good possibilities. It is somewhat the dilemma of the fictitious mule who starved to death because the beast, standing between two equally tempting bales of hay, could not decide which way to turn. Let there be no such nonsense here. Let both statements be promptly chosen.

"All that we see," says Newman in the first, "is destined one day to burst forth into a heavenly bloom and be transfigured into immortal glory."[39] In the second the idea remains under a different phrasing, though not altogether different. The meticulous stylist didn't seem to mind repeating himself on a subject which held for him an abiding charm. The key words return: "This earth, which now buds forth in leaves and blossoms, will one day burst forth into a new world of light and glory" — a glory, the author goes on to say, alive with active angels.[40]

They are here now, already present to the world before its glorious transmutation, swarms of them, coming and going, doing their assignments from the Most High. Only, we do not see these gorgeous carriers of grace who see us. They hear the liturgical call to them from choirs of chanters on earth: "Praise the Lord from the heavens, praise him in the heights! Praise him, all his angels!"[41] It cannot but be a superfluous call since they have been doing that from the moment of their creation.

Do they really run the universe? The Church leaves it

an open issue, which Cardinal Newman felt she would in due time affirmatively close. But already a fair number of her greatest theologians, not a few of her mystics, practically all of the Fathers, could in their day with so much sharper meaning address the sun and moon, the shining stars, the sailing clouds, seas and rivers, mountains and hills, fruit trees and cedars, frost and snow and ice, and the rest of the inanimate items of Psalm 148 and the Canticle from *Daniel*, because they knew their apostrophe was not a mere show of rhetoric and nothing more.

Would that St. Augustine were back on earth! If only long enough to refute with his keen insight into error the Teilharian pantheism which has befuddled the modern mind. That can be no true explanation of the universe which identifies and equalizes its Creator with the created. He is, and has been from eternity what he will forever remain, Absolute Being. Nothing coexisted with his Triune Majesty from the beginning, who had no beginning. If the universe seems too complicated a harmony of activities to operate without intelligence, there is no need to violate the truth. Simply believe with St. Jerome that inanimate nature does what God gave it the power to do autonomously. Or accept the patristic alternative.

The angels could do it.

* * *

Notes

1. *The Wall Street Journal*, April 2, 1971.
2. *De diversis questionibus octoginta tribus.*
3. *Summa Theologica*, Pars Prima, q. 110, a, 1.
4. On Habacuc I, 14.
5. *De Genesi ad litteram* VIII, 24, 45.
6. *A Dictionary of Angels* by Gustav Davidson, Introduction XX, The Free Press, N.Y.
7. *Christian Crusade Weekly*, Feb. 4, 1973 & *The Fatima International*, Mar. 13, 1973.

Angels in the Universe

8. Hebrews 1:7.
9. Acts 27:18-24.
10. Daniel 3:26-27.
11. Daniel 6:22.
12. Matthew 28:2.
13. Genesis 32:25.
14. Psalm 78 (77):49.
15. 2 Samuel 24:15-16.
16. "Our Friends the Angels," *The Register*, Oct. 1, 1967.
17. Claudel: *Présence et Prophétie*.
18. "Some Reflections on the Angels," *Homiletic & Pastoral Review*, June, 1973.
19. *Parochial and Plain Sermons*, Vol. 2, "The Powers of Nature."
20. *Ibid.*
21. *Apologia Pro Vita Sua*, Chapter I, "My Religious Opinions to the Year 1833," Longmans, Green and Company.
22. Francis Thompson: "The Kingdom of God."
23. Daniel 9:21; 10:5.
24. Judges 6:19-21.
25. Tobit 5:4-6; 12:11-15.
26. Matthew 18:10.
27. *Parochial and Plain Sermons*, Vol. 4, "The Invisible World."
28. *Parochial and Plain Sermons*, Vol. 4, "The Greatness and Littleness of Human Life."
29. Luke 21:25-28.
30. 2 Peter 3:10.
31. Isaiah 24:3.
32. Genesis 19:13.
33. Matthew 25:31; 24:29-31.
34. Isaiah 66:22.
35. 2 Peter 3:13.
36. Revelation 21:1.
37. St. Thomas Aquinas: *de veritate*, q. 5, art. 8, ad 4.
38. Isaiah 30:26, which St. Thomas quotes in his *Summa*, IIIa Suppl. q. 91.
39. *Parochial and Plain Sermons*, Vol. 4, "The Greatness and Littleness of Human Life."
40. *Parochial and Plain Sermons*, Vol. 4, "The Invisible World."
41. Psalm 148.

14.
Satan Educates a Teacher

IT will always read like a nightmare of unreality. Yet believe it we must. It happened. Just when the American news media were discovering the Devil in the late 1960's and featuring him thereafter, the more fashionable catechisms for Catholic schools had apparently lost all knowledge of the damned old troublemaker. The cover of the now defunct but then popular *Look* magazine, under the date of August 24, 1971, carried the picture of a self-acknowledged high priest of Satan. To rate such attention, Anton La Vey had to be very much in the news. More newsworthy still, Satan himself made the cover of *Time,* June 19, 1972, as an ugly, black-hooded somebody, whose sinister face looked more animal than human. Lest his identity be mistaken, there stood beneath the portrayal the clear-cut caption: Satan Returns. *Newsweek,* less than a year earlier, July 19, 1971, had run a feature article under the title of "Satanism: Rosemary's Babies."

It was a period when the Devil had come out of hiding and films like *Rosemary's Baby* acknowledged him. Michael Warneke, a former diabolist with a congregation of 1,500 disciples in southern California, found a ready audience from coast to coast for his lurid confession. And what did he confess? Such tidbits of cruelty as breaking the fingers of a kidnapped young woman until she yielded to the ritualistic orgy he was conducting in honor of Satan. Another devotee of the arch fiend was reported far and wide to have slaughtered a social worker near Yellowstone Park, ripping open her body and cutting out the heart which he ate while it was still warm. At the time of his arrest, he had in his possession as a keepsake some of her bones.

The Citadel Press in New York, a leading publisher of occult books, made a considerable profit from its *Studies in Ferocity, Witchcraft, Satan and Witchcraft*. Diabolism had become a popular demand. And yet all this while, when the the country at large was being alerted to "the evil one" of Scripture, the catechisms most widely used in Catholic schools excluded the Devil completely. Much to his infernal satisfaction, he got no mention from them. The leader of hell's angels can work to easier advantage when he is taken for a nonentity, for then his machinations are not suspect.

But he need not take pride in the snub. It was no distinction. Michael and his good angels received no mention either — along with how many other doctrines of the Faith. The Holy See tried to correct the outrage, issuing in the spring of 1971 a directory that expected Catholic dogmas to be found in Catholic catechisms. Some of our diocesan schools, if they had been using faulty ones, now changed over to faithful texts already on the market. In Buffalo the chancery insisted on this. The Confraternity of Christian Doctrine up there refused to comply. Bishop James A. McNulty promptly abolished it and replaced it with the Religious Education Office. He had the noblest of motives: "to keep our Catholic schools Catholic in doctrine, morality, virtue and good manners."[1]

But mostly the counterfeits remained in undisturbed use. I wish it were not true, yet it is: they remained. At present,

Satan Educates a Teacher

years after, with some but not nearly enough revision, they are still going strong. They have wrought untold damage, depriving God knows how many children of sound doctrine while worrying God knows how many parents and others responsible for the religious training of these children.

In the light of the following crisis, which overtook a CCD teacher, we may judge the travesty of the evasion more easily and decisively. To particularize a general calamity is to sharpen its relevancy. Nor in her disillusionment, it is only fair to add, did the personable young teacher take the initiative. Give the Devil his due. He shocked her into it.

This is what happened:

Looking up from her newspaper, she gave out nervous little cries not unlike the bleats of a lady in a restaurant when the waiter behind her has accidentally spilt a dash of ice water on her neck and she feels its cold trickle going down her back. But the teacher from the Confraternity of Christian Doctrine was sitting in no restaurant. She was sitting in a school library, reading the *New York Times,* never looking away from it without returning her fascinated gaze to the grisly report until its end.

It covered half the front page of section 2, set off by pictures of three youths involved, and, in need of further space, continued on a subsequent page. It named names. It quoted witnesses. It filled in the particulars, which ought to have come as no great shock, since the headline should have predisposed one to expect the worst. For reasons of her own, however, the CCD teacher did not expect so gruesome an outcome of the bold-faced caption: Satan Cult Death.

The headline was telling the truth. That was what the tragedy turned out to be: a death, involving both murder and suicide, just to please the Devil. The murdered youth, only a year out of high school, assisted in his own drowning. Confident that his death by a self-willed violence would in the after life qualify him to take charge of forty legions of the damned, as their captain under Satan, he started already to issue orders.

The boy had earlier driven out of Vineland to a pond in the sandy terrain of southern New Jersey, with two close friends, one eighteen, the other seventeen, and there, after performing a "satanic ritual," he ordered them to bind securely with adhesive tape his hands and feet. Thus readied to go, he invited his accomplices to push him into the water. They obliged. Watching him sink, they knew they had helped the young man to achieve an ultimate ambition in life: he drowned in Clear Pond, near Millville — for the Devil.[2]

In the school library, awaiting her turn for class in the auditorium, the Confraternity teacher folded her newspaper. She must steady herself. Her quivers of incredulity, which had shaken her dignity of person like a seizure of hiccups, were not for the children to see. It was bad enough that her fit of nerves had drawn the notice of two witnesses, who looked on from across the library's wide reading table but as complete strangers were restraining their curiosity to a polite silence. She put the *Times* down alongside her text book on the table, giving the catechism a quizzical stare as she folded her arms. Her watchers could see that the young lady was in no hurry to take it up.

She taught the lower grades from it: a catechism that makes no mention of the Devil, or original sin, yet having to say something of man's evil tendencies attributes them to nothing in particular. The once-a-week teacher, as this social worker liked to refer to herself, had accepted the evasion, enjoying an inner glow of superiority in that she was with it — the new method of omission. Her airy sense of being with it was now deflated. Never having questioned the honesty of a text which the parents of her pupils had a right to presuppose a guide in Catholic doctrine, the unwary agent in the fraud had just begun to see through it. She felt taken in. Her angered misgivings would not relent. She who had

Satan Educates a Teacher

of late not allowed the Devil a thought, could now not get him out of her mind.

There was no mistaking, from the report, his evil influence. His "Satanic Majesty" dominated the turn of events. The willing victim of the gruesome drowning, whose forename was Michael had failed to cultivate the aid of his angelic namesake; he had, instead, interested himself in witchcraft, spiritism, sorcery, demonology. His private collection of books, found by the police in the boy's room at his home, gave proof of that. The entire inquest confirmed the proof.

All the pieces of evidence fitted together. Girls from his high school, admitting an uneasiness in his presence, described the handsome youth as "eerie." His closer acquaintances, far from resenting the inquiry, glibly replied that Mike had been attending with others (as many as from 80 to 90 others) regular services to the Devil's honor. He even on occasion conducted the services. Nor did he shrink from the rubrical demands. His own favorite form of ritual sacrifice, before his suicide for the hell of it, consisted in the sadistic hilarity of shaking hamsters to death in a wooden box studded with sharp nails and then smearing their blood on his sleeves. This gave the celebrant a thrill. It pleased the Devil.

All this stayed in her mind as the Saturday-morning teacher tried to push it out. A modernist of her self-assurance, who must shortly face her class, must not let the children see it shaken, according to her own later admission. The effort, bringing to her comeliness a statuesque calm, did not last beyond half a minute. Then, in a vigorous double gesture, she unfolded her arms and picked up the provocative book, not to open it, but to give it a soft snort which struck one of her observers as comical for having emerged from the coolest-looking nose.

It was a snort of genuine resentment. Against what? She herself would supply the answer, to the principal's face, in her subsequent excoriation of a manual of Christian doctrine that lacks relevancy to Christian doctrine, that along with the Devil leaves out the Commandments and the Fall and the corresponding need of Redemption. And to what purpose? To achieve the dishonesty of a Pollyanna insipidity.

But now, briskly, the bell began to ring through the corridors. Not so briskly the CCD teacher rose to her feet. She stood, hesitant, wobbling momentarily on a pair of uncertain legs. Was she at all ready for class? With a courteous nod to her two witnesses, whose mounting curiosity had not eluded her notice, she walked to the door. Leaving the *Times* on the table, she had taken the catechism with her. And as her erect figure turned into the corridor, a final glimpse showed her lips twisted in a scowl and a resolute hand wagging the book lightly up and down as though getting up momentum to throw it — at who knows what?

Her education in diabolism, just begun, was to continue through the next months. The subject intrigued her. She had herself been taught from a catechism that knew better than to omit the supernatural world of angels, whether of heaven or of hell, and her belief in both had remained undisturbed until in recent years it suffered from the insidious propaganda of the workshops she attended. No one there had ever asked of her a denial. The lecturers only raised questions, sowed doubts in her mind, in order to leave the impression that the updated scholar of Scripture now has a more enlightened explanation of its numerous angels than to accept them as real persons. The brainwash attempt did not fail. For the Confraternity teacher, while not denying them, did relegate these holy and unholy spirits to the subconscious caverns of her mind. She became unaware of them.

The *New York Times,* of all agencies, brought the Devil sharply back into her conscious mind. Its report of his malignant influence, in a section of southern New Jersey, reactivated her faith in the prince of devils. The facts left no doubt of his ugly reality in the lives of teen-agers who, al-

Satan Educates a Teacher

legedly with the help of drugs, had converted to his cause.

She would read plenty else in her research into Satanism, books and pamphlets and encyclopedic accounts, along with additional reports from the news media. It would particularly horrify her that in San Francisco, behind the closed doors of the Church of Satan, his worshippers would take off their clothes to attend their black mass in the nude so as to participate adequately in the elaborate orgy which accompanied the ritual. For that matter, at about the same time, she went into a neighborhood theatre to see for herself a black mass in the motion picture, "Witchcraft 70." A supposed documentary, the ceremony in the most lurid of settings travesties the true Mass in remembrance of the Last Supper. There is an altar, with the usual lighted candles and a celebrant and servers. But the servers are naked girls and on the altar lies a naked woman on whose bosom, in a brazen misuse of so noble a creation, stands the chalice. The prayers chant the praises of Satan.

If in the course of her education the Satanists could no longer shock their researcher, the ingenuity of their malice did continue to surprise her. She learned from the written admissions, for example, that they much prefer to have for their celebrant of a black mass a genuine priest who has defected but nonetheless has retained his power to consecrate bread and wine into the Real Presence. For which act of treachery (need it be added?) the contemptible wretch receives his thirty pieces of silver many times over. When such a Judas Iscariot cannot be hired, there remain other ways of compounding insult with injury in this fiendish abuse of the Eucharistic Christ.

The children's religion teacher, out of many instances, would afterwards pick this one to relate. Her information she found in the writings of Father Mateo, the world-famous apostle of the Sacred Heart, who in telling of a convert of his from Satanism does not, for an obvious reason, reveal the man's name. The man, a lapsed Catholic who joined a Luciferian Lodge, made a practice of going to church to receive Holy Communion for his own sinister purpose. No sooner had he received than he would remove the Divine Wafer from his tongue to his pocket, keeping the adorable Host there until he could deliver what he admitted to be "the actual Christ" to this or that diabolist group for use at their black mass. The man had not lost his faith; he perverted it, still believing in the Blessed Sacrament not out of love but hate. Doesn't the Devil himself believe?

What struck the growing authority on Satanism more and more forcibly as she delved into its subhuman perversities was its obsessive lust, its debauchery, its degrading of sex, with a flair of sadistic cruelty. She followed with an interest at high pitch the daily reports on the trial of a self-confessed diabolist from Miami, named Kim Brown. For her act of manslaughter this seventeen-year-old girl received from the court what she herself considered too light a sentence, which she forthwith attributed to "the intercession of Satan." She had deliberately stabbed to a slow death an enfeebled senior citizen who could not resist, and she took pleasure in the act and now pleasure in the memory. "I really enjoyed killing him," said the murderess without a qualm. Then to the reporters she added with the air of a boast: "I even had a fine sexual experience doing it."[3]

Later the same year the Confraternist chanced upon another bit of evidence which was, to her research in the occult, the clincher. She had gone to her hairdresser's for a routine treatment, but while waiting her turn caught sight of a magazine lying open on a table. More specifically, she caught sight of a heavily framed insert on that open page and its still heavier headline: *The Influence of Satan*. She had the magazine in her hands at once, noticing that it was an advance copy of *Esquire* for November, 1971. She wondered what it was doing in a women's salon. But there it was, in her hands, with its inserted summary of the different satanic cults in the world, identified by name, given to hellish

Satan Educates a Teacher

rituals, to sado-sodo sex magic, to torturing, mutilating, blood-drinking, killing for the sheer joy of it, psychedelic vampirism, and the rest of it. These cultists idealize evil, observing the commandments in reverse, such as "Thou Shalt Kill."

Yet the insert was only incidental to the lengthy article, into which it was placed, framed off by heavy black lines, on page 109. The article itself began on page 105 and covered in full or in part seventeen pages all told. It was a carefully written exposé of the sex maniac, the mass murderer, the "hippie satanist," Charles Manson, who ran a commune of fornicators, thieves, torturers, throat slitters, and fiendish killers. They were known as Charlie's family, a select assortment of young men and about twenty girls, who did not object to being called "Satan's slaves." The term allows of a double meaning: slaves not merely of the Devil but of his stand-in Manson as well. A misogynist, Manson would in a fit of rage beat the girls mercilessly, favoring over the others "Snake" — the community's name for Dianne Lake — who became Charlie's punching bag. The threat of having their breasts cut off intimidated the more venturesome chattels into a proper servility. They were all encouraged to promote infant sexuality, one of the mothers among them admitting without shame that she practiced fellatio on her baby son.

Enough of that! It sickens unto nausea. It does, however, serve a worthy purpose. "Charlie and the Devil," by Ed Sanders, has implicitly shown up for the escapists they really are those educationists who would disallow to children and youth a forewarning of the arch instigator of evil when they must find their way in a world so palpably suffering from his malevolence. The inhuman slaughter of Sharon Tate, with her undelivered baby, and the other victims, and then the vile desecration of their bodies, all of which the news media publicized: all this the erudite article in *Esquire* reported anew in order to get behind the ugly evidence to the diabolic motivation.

Ever more and more, pro or con, diverse groups are taking an interest in the Devil, but not the modern Catholic catechists who ignore him with other realities of the Faith. They evade or tone down certain revealed truths, like sin, like hell, like the last judgment, in favor of a humanistic mishmash that outdoes the vapidities of Little Lord Fauntleroy. Why? After the urgent directives from the Holy See to the contrary, after so much evidence of Satan in broad daylight, why? The question still puzzles a teacher who once joined the Confraterity of Christian Doctrine to instruct children from a text which gave the snub to Catholic doctrine (and after a revision has yet to do it justice).[4]

The discrepancy, while still puzzling, bothers her no more. It hasn't bothered her, in fact, from the day the *New York Times* alerted her, out of a mental sleep, to diabolism in south New Jersey and she went on from that to her immediate study of the subject. It did indeed bother her at the time — for about half an hour — when she sat in the school library a distraught teacher who felt herself a sudden impostor.

But she left the library at ease, angry, yet free of tension, her mind made up. She did not hurry, she did not go, to her class. Carrying her catechism, she strode with conviction through the corridor to the nearest incinerator shoot and tossed it in. As she heard it hurtling down to the furnace, the scowl on her face turned into a smile.

Then, according to her own account, she walked into the principal's office and resigned at once as a CCD teacher until such time as the Confraternity of Christian Doctrine stops ignoring doctrine. And she added:

"I threw my catechism down the incinerator."

"Why, in God's name why?" asked the principal badly shaken.

"That's where trash belongs."

Notes

1. *The Wanderer,* Sept. 9, 1971, carries in its entirety the bishop's pastoral letter to the diocese explaining his decision. His action received a lengthy report from the *Buffalo Courier Express.*
2. The *New York Times,* July 6, 1971.
3. Cf. *The Mindszenty Report,* July, 1972.
4. Cf. Msgr. Eugene Kevane: *Authentic Catechetics?* An analysis of the Proposed National Catholic Directory. Notre Dame Institute Press, Middleburg, Va. 22117, July, 1975. Also: *Pro Ecclesia,* January, 1979, The Catechetic Corner. Here James Likoudis writes: "In this column we have often noted the dangerous impact of the 'New Catechetics' in eroding the faith and morals of millions of Catholics mesmerized by whatever passes itself off as 'New.' The ruin caused by the 'New Catechetics' with its doctrineless Creed, its manipulative methodologies, and its permissive morality is all about us. Catechisms and other religious education materials influenced by the current wave of neo-Modernism remain, however, in extensive use in my diocese, as in many others."

15.
The Iconoclast Has Returned

THAT extreme form of naturalism which ignores Satan, when it doesn't take the trouble to deny him, would like to abolish hell from the human mind — and heaven too. It disbelieves in the eternal world of the blessed and the damned, and of course has no use for any graphic reminders of them. It therefore understands and fosters the animosity of those Christians and pagans who would destroy, if they could, all the statues or pictures of the saints and the angels, of even our divine Lord and his beloved mother. In the present naturalistic climate we need not be surprised, then, that iconoclasm has returned to fashion — and so flagrantly as to alarm most naturalists.

The iconoclast at St. Peter's in Rome, who in May of 1972 jumped the protective railing to hammer away at the Pietà, shocked the world. His senseless attack, no less than fifteen blows, broke off the graceful left forearm of the Madonna, smashed the tip of her delicate nose, chipped her left cheek and inflicted an ugly nick on her veil. Outrageous as such damage was, the vandal did worse. He shattered an eyelid of the most pathetically beautiful pair of eyes ever done in marble, annihilating at a stroke this mother's exquisite look at death in her arms, a look which holds back the tears in an ache of resignation.

Stanley Eames, who eight years earlier saw the masterpiece at New York's World Fair, spoke the mind of the civilized world in his appraisal. He said that if he had not been moved along on an insensible escalator, he would have stood his ground there at the Vatican Pavilion, transfixed, for heaven knows how long. On that mother's face, so he accounted for his enchantment, "is carved all the love and all the grief ever written on the face of a woman." And after the escalator had taken him from the finest exhibit at the fair, it occurred to him that when the other exhibits will have been forgotten "the Pietà will speak still, as long as its stone endures."

But its stone cannot endure the hammer of the iconoclast. Fortunately, the damage done was so thoroughly and meticulously repaired that it would take an expert at close range to detect where the blows had fallen. All the same, had that maniac not been stopped by an onrush of indignant witnesses, the Pietà would have been reduced to a heap of rubble which no team of technicians could possibly reassemble. Only another Michelangelo, if even he, could reproduce a perfect duplicate. The noblest chef-d'oeuvre of its kind barely escaped annihilation.

"The incomparable work has been happily restored," said Pope Paul to the crowd who had just watched him unveil the Pietà to public view once again — though now from behind a wall of bullet-proof glass fifteen-feet high.[1] This transparent barrier stands there, a necessity against the threat of a revived mania to do away with sacred images, which would also do away with churches worthy of them. Laszlo Toth, the most publicized because of his attack on a unique masterpiece, the Pietà, is but one of many. When in San Francisco its new cathedral was dedicated to the glory of

God, a hostile group (who evidently thought the Most High unworthy of the costly edifice) picketed it. They were ill disposed toward its exterior and interior magnificence.

In France, in Italy, and elsewhere, civil authorities have felt obliged to protest the indiscriminate hacking from historic shrines truckloads of crucifixes, stations of the cross, statues, mosaics, ornate tabernacles with matching candelabra, and the rest. They had in mind, from a sheer sense of patriotism, to shame Catholic pastors out of their reckless impoverishment of Europe's treasury of art.[2] An ironic interchange of values between Church and State, would you say? Call it what you will, irony it is.

Meanwhile, it must not be thought that the world's spiritual leaders bore the despoliation in silence. Pope Paul VI, for one, came out with his memorable defense of St. Peter's in Rome and of all the other magnificent churches which have in their tabernacles the adorable Sacrament. "The exterior grandeur which meets the eye is not an empty show." To think that, he said, "misses the point." Rather it is a chorus of many things singing of the supernatural, a symphony of beauty that fills the attentive soul with the wonder of holiness. For all around are statues of adoring saints and angels and their superangelic queen, stained-glass scenes from the life of Jesus, paintings that try as best they can to depict to our fallen human race the transcendent glory open to its choice. The Vicar of Christ declared the whole of it an expression of faith, "not only legitimate but necessary to the nature of man" who needs such timely hints of God's infinite majesty. The exhortation ended with a warning to the faithful not to take false scandal from the costly architecture and furnishings of churches which are but doing honor to the Real Presence.

These sentiments were obviously not shared by the then Archbishop of Venice who urged his priests to sell the art treasures within their churches and hand over the money to the poor. Heedless of the papal instruction, he did not seem to realize that his campaign for the poor was really doing the poor a disservice. It was depriving them of those reminders in their familiar shrines of a better world beyond time awaiting their homecoming: reminders for which they hunger with a greater need than for bread. As Father Edward P. Atzert with singular insight remarked at the time, "It could very well be that the poor of some Venetian village, after they have eaten their pot of beans, will be hungry again and spiritually hungrier still for what was taken away. Then, as they trudge along the road to their denuded church, there will pass by one of the archbishop's subjects driving the family's second car, a Lancia, to her summer villa where she will serve expresso and a dolce out of the lovely ciborium she got at the church auction."[3]

Surely the poor made up the majority of the rioters who swarmed as unarmed crusaders into the streets of Constantinople in 726. What provoked their uprising? To begin at the beginning, Bishop Xenaeas of Hierapolis, a Nestorian who considered Christ the Incarnate Son of God a merely human person, had incited Emperor Leo III to order his soldiers to go into churches, not to pray, but to rip down icons and shatter statues and let no "idolatrous" image escape destruction. They did more than invade churches. A group of the marauders climbed the very portal of the imperial palace and, from the summit of its arch, tore away a revered picture of Jesus the Savior of the world. That sacred fixture, so prominently on display through the reigns of monarch after monarch, had been the pride of Constantinople. It still was. Men and women, and children sufficiently mature to understand the malice of the act, had now taken all they intended to take inactively. Their seething resentment burst into fury. They crowded the streets, clamoring for a stop to the atrocities.

The fanatics, not satisfied to strip the churches of all religious images, went on to seize and sink into the sea as many relics of the saints as they could seize. They did not

The Iconoclast Has Returned

like the saints, and in their frenzy to kill every mention of them rejected from the Apostles Creed the doctrine of "the communion of saints." Their frenzy betrayed an especial hatred for the veneration paid to Mary the Mother of God. It damned what it called the idolatry of giving to any of Christ's images such honor as presupposes his divinity. Yet what should we expect? The leading iconoclasts showed clearly in their argument an Arian-Nestorian bias against the co-equality of the Incarnate Son with the Father.

The Paulicians, of all these wild inconoclasts, added a new dimension to the denial of Christ's divinity. They professed a Manichaean dualism: the spiritual alone commanded reverence, whereas matter was intrinsically evil, including even the adorable Body of Christ and of course icons, statues and relics. The Paulicians, who had made their presence felt in Constantinople a century before, led the other image-breakers in persecuting the faithful. Their ferocity, which had his army's backing, pleased the emperor. Bishops or pastors who resisted the madness were deposed, often exiled, some of them tortured to death. Abbot John of Monagria, refusing to trample an icon, was tied in a sack and tossed into the sea. Andrew of Crete, an apologist for images, received for his eloquence a whipping to death. Entire religious comunities suffered martyrdom.

The frustration of the faithful laity meanwhile mounted. More and more of them met violent deaths. The army had weapons; they had none. But the survivors, seeing in their churches a stark absence of icons and in their place irrelevant pictures of flowers and fruit and tropical birds, did find some relief from their frustration in humor. The records bristle with fierce jokes. It amused the devout, while saddening them, that their churches no longer looked like churches but more like floral shops, grocery stores, peacock sanctuaries.

From the start of the persecution the Patriarch of Constantinople, Germanus by name, a true shepherd to his flock, defended their protest, encouraged it, directed it. For which the emperor forced him into exile. Although his old body could be jostled about, the intrepid bishop would not yield. He availed himself of a final resource, doing what St. Athanasius and St. John Chrysostom had done as abused patriarchs in their day: he appealed the case to the Holy See. Decrying the outrage upon the churches, denouncing Leo the Iconoclast for his fanaticism, he implored Pope Gregory II to countermand the imperial edict against images.

Before the patriarch's letter arrived at the Vatican, Pope Gregory had received one from the emperor. It reeked of insolence. It demanded that His Holiness support the imperial edict; that he forthwith order all religious statues and paintings in Rome to be demolished; that he evoke an ecumenical council and have it issue a decree against "image-worship." There followed a threat. Unless the Holy Father complied, he, Emperor Leo III would ride into Rome and with his own hands break to pieces the great statue of St. Peter: the same bronze figure seated in a chair and holding the keys of the kingdom, which now graces the nave of St. Peter's Basilica.

The Holy Father did not become frightened at those demands, nor at the additional threat of exile and imprisonment if he allowed the statues in Europe to stand. As it turned out, no hammers touched them. A large supply of hammers did indeed lay ready for use in their crates, but there they stayed. Their intended users could not get into Rome. For a popular uprising repelled the emperor's invading army on the Italian peninsula while his fleet foundered in the Adriatic.

In his written reply to the emperor, Pope Gregory II defended the use of images to promote devotion; stressed the radical difference between these and idols; admitted something of a shock that a Christian monarch could not grasp the difference. An ironic humor flavored the papal reply. What would it profit Caesar to capture the Pope? It would

The Iconoclast Has Returned

not coerce the West or the East into accepting iconoclasm. It would only strengthen in the faithful their loyalty to the See of Peter.

Leo the Isaurian got the council he had demanded, though not on his terms and a good forty-five years after his death. Another than Gregory II sat in the Chair of Peter at the time of this Second Nicaean and Seventh Ecumenical Council, which reaffirmed the age-old defense of the veneration of holy images and condemned as an intolerable heresy iconoclasm. Pope Adrian I, whose two legates represented him among the assembly of some 300 bishops, enjoyed remote control over the council through them. Their signatures always came first on the finished documents and their names came first in every roll call. The Roman See, commanding a primacy of respect, received it.

The eighth and final session did not take place in Nicaea but in the imperial city of Constantinople. The shift of location, out of deference to Empress Irene, allowed her to attend the grand finale at her convenience. She affixed her signature to the canons, the anathemas, and the citations in praise of Germanus, John Damascene, George of Cyprus, the three saints historically identified with the condemnation of the savage heresy. Acting as regent for her underage son, Empress Irene made the most of her opportunity to swing the enormous power of the state away from the destructive madness of the iconoclast and back to sanity. She had seen heaps of sacred art burning. She had sickened at the reports of torture inflicted upon the devout who venerated images. She ordered the icons back into the churches, and I suppose the banana trees and onion beds and occupied bird cages out.

Actually the Church had condemned iconoclasm a century and a quarter before Nicaea II. Pope Gregory the Great, her supreme pontiff from 590 to 604, did not allow the first outbreak of the mania in his day to gather momentum. He squelched it without delay. This is what happened. Bishop

Serenus of Marseilles had ordered all the paintings in the churches of his diocese to be confiscated, which they were, and to be destroyed, all of which were not. The Holy Father intervened. "Put the paintings back," the mitered iconoclast was told in effect, "or else!" He had those of them not destroyed put back.[4]

Pope Gregory I in his famous letter to Bishop Serenus went on to explain: "Not without reason has antiquity allowed the stories of saints to be painted in holy places. We do indeed praise you for not allowing them to be adored, but blame you for breaking them. For it is one thing to adore an image; it is quite another thing to learn from the appearance of a picture what we must adore. What books are to those who read, that is what a picture is to the illiterate who look at it. In a picture even the unlearned may see what example they should follow. Those who cannot read words can nonetheless read a picture."[5] Agreeing with which, another great defender of the Faith, Arnold Lunn, has seen fit to call the stained-glass windows of a medieval shrine "the Bible of the poor."[6]

The iconoclast does not die easily. And he does not stay dead. If Pope Gregory I laid him to rest in his day and Empress Irene with the aid of an ecumenical council in hers, yet half a century after her death he revived with his usual vehemence. He emerged from his dormancy to start the familiar process over again: to destroy sacred art for as long as he could and then, as always before, suffer a setback into dormancy. The Fourth of Constantinople and Eighth Ecumenical Council was driven by his ferocity to condemn him anew.[7]

He was certainly back at his mischief in the sixteenth century, much to the loss of great architecture, as the ruins of Tintern Abbey and the vacant niches in magnificent cathedrals testify. The Reformers hacked away at carvings and pounded statues with the same ferocity as the iconoclasts of old had split icons. Were they under an influence they did

The Iconoclast Has Returned

not suspect? An expert on the subject in his research does not openly say. Emile Male is content to record the facts, such as: "In a picture of the crucifixion Christ had been torn to shreds, while with diabolic irony the figure of the bad thief had been left intact. In a reredos devoted to St. Michael, the archangel had been destroyed while the demon at his feet was spared." But why go into sickening detail? Let it simply be added that the Council of Trent, in its twenty-fifth session, reasserted the condemnation of Nicaea II and Constantinople IV.[8]

Where did the Reformers ever get the idea that the early Christians did not allow in their places of worship statues and paintings of Christ our Lord, or of his mother and other saints, or the angels? The catacombs give the lie to so strange a fallacy. If few statues have been unearthed there, wall paintings which do not take up added space abound. An album of murals from the catacombs, photographed by archaeologists, shows portrayals of Christ crowned with thorns, Christ raising Lazarus from the dead, Christ instructing the apostles. But the favorite subject in that album is the portrayal of Jesus the Good Shepherd, which outnumbers any other. The same album includes pictures of the Annunciation; and along with Mary and Archangel Gabriel both St. Peter with his keys and St. Michael with his sword are well represented. Christian art had its origin in the catacombs.

The discoveries of archaeology since the Reformation have nullified the claim that the early Christians neither had nor desired to have religious images to venerate. Even if the Reformers did not have the advantage of these later discoveries to enlighten them, they did have the contemporary records to consult — and did not. The historian Eusebius makes quite a little ado over some antique statues of Christ found at Caesarea Philippi. St. Paulinus of Nola, after buying for the churches in his city mosaics depicting scenes from the Bible, then wrote an appreciative poem about them. St. Basil in a homily on St. Barlaam wishes aloud that some artist would produce a painting of the martyr, which would do him greater justice than words. A renowned statue of the Good Shepherd, from as far back as the first quarter of the third century, now belongs to the Lateran Museum: but it was already available to the Reformers, if they had cared to look.[9]

When one reviews the history of iconoclasm, its recurrent outbreaks of hostility toward the treasures of art, one cannot but realize that it has been fostered by the misguided who deny by whatever twist of argument the divinity of our Incarnate Lord. They in particular detest angels of art adoring the Sacrament Most Holy, which to them means kneeling or bowing or praying with folded hands to mere bread. From this, however, the conclusion must not be drawn that pastors who empty their churches of statuary and paintings and expensive tabernacles have lapsed into heresy. Their motive may be nothing worse than an innocent dislike of ornament, of what they call tawdry and gaudy unnecessaries. Be that as it may, iconoclasm does have a history of tying in with heresy. Against it the Church has preached her sanity of doctrine through the ages even when her audiences have only too often suggested (is it uncharitable to be honest?) wild packs of lunatics.

The Church still remains firm under the pressure of a milder revival of image-hatred. Junk yards as well as shops are overcrowded with Holy Family statues and other hallowed castoffs. Sanctuaries where rich draperies used to hang now have on display ragged banners with such devotional scrawls as "Luv is life in a nutshell" and "Get with it, Christian" and, believe it or not, "To each their thing, that all may pull the load." The exchange, from artistic or even inartistic images of the blessed to pert slogans scribbled on burlap, could hardly be considered an advance in taste. To look around in a modernistic church, after a visit to some old cathedral, is to share the feeling of the critic whose appraisal of an exhibit of abstract paintings amounted to six words: "Would that my eyes could vomit!" Anyhow, Vatican Council II in accord with tradition has sanctioned anew the cult of images, the beautifying of God's houses of worship.[10]

Pope St. Paschal I, learning in a vision the exact whereabouts of St. Cecilia's tomb in the catacombs, went there personally to find indeed the youthful body of the martyr in a cypress coffin, incorrupt after six centuries, richly clad, lying on its side, the delicate neck still showing the ugly cut of the sword, the face turned downward on its forehead. Thinking to himself that this is the position in which the little saint had breathed her last, the Holy Father could not hold back the tears. Defiant of the reactivated iconoclasm of his day, he made sure no relic-snatchers would get their hands on this sacred body. He had it transferred to the Basilica of St. Cecilia in the Trastevere section of Rome, where it was reverently placed in a crypt.

What Pope Paschal saw through tears of holy joy at her original tomb in 822, exactly that is what Cardinal Baronius and countless other viewers beheld almost eight centuries later, in October of 1599, when the Basilica of St. Cecilia was undergoing a renovation and in the course of the work her casket was brought out of its crypt and again opened for public veneration. The body still looked after all that time perfectly intact, firm and youthful, and had the same position, just as Pope Paschal had beheld it in the catacombs. The great sculptor Maderno, while its casket remained open for weeks, did more than view the miraculous corpse. He started to do his replica of it in marble.[11]

His masterpiece is now on display to the public, so that visitors to the Roman Basilica of St. Cecilia may still see under the main altar, if not her real corpse, at least a statue of true likeness to it: the molded form of a girl in her late teens or early twenties, lying sidewise in death, the visible half of her face and neck retaining an adolescent freshness and rendered the more poignant by that unsightly gash from a sword which had meant to behead but out of pity relented. The statue, a copy of reality, must of necessity stir the sense of awe in any viewer — who is not an iconoclast. Pray God that no hammer ever touches this marble facsimile of a saint's incorrupt remains: remains now asleep in a consecrated crypt, awaiting the Resurrection.

* * *

Notes

1. Cf. *Time*, April 9, 1973.
2. Cf. André Chastel: "Mort aux retables" in *Le Monde*, Feb. 17, 1965.
3. Cf. CUF Newsletter for the New Jersey Area, June, 1976.
4. Cf. Hardouin IV, 306. Poulet-Raemers: *The History of the Catholic Church*, Vol. I, Part II, Second Period, Section I. Adrian Fortescue: The Catholic Encyclopedia: "Iconoclams" & "Images," Encyclopedia Press, Inc., New York, 1913. Ludwik Nemec: The Catholic Encyclopedia for School and Home: *"Iconoclasm,"* McGraw-Hill Book Company, 1965.
5. Ep. IX, 105. P.L. LXXVII, 1027.
6. *Within That City,* Chapter XI, Sheed & Ward, 1938.
7. Cf. Denzinger 337.
8. Cf. Denzinger 986. Emile Male, eminent French art historian: *Religious Art*, The Noonday Press, a subsidiary of Farra, Straus and Cudahy, New York, 1949.
9. Eusebius: *Hist. eccle.* VII, XVIII. St. Paulinus' Poem, P.L. LXI, 884. St. Basil: Or. in S. Barlaam, P.G. XXXI, 488-489. The Good Shepherd statue: Kraus, I, 227.
10. *Documents of Vatican II*: Liturgy, Chapter 7, "Sacred Art and Sacred Furnishings."
11. Cardinal Baronius: *Annales* ad e. 821, n. 13 seqq. Antonio Bosio, explorer of subterraneam Rome: *Historia passionis S. Caecilia,* Rome, 1600, 153 seqq. Ludwig von Pastor: *The History of the Popes,* Vol. XXIV, Chapter XII, B. Herder Book Company, St. Louis, Mo., 1933. J. P. Kirsch: The Catholic Encyclopedia: "Cecilia," Vol. III.

16.
Why Begrudge God Beautiful Churches?

THE new assistant, mounting the rectory stairs, paused at the landing to view an enormous picture hanging there on the wall.

It was a portrayal of Constantine leading a cavalry charge to victory. In the forward rush of horses, two of the riders each hold aloft a triumphant cross, the emperor himself holds a spear poised for action, while from the rear a trio of trumpeters urges on the advance. In the sky above flies along a bevy of angels, one of whom carries a drawn sword, and another, turning an alert eye on the imminent clash of armies below, points out with a determined finger the opposing commander. Whether the angelic sword or the imperial spear is to strike down the tyrant Maxentius, known to have fallen from his saddle at the Milvian Bridge into the Tiber, the picture does not decide. Its message, however, is unmistakably clear: should the badly outnumbered soldiers of Constantine need reinforcement, the angels are there to supply it.

The magnificent design, which ought to have pleased, left

its observer cold of eye. That the original of this elaborate print had been sketched by the great Raphael and executed by Giulio Romano for a Vatican fresco, even if the young assistant had been told, would not have softened the frown on his face. He knew well from his kind of reading how to react to all such exhibits of triumphalism. "Disgusting!" he said aloud, following instructions, and suggesting by his vehemence what must surely happen to the unpardonable work of art — if ever he became the pastor.

The parishioners may thank God that he wasn't. Not that it could matter to them what samples of art would go from the rectory if the new priest did become their pastor: but would he stop there? The adjoining church, after all, offered by far the richer temptations to one who regarded the haloed statue an indecent flaunt of piety and looked at stations of the cross as though they were a stench to the eye. Would such a pastor allow the noble figure of Mary, trampling the serpent of Eden, to remain the honored occupant of a sanctuary niche? Might not the niche itself, once devoid of the statue, have to be curtained over to hide its mosaic inlay of rejoicing cherubs? But then, why bother to select the likeliest of the statues or mosaic inlays to go when all of them, a general annoyance to the iconoclast, must receive from him a common ride out to the city dump?

The ceiling fresco over the sanctuary, depicting the angelic battle between Michael and Satan, would present somewhat less a difficulty. It would require no removal. An overlay of coarse paint could in easy sweeps of the brush conceal from the parishioners the colorful scene of the Prince of the heavenly host tumbling the hideous Devil into the flames of hell. The concealment would nicely contribute to the updated objective: to keep the praying mind a blank, suggesting to it no ideas, rescuing it from all the visual aids to piety.

The craze for substituting sacred art with none at all has for its apologists a new breed of iconoclasts who would

Why Begrudge God Beautiful Churches?

justify it from Scripture, yet cannot. Nor does it seem to bother their consciences, or perhaps they do not know, that their craze has been condemned by Councils: Nicaea II, Constantinople IV and Trent. For that matter, Vatican II which they misinterpret at random has this to say: "The practice of placing sacred images in church so that they may be venerated by the faithful is to be maintained."[1]

But it must not be supposed that only the young cherish a contempt for the artistic embellishment of churches. At the dedication of his own made-to-order church, a pastor old enough to know better delivered the homily (which is what the program called it). He explained the building, its emptiness of design, the severity of its barren achievement. He boasted of its not having a single piece of statuary and certainly no stained-glass windows, nor even an ornate tabernacle, "because," he quoted from his script, "any exhibition of that kind disregards the Bible's strict demand for purity of devotion which must always come from the heart and not from external objects."

Did this master of the non sequitur believe what he was saying? Could he have believed his inference from a premise not there? Did he really mean to infer that a devout look at a finely wrought pietà could only leave the heart unmoved because what the eye sees, since it is an external object, cannot touch the heart? The confused speaker might as well have said that the crucifix which drew sobs from Francis of Assisi made a hypocrite of the saint. One wonders, did the unrealist who would deny to the heart its external influences ever hear of love at first sight?

One must also wonder if, in this church of his designing, the pews were allowed to keep their padded kneelers merely as a concession to custom. There was no mention by him, nor suggestion, that the building had been erected to house the Real Presence, before whom the parish should find it a privilege to kneel in prayer. The tabernacle itself stood off to a side of the sanctuary, an unadorned box of steel, lacking even the proper lustre. The whole environment lacked reverence.

To shame such pastors who in France had stripped their churches of ornament, Thomas Molnar reports, "one tabernacle was widely shown in French picture magazines as serving now as a doghouse in the new owner's garden." It was a precious tabernacle from the Middle Ages, which shared the fate of many a junk pile of equally precious retables, candelabras and statues. Urged on by outraged connoisseurs, the government from a sense of patriotism and not religion finally called a halt to this vandalism which was impoverishing the national treasury of art.[2]

But where did the pastor, who is our concern, come by his notion that Scripture requires in a church a dearth of ornament? His audience, he must have noticed from the pulpit, did not seem to believe him. Not a few of them, apparently sensing the contradiction between what he was saying and what the liturgical readings had said right before, sat squirming in their pews. When not quoting it, he did no more than paraphrase the architect's own foreword in the brochure handed out for the occasion, which the people could read for themselves. And this added another touch of uneasy humor to their discomfiture.

Whether or not the pastor had listened to the prescribed first reading from the Old Testament, the lector had given it a fine rendition. He related with sonority the action of a great moment, which the centuries had waited for, and which Solomon's now completed temple stood ready to receive with open doors. "So the priests brought the ark of the covenant of the Lord to its place, in the inner sanctuary of the house, in the most holy place, underneath the wings of the cherubim. For the cherubim," the text went on, staying with the idea to stress the propriety of it, "spread out their wings over the place of the ark."[3]

These air-borne angels, poised in meditation over the ark, were pygmies compared with the two standing guard on each

Why Begrudge God Beautiful Churches? 197

side, looking straight ahead, and having a combined wingspread as wide as the sanctuary itself. In other words, the right wing of one touched the wall while its left wing touched the right wing of the other giant whose left wing reached to the opposite wall. The two of them stood fifteen feet tall on a golden floor, themselves overlaid with gold, facing the nave as if to see to it that no unordained intruder dare enter the holy of holies through the curtain that had its own share of cherubim stitched into the rich material.[4]

The temple's many angelic statues out in its large public space, whether carved to the walls and doors and pillars or moulded in the round, all sparkled of God. Solomon considered nothing too costly to go into the enrichment of this magnificent house of God. The vestibule "he overlaid . . . on the inside with pure gold. The nave he lined with cypress, and covered it with fine gold, and made palms and chains on it. He adorned the house with settings of precious stones."[5] Nor was Solomon, in doing so, indulging a personal whim of grandeur. He was following instructions. The kind of temple he built for the Lord in Jerusalem on Mount Moriah, he proudly acknowledged at its dedication, had been the Lord's idea from as far back as the time of Moses. A higher than human architect dictated the designing and its rich embellishment.[6]

The pastor, then, who stands in his pulpit to denounce all adornment in God's houses of worship has not a shred of justification from Holy Writ. To have read with an attentive mind *Exodus, Leviticus,* the first book of *Kings,* the second book of *Chronicles,* is to know better. To recall from the Gospel the protest of Judas Iscariot that Mary Magdalene spent far too much on her ointment for Jesus when the money might have been given to the poor; to remember the Lord's quick rejection of the complaint and his warm approval of the deed; this ought to shame any propagandist for cheaper and plainer churches into an attempt to find another source for his nonsense than the Bible.[7]

Surely the homilist who makes a boast of having installed in his church the plainest of tabernacles cannot from Scripture vindicate his action. He cannot find what is not there: namely, texts in favor of stinting Almighty God of his due glorification on earth. The ark of the covenant, for which the tent and afterwards the temple were erected to afford it a home, were ordered by God himself to be built of no cheap material. Apart from the cherubs of hammered gold that were to surmount it, the ark proper enjoyed an enrichment of its own. "You shall overlay it with pure gold, within and without shall you overlay it, and you shall make upon it a molding of gold round about."` Yet the ark barely rates comparison with the tabernacle that encloses, not just tablets of the Law, but the living Presence of God's very Son. The Fathers of the Church understood the analogy for what it was worth. Why should not the pastor in question have?

A prefigurement of the tabernacle, the ark again by divine decree was to have a lamp burning before it all day and all night in recognition of God's covenant with man. But suppose we let the Lord speak for himself, to Moses: "Command the people of Israel to bring you pure oil from beaten olives for the lamp, that a light may be kept burning continually. Outside the veil of testimony, in the tent of meeting, Aaron shall keep it in order." The lampstand itself, to satisfy the divine command, had to be of pure gold." Need it be added, as a corollary, that the Blessed Sacrament merits better than a shabby sanctuary lamp?

There is an ugly tendency among the seekers of a naturalistic utopia on earth to minimize and even ignore, if not deny, the sovereignty of God in the scale of human values. It shows to an extreme in atheistic modern art, which is to be expected. But it has also been forced upon churches supposed to be Catholic, depriving them of whatever adornment made the medieval cathedral holy, disallowing all such reminders of the Most High as the spire, the sharply defined sanctuary, the worshipping statue of saint or angel, the fres-

Why Begrudge God Beautiful Churches? 199

co that speaks to the soul, however imperfectly, of the transcendent mysteries of faith. This ugly spirit of belittling his Creator to extol man stands brazenly exposed for what it is in the smart aleck taunt: that if you can't recognize Christ in some neighbor singing a Sunday hymn off key in your pew, then neither will you find Christ in "a thin slice of dried paste locked in a gilded safe beyond the barricade of a communion rail."

A church which is to have in its keeping the Blessed Sacrament, if built along the lines of a sectarian meeting hall which lacks a sanctuary and invites socializing together at prayer instead of praying together to the Eucharistic Christ for his own preeminent worth — such a misconstructed church may not show the positive impudence of that unprintable but printed blasphemy. Yet it does, by default, slight the Adorable in deference to the subordinate worshipper. It lacks balance. It misses inexcusably the priority so evident in the double commandment to love God first and foremost and then, as an overflow from this, to love one's neighbor as oneself. It certainly has missed the secret of those sturdy parishioners of the Curé of Ars who in their poverty found a wealth of satisfaction in procuring for the sanctuary of their church the rarest of flowers, the neatest of altar linens, a resplendent tabernacle, the costliest of sacred vessels. The spiritlessness, that would deny the Lord a proper show of generosity in churches that house his Real Presence, ought to learn a lesson from Palm Sunday. There were those in the crowd that day, the prototype of a sad modern breed, who recoiled from the enthusiastic outburst of faith: but the Divine Subject of the demonstration did not discourage it. He didn't think the demonstrators, in waving their branches and spreading their garments on the road and shouting their hosannas at his approach, were overdoing a good thing. Rather, he repelled the protest. "I tell you," he said aloud, above the din of the devout merrymakers, "if these were silent, the very stones would cry out."[10]

Eventually they did, in Gothic architecture. Chesterton reaches his triumphal best in telling of it. In more than one book he touches on the subject, obviously enjoying it. He glories in the sculptured jubilee of angels crowding together, wherever they can find a suitable place on the front of great shrines, either to sing ecstatically to the Most High or to vociferate their defiance at the diaoblic gargoyle. From the impulse of Christian mirth, writes Chesterton from the same impulse, "arose like a clamorous chorus the facades of the medieval cathedral, thronged with shouting faces and open mouths. The prophecy has been fulfilled: the very stones cry out."[11]

The strangest ironic twist in the argument of certain deflators of God's glory in art and architecture, which they dismiss as triumphalism, is their taking for granted that Scripture supports their fallacy. Like the iconoclasts of old, they cannot have read its books with an open mind. Brazen idols it does most emphatically condemn. The very first command of the decalogue forbids the forming of graven images of animals and whatever else for the purpose of worshipping them as gods. However, if I may repeat, the Most High who dictated that commandment also ordered the shaping of angelic images to decorate his temple. The essential difference becomes clear at a glance: the molten or embroidered cherubim are fixed in the act of adoration, which has to mean that they are there not to be adored but to acknowledge the one true God. The same applies, in later times, to the statues and pictures of the saints.

The young priest, who sneered at that painting of Constantine's victorious charge under the protection of angels, would have an impossible task explaining in his favor many a sacred text. Did not Joshua enjoy a like protection? Scripture thinks so. "When Joshua was by Jericho, he lifted up his eyes and looked," and what did he see? An angel with a drawn sword in hand. And what did the angel say? "As a commander of the army of the Lord I have now come."[12]

Why Begrudge God Beautiful Churches? 201

The artist, who painted a flight of angels as allies watching over the rush into battle of the imperial cavalry, had done no more than take his idea from the inspired record.

Since the Bible is proud of showing off heaven's angels and gloating over the fallen devils of hell, one would think that the designers of at least the churches enclosing the Real Presence would follow suit. Oh, but that would be violating a modern dogma of fashion. This nervous avoidance of the Faith in triumph, which finds its apogee in art's portrayal of St. Michael with uplifted sword, betrays a mentality that has no encouragement from Scripture whatsoever. Surely the luminous angels who crowded into the Bethlehem skies to serenade the Birth of Christ hadn't realized their triumphalism was in bad taste. They went on singing the glory of God and God's goodness to man as naturally as the sun shines: their presence resounded in the night and shone more brightly than day.[13]

Can they have been wrong? Can art in many a famous reproduction have been in error for showing them off so unashamedly triumphal? But in God's name let the inquiry be turned upon the provoker of it. Can he of such stolid taste be right, who would have us cool our fervent love of the All-Lovable, restrain our irrepressible joy in him, and empty of all beauty the churches in which he dwells among the children of men to the end of time?

As Pope Paul said, the Holy See has never forbidden to churches under its jurisdiction an architectural beauty because the Eucharistic Christ, whose homes on earth they are, deserves the best. With which, Pope John Paul must surely agree. He has with an unwavering zeal reaffirmed the replies of his predecessor to the would-be wreckers of the everlasting Faith, who have now turned their criticism upon him. And yet, *mirabile dictu,* these dissenters did find one statement from his many public utterances to praise.

It was his admission of a flaw, on the part of the ecclesiastic authorities, in their handling of the Galileo case.

Notes

1. "Constitution on the Sacred Liturgy" from *Documents of Vatican II*.
2. "Ecumenism or New Reformation" (ch. IV), Funk & Wagnalls, 1968.
3. 2 Chron. 5:7-8.
4. Ibid., 3:10-14.
5. Ibid., 3:4-5.
6. Ex. 25:1-8.
7. Jn. 12:1-8.
8. Ex. 25:11.
9. Lev. 24:1-4.
10. Lk. 19:40.
11. *Orthodoxy*, ch. VII, Dodd, Mead & Company, New York, 1908.
12. Josh. 5:13-14.
13. Lk. 2:13-14.

17.
How Wrong Was the Galileo Verdict?

At last it happened. Some of the bitterest critics within the Church all of a sudden found an utterance from Pope John Paul II to their liking. They had been blasting away at his immovable stand on celibacy for the clergy, on the impossibility of ordaining women validly for the priesthood, on the intrinsic evil of abortion. Then on November 11, 1979 the strident voices went soft with praise for a change. A widespread news release of that date quoted the Supreme Pontiff as having lauded the genius of Galileo while admitting the flaw in his condemnation.

As to the first half of that double statement, who wouldn't praise the genius of Galileo? He invented the thermometer. He took the deficient telescope of a Dutch optician, Lippershey, and made it a proficient instrument for searching the heavens. More than any other scientist, he merits the title of "father of dynamics." On the other hand, his genius could go wrong and sometimes did. He offered a proof for the earth's rotation on its axis from the daily movement of the tides, which science finds no proof at all. He ridiculed Kepler's proposition that the moon exerts an influence on the tides, which science holds in respect today. And his idea of comets, as if nothing more than atmospheric reflections like halos and rainbows, Tycho Brahe disproved. Notwithstanding these miscalculations, Galileo remained a genius whom Pope John Paul was being characteristically honest in so appraising.

In admitting the error of the Inquistion, the Holy Father was again right. The condemned, to be sure, may not be freed of blame. He charged the Bible with an untruth for saying that, to accommodate the Israelites who needed the time to rout their enemy, "the sun stood still."[1] He brazenly repeated the charge, now including other similar texts, to become a public scandal. Unfortunately, the censure took on an erroneous wording. In a laudable attempt to safeguard the inerrancy of these texts the ecclesiastical authorities made 'the mistake of interpreting them literally. Having done which, the tribunal had no alternative but to forbid Galileo from flaunting his theory as knowing better than Holy Scripture.

The Congregation of the Index in its 1616 censure allowed the defendant to hold his theory on the condition he would use it as a working hypothesis, only forbidding him to boast of its being an established certitude, which it was not.[2] Scientists and philosophers and literary lights of the day found this more than fair. They considered it a bending over backwards to oblige an upstart in their midst. They mostly disbelieved, and some of them denounced, his demand that "the sun is the center of the universe."

Tycho Brahe felt a repugnance toward it. Francis Bacon ridiculed it. Michel Montaign likewise laughed it to scorn. René Descartes in a letter to Mersenne declared it unworthy of serious attention. Blaise Pascal deemed it "wise not to sound the depths of the Copernican system" — which has to mean the Galilean as well. And Dante, for his part, beautified his warning in a much-quoted tercet from *The Divine*

How Wrong Was the Galileo Verdict?

Comedy. As for poet and critic Alessandro Tassoni, he hit the popular fancy with this test which was supposed to make nonsense of the theory: "Stand still in the middle of a room, and look at the sun through a window opening toward the south. Now, if the sun stands still and the window moves so quickly, the sun will instantly disappear from your vision." But the sun does not instantly disappear. Ergo.[3]

Nor did the contemporary scientists take to the arrogance of one who strutted about as the orginator of the idea when they knew that Galileo knew he was a Johnny-come-lately. Pythagoras had the idea first. A century and a half later Aristotle contradicted him to designate the earth and not the sun the pivot of our planetary system. Afterwards Ptolemy, adopting the Aristotelian theory, made it the acceptable working hypothesis for astronomy. So it remained until the age of Galileo.

But it was not Galileo who reintroduced the Pythagorean contralization of the sun to astronomy. It was Nicholas Copernicus, a Catholic priest, who was not surprised to find his fellow scientists hostile to the change of view. Anticipating their hostility, he had delayed publishing his monumental *Revolutions of the Heavenly Spheres.* After years of delay, yet only under the urging of Cardinal Schomberg and Bishop Tiedemann Giese did he finally publish the book, dedicating it to Pope Paul III. But the point is, Copernicus was openly teaching the theory twenty-some years before Galileo Galilei was born.

Galileo of course shares with Pythagoras and Copernicus the conviction that the earth follows a circuit around the sun, which remains fixed in the center of the planetary system. Yet he, too, hesitated to publicize his conviction. Why the hesitancy? From fear of the scientists, he has told us, not the Church. He didn't want to be hissed off the stage, is how he explained his fear of them.

From another source did he run into opposition. Martin Luther in his *Table Talk* writes of Copernicus in words that could no less easily apply to Galileo: "Men pay heed to an astrologer who contends that it is the earth that moves, and not the heavens or the firmament, the sun and the moon.... This madman would subvert the whole science of astronomy; but Scripture tells us that Joshua bade the sun and not the earth to stand still." There the Reformer falls into the same trap which caught the Holy Office unawares. He unnecessarily interprets the text *ad literam*.

A second early Reformer, Melanchthon by name, widens his denunciation to include both Copernicus and Galileo and, inferentially, all their followers. In *Principles of the Science of Physics* this "scribe of the Reformation," so called from his fluent pen, expresses Luther's displeasure in equally indiscreet language: "The eyes testify that the heavens revolve every twenty-four hours; and nevertheless some men, either from love of novelty or to parade their genius, insist that the earth moves, and that the eighth sphere and the sun do not revolve. Every true believer is obliged to accept the truth as revealed by God, and to be contented with it."

To linger upon these insufficiently known facts of the case has become a necessity from the malicious charge of hostility to science which certain of her dissidents are now imputing and restricting to the Catholic Church. It is insidious of them to quote Pope John Paul's admission of a faulty censorship without stating the leniency of the judges and with never a word about the circumstances. To his dying day Copernicus had drawn from the Holy See no protest to his theory and in 1615, a year before Galileo would use it to sneer at the Bible and thereby provoke his trial, Cardinal Bellarmine as secretary of the Holy Office remarked with admirable poise: "If ever the Copernican theory be really demonstrated, we must then be more careful in explaining those passages of the Scriptures which appear contrary to it. We must then say that we do not understand their meaning rather than declare a thing false which has been proved true."[4] Does that statement indicate the slightest opposition to science?

It reflects the traditional conviction of the Church: that between Science and the Faith there can arise no genuine conflict since Infinite Truth is the source of both. A conflict arises only from a misunderstanding on one side or the other, or both. That Galileo falsely accused the Bible of ignorance for having the sun move is alone what brought him, let it be repeated, before the ecclesiastical authorities. Had he not dragged theology into his dissertation, they would have left him unmolested. That he acted too aggressively sure of his Copernican claims without convincing his fellow scientists pretty well defines their sentiments. The infuriated astronomer retaliated by calling the latter "mental pygmies." Were they really such nitwits? Granted that the earth does the moving around and not the sun, Galileo based his argument for it on inconclusive grounds, which are now rejected. His moons of Jupiter, while overthrowing the Ptolemaic system did not win for him a monopoly on the truth. Other feasible explanations remained available.

Einsteinian relativity, to take an example, cuts Galileo's claim of an indisputable certitude for his theory down to a mere hypothesis, which is all his ecclesiastical judges had done. They allowed him to teach his system so long as he refrained from calling it the only possible solution. With which, in contrast to the carpers within the Church, Morris R. Cohen fully agrees. His book, *Studies in Philosophy and Science,* boldly asserts that the "later theory of relativity reopens the issue between Galileo and those who condemned him for saying the earth is in motion." Have a good second look at *reopens* before going on to the author's reason for having used the word. If all motion is relative, he argues, it is just as true to say that the sun moves around the earth as to say that the earth moves around the sun.

Moreover, aside from the relativity theory, astronomy now has proof that the sun does for a fact move in space and while moving in space turns on its axis, while at the same time the spinning earth follows its fixed circuit around the sun. Galileo did not know that. He insisted to his judges that Holy Scripture had to be wrong in saying "the sun stood still" because this unmistakably means that the sun had been moving, which, according to the overconfident defendant, the sun doesn't do. Modern science knows it does.

For that matter, Thomas Huxley already in the Victorian Age knew how wrongheaded Galileo could be. In a letter to St. George Jackson Mivard, a fellow biologist, he wrote: "I looked into the matter when I was in Italy and I arrived at the conclusion that the Pope and the College of Cardinals had rather the best of it." Sherwood F. Taylor goes further. To gather material for his book, *Galileo and the Freedom of Thought,* this rationalist had to do a great deal of research. His honest study of the facts, which caught his prejudice by surprise, led him to a rectory. He became a Catholic.

Galileo, summoned to Rome by the Holy See, was received cordially. He enjoyed a reasonable hospitality throughout his trial. His judges, eleven theologians from the Holy Office, first examined his *Letters on the Solar Spots* and found a statement therein "absurd and false in theology, and formally heretical, because it is expressly contrary to Sacred Scripture." The statement insisted on the immovability of the sun around which the earth did the moving while spinning on its axis, whereas Copernicus had been satisfied to propose the same as a mere theory. On March 5, 1616, the Congregation of the Index decreed a condemnation of it to the defendant's face, forbidding him to promulgate it any further as a certainty. He promised to abide by the verdict, which he did for a while and then did not.

It was a bad decision, in that it insisted upon a false interpretation of the texts under review. There were those of the Inquisition who in a flare of temper betrayed an attitude which might in all fairness be interpreted thus: even if it were true that the sun does not move, Scripture in a number of passages says it does, and that settles it. Excuse the decision, whoever will, on the grounds that it was motivated by a sincere desire to uphold the honesty of the Bible — but this cannot change its having been an easily avoidable blunder. The theologians should have known from St. Augustine and other reliable exegetes that the sacred text, using the resources of rhetoric, often departs from the literal. It often describes what is seen just as it appears to be, not necessarily as it is. "The sun rises and the sun goes down, and hastens to the place where it rises" does not jeopardize God's word. And for this reason: old Ecclesiastes, whether in his conviction a Copernican or a Ptolemaist, or neither, was speaking of a phenomenon as it looks to the eye.[5] The same may be said of the inspired writer who, in accounting for what seemed to be an exceptionally long day or what may indeed have been a miraculously long day, was simply recording the visual impression that — to delay its setting — "the sun stood still." The words *sunrise* and *sunset* remain in the dictionary because they enjoy popular usage, even in scientific journals.[6]

The decision of the court, based on faulty exegesis, did not militate against the doctrine of papal infallibility. It lacked the ratification of Pope Paul V, who would not sign the decree. He must have been disappointed with it, and there is equal reason to believe that Robert Cardinal Bellarmine was. The supreme pontiff certainly wrote these words to Cardinal di Zoller: "Holy Church had not condemned the opinion of Copernicus, nor was it condemned as heretical" when declared a fixed truth, "but only as rash." His Holiness then added: "If anyone could demonstrate it to be necessarily true, it would no longer be rash."[7] Well, in the nineteenth century, Faucolt did finally prove to the satisfaction of science the earth's double movement, on its axis and around the sun, only now to have Einsteinian relativity throw new light on the issue. What matters is, the court's unratified decision did not involve, did not compromise, did not so much as touch papal infallibility.

For having broken his pledge not to put forward his theory as the sure truth, which through the interval of sixteen years he ever more vehemently did, Galileo was called back to Rome in 1632 to face again the Inquisition. Pope Urban VIII, familiar with the defendant's polemic masterpiece, *The Essayist,* nonetheless extended to him a generous hospitality. All that once fashionable talk about the poor man's being locked into a jail cell with iron bars across the only window, and regularly brought out to undergo torture, shows the desperation of a malicious propaganda. A tribunal of ten cardinals did of course sentence him to imprisonment, but, in the way he fulfilled his sentence, a more accurate word would be *retainment.* He spent the first three weeks of it in a commodious apartment at the Vatican, with a servant. After that, to quote his Protestant biographer von Gebler, "he was allowed to use as his places of confinement the houses of friends, always comfortable, and usually luxurious."

For that matter, three of the ten who formed the tribunal would not sign the sentence. Nor would Pope Urban VIII, which left it without papal sanction. What is more, when the tempestuous scientist lay dying, he received from the Holy Father a personal blessing. Still more, when his corpse lay in state, there came from the Holy See a permit to entomb the body in Holy Cross Church, in the Florence Galileo had so much loved.[8]

Cardinal Newman, remarking in his *Apologia* that the Catholic Church has followed a policy of keeping clear of conflicts with science, then takes for his proof of that policy "the one stock argument" against it, "the constantly cited case of Galileo." He immediately comes in with his point: "Exceptio probat regulam."[9] And what a weak exception to the rule it is when neither Pope Paul V nor Pope Urban VIII finally supported the censure as worded and when scientists

How Wrong Was the Galileo Verdict?

themselves have found the defendant indefensibly brash.

Lovers of the Holy, Catholic, Apostolic Church — like Newman and most assuredly our gloriously reigning John Paul II — would see in the final refusal of the two popes to sign badly worded documents, not an accident, but the sure guidance of the Holy Spirit. Why do not the present malcontents within the same lovable Church share such favorable sentiments? Why do they not learn the facts of the Galileo case instead of spouting off their ignorance of them at the expense of the divinely founded institution they apparently do not love but will not leave? Why, indeed?

God knows the answer, whatever it is.

* * *

Notes

Cf. *Encyclopaedia Britannica*, Vol. 9, Galileo.
The Catholic Encyclopedia, Vol. VI, Galilei.
Reuben Parsons: *Studies in Church History*, Vol. IV, Ch. IV, Galileo.
Sherwood F. Taylor: *Galileo and Freedom of Thought*.
1. Josh. 10:13.
2. Date of Censure, March 5, 1616.
3. Reuben Parsons: *Studies in Church History*.
4. Robert Cardinal Bellarmine, canonized saint, Jesuit scholar, made the remark to a foremost scientist of the day, Foscarini, in a letter.
5. Eccles. 1:5.
6. Pope Pius XII in the encyclical *Divino Afflante Spiritu* points out that profane literature as well as everyday talk uses figures of speech and may describe what is seen as it is seen ("as it appears to the senses"), not bothering about the literal truth. He draws his inference: "When then such modes of expression are met within the sacred texts, . . . justice demands that they be no more taxed with error than when they occur in the ordinary intercourse of daily life."

7. Sherwood F. Taylor: *Galileo and the Freedom of Thought.*
8. One of the seven cardinals who signed the sentence, Anthony Barbarini, tried his utmost to have it remitted.
9. *Apologia Pro Vita Sua,* Chapter V.

18.
Pope Paul Lived and Died a Martyr

OUR LADY OF FATIMA foretold it. She did not mention his name. But she did have in mind a definite person. In speaking of the dark future to her visionaries, she said that "the Holy Father will have much to suffer." The prediction especially fits Pope Paul VI.

On the occasion that he opened the Holy Year at St. John Lateran's in the November of 1973, the aging pontiff sat down to preach a homily from no prepared text — rather from a grieving heart. "Who is speaking to you?" he leaned forward from his cathedra to say. "A poor man. A phenomenon in smallness. I tremble, my brethren and children, I tremble to speak because I am feeling things to say that are immensely larger than I am."

Then into his voice came a ring of conviction that did not remove its quaver. "I am announcing to you the word of Christ. I have been sent by him. I am the successor to St. Peter. Accept me. Don't despise me. I am the Vicar of Christ. I am speaking to you in his name, and therefore I ask you to show respect — not so much for me as for my word."[1]

That pitiable appeal had in it the remembrance of many a rebuff from dissenting priests who had brazenly belittled the authority of Pope Paul after his *Humanae Vitae,* an encyclical in defense of human life against its abuses. His reminding them that he carried the keys of Peter did not deter them, for in the reminder they either did not grasp or did not want to grasp its doctrinal import. They went on talking as if his authority must come to him from the people of God, for whom they pretended to speak. They seemed to think that, since his legislation lacked popular approval, it could have no validity.

Nothing could be further from the truth. Our Lord did not hold a meeting with the apostles to determine their choice of a primate. He picked one for them. He had not gone loitering among the disciples to gather their recommendations for a candidate. He made His personal selection of Simon Peter without consulting them. The people of God were not then (and in the election of any new pope are not now) given a vote. Let those who will, bemoan the action as monarchial or denounce it for being out of fashion with the progressive liberalism of the day. Only, let them not forget that this is what the Founder of Christianity did.

The Christ of the Gospels, who with infinite compassion taught the multitudes, reserved most of his instructions and of course his special instructions for the select few. He founded a hierarchy. By word and deed He made it clear that his priests were to be not only of the people but canonically distinct from them. Accordingly, unlike the modern movement that would reduce the priesthood to an institution of social workers, the *Acts of the Apostles* presents the chosen of the Lord preaching his doctrines, conferring upon the faithful the sacraments, doing for the people what they alone were ordained to do. They obviously didn't think it necessary to promote the social betterment of their converts before enriching their souls. They simply followed the procedure of their Divine Exemplar who administered spiritually to the poor while they were still poor, whether they were ever to be materially better off or not. He never did make bodily comfort a prerequisite to salvation.

Pope Paul had for Holy Orders a right appreciation. From the start of his pontificate he insisted upon the dignity of the priesthood, the episcopate, the papacy. He would have the priest act like one, talk like one, dress like one. He would have the bishop not cringe before the heretical uprisings in his diocese but use his high authority to explain and extol the doctrines under assault. Nor did he ever feign a false modesty to play down his own higher authority. At every opportunity he asserted it. He certainly reminded an international group of theologians at Rome on October 6, 1969, that his primacy derives from Christ and is "essential to the government, stability, peace and unity of God's Church." Attack that, he warned, and you attack the Church and must answer to God.

At the world synod of bishops a week later in the Sistine Chapel the firm but gentle pontiff stressed the point. "Let us reflect," he began. "There exists between us, who have been chosen to succeed the apostles, a special bond, the bond of collegiality." Together they shared a responsibility, though not coequally. His exceeded theirs. And so he said of himself in the customary papal plural: "We must remember our supreme responsibility, which Christ wished to entrust to us when he gave Peter the keys of the kingdom and made him the foundation of the edifice of the Church, committing to him a most delicate charism, that of strengthening his brethren."[2]

It was during this synod at Rome that a demonstration occurred that did not belong to it but cannot be disassociated from it. The bishops did not witness the demonstration. But Pope Paul did. He inspired it. While elsewhere at the Vatican they were engaged in one of their routine sessions, which normally the Holy Father would have attended, he stood before a packed audience in St. Peter's Basilica and had no more finished his address than the crowd broke into wild applause. It did not sound out of place. Why should it? With the environment it partook of a sacred character. It was a resounding act of faith.

The address, just another of the weekly allocutions to a general audience, owed much of its supercharged interest to the advance gossip about the synod. News releases out of Rome had insinuated that a dominant clique of attending bishops would trim down papal authority to an equality with theirs. Then after the first session a syndicate distributed to the press an alarming picture, with a commentary to go with it. The picture showed an unsuspecting cardinal at a lectern, snapped from the rear, and at such an angle as to make of him an over-powering figure talking down to a meekly seated, remote little pontiff. The photograph without the commentary could not so grievously offend. The combination did.

It stung the faithful. Given wide publicity and practically the status of a foregone conclusion, the innuendo rankled. And so indeed, when an aggrieved multitude converged on Rome and crowded into St. Peter's to hear the Holy Father reassert his irreducible primacy and plead for harmony in the Church under his supreme guidance, it was but natural for these people without a common vernacular to respond as they did. With the aid of interpreters among their national groups, they had promptly understood the papal message and in a frenzy of relief demonstrated to Pope Paul their reverence for him as the Vicar of Christ. They broke into applause.

Then there suddenly came to their lips the timeliest words of a common idiom. They had known Gregorian chant from years of use in their various countries, and when some inspired voice in their midst had lifted well above the applause the shrill intonation of *Credo in unum Deum,* it was all the cue the other hundreds of voices needed. The hard hand-clapping stopped, not from being tired out. In full vigor it

Pope Paul Lived and Died a Martyr

simply yielded to a superior form of acknowledgment: and St. Peter's spacious interior thundered with song, the Latin sonority of the Nicene Creed.[3]

The synod continued through its weeks of discussion, but any exploring to widen collegiality had been done within doctrinal bounds. Leon Joseph Cardinal Suenens spoke the mind of the many attendants in his retort to the press: "There are no heretics here." None questioned the primacy of one among them, and only one. They affirmed it, devoting the final session to the theme of unity "with and under" the Roman Pontiff. As once at Chalcedon and again at Constantinople, so now the assembly of bishops recognized in the message of their primate the voice of Peter. The synod ended in a tribute to "the Pastor of the Universal Church."[4]

The 1969 display of faith at St. Peter's, on the part of the laity, deserves comparison with the demonstration at Ephesus during the great council of 431.

The first session of the council, which lasted a day, took place in the cathedral proper. By sundown a great throng had gathered around it to await the news that could not have better relieved their tension, had it come to them directly from heaven. They were disturbed that no less a dignitary than the Patriarch of Constantinople had forbidden them to call Mary the Mother of God, and that in defiance of the Holy See he refused to recant while flaunting his own magisterial authority before their qualms of anxiety. They had endured months of suspense. But learning now that the council had condemned his error by an overwhelming vote and the thunderous cry of "Anathema to Nestorius!" they let go a tremendous shout of their own. Whoever eschews triumphalism will take no satisfaction from the behavior of the Ephesians on the night of June 22, 431. They paraded the streets until the hour of dawn, singing and dancing as they went. They would stop here and there to serenade the residence of some visiting bishop. It was a holy rejoicing. For its justification lay in the beautiful inference, which poor

Nestorius could not perceive: "Mary is the Mother of God because she is the Mother of Christ who is God — and through her our Brother." There was in the hilarity a noble pride.[5]

A foremost item of interest about the council at Ephesus, like every other ecumenical council, was its deference to the Holy See. The Patriarch of Alexandria assumed the presidency of the first session with the understanding that he was "filling the place of the most holy and blessed Archbishop of the Roman Church." During the day-long session, whereas a hundred and twenty-six other speakers were heard from, none could match the eloquence of the presiding genius who opened his introductory address with a sigh of relief and the words: "I see here a joyful company of Christian men met together in ready response to the call of Mary, the holy and ever-virgin Mother of God. The great grief that weighed upon me is changed into joy by your presence, venerable Fathers. Now the beautiful saying of David the psalmist, *How good and pleasant it is for brothers to live together in unity,* has come true for us.

"Therefore, holy and incomprehensible Trinity, we salute you at whose summons we have come together to this church of Mary, the Mother of God."

Whereupon, there in her cathedral, St. Cyril of Alexandria sounded her praises in an oration that awed his audience like great music.[6]

He guided the discussions in accord with the directives he had received from Pope Celestine in their correspondence. As in the preceding century Athanasius depended upon the support of the Holy See to turn back the encroachments of Arianism, so now Cyril needed the same support to fight off Nestorianism, an insidious derivative of the former heresy. Neither of these great Eastern expositors of pure doctrine could have prevailed without the approval of the Apostolic See. "Take care," wrote St. Catherine of Siena to Pope Gregory XI, "that I do not have to complain about you to Jesus

Pope Paul Lived and Died a Martyr

crucified. There is no one else I can complain to, for you have no superior on earth." And this primacy of spiritual power, however unworthy its possessor at any given time, has under the guidance of the Holy Spirit proved to be through the ages the ultimate security against corruption of the Faith.

The jubilant crowd singing their *Credo* before Pope Paul in St. Peter's Basilica on that October day in 1969 cannot but have had it in their minds that here was God's vicar on whom they could rely to defend the changeless doctrines of revelation from modern assault. Insofar as the New Theology has presented original insights into old truths, which must deepen an appreciation of them, just so far does it have respectability. However, it has only too often in its better known proponents served no such purpose. Their explaining truths away, under the pretence of bringing them up to date, does not revitalize but destroys them. The pretence could not do else than offend the faithful for the reason that false notes from a symphony must offend the ear sensitive to music.

The international group who came to St. Peter's to find reassurance from the Holy Father, let it be remembered, may have needed that reassurance. They had been exposed (as who wasn't?) to a spate of double talk from innovators discrediting Original Sin, our First Parents, the Ten Commandments, the Real Presence aside from the Mass, the Mass itself as a Sacrifice, the Omniscience of Christ from the moment of conception, the scriptural account of the Divine Infancy as so much *haggadah midrash* instead of history, the inviolate virginity of Mary, the reality of Angels, of Purgatory, of Hell, and, needless to add, the full authority of Peter in his present successor. From Pope Paul meanwhile, as fast as the misinterpretations could propagate, the rebuttals came. His voice spoke out vigorously for the unchanging truths. Ridicule could not silence him. But Satan knows it tried. The devil also knows to his disappointment that those who mean to die in possession of the Faith have everywhere hearkened to the Holy Father with a relieved sense of joy. They have recognized in his vicarious voice, so distinct from the babel of contemporary prophets, the guidance of the Good Shepherd.

No segment of the faithful could have better expressed the conviction that Pope Paul with the fortitude of his patron would withstand the infidel, than that group of admirers who sang to him the Nicene Creed. The fathers at Ephesus recited, no less appropriately, the selfsame Creed to open an ecumenical council that would promptly carry out the behests of the Holy See to safeguard the distinction that, while in Christ Jesus there are two distinct natures, they subsist under the unity of one Divine Person. The council in a befitting act of gratitude eulogized Pope St. Celestine for not allowing Nestorianism to deprive the Faith of an endearing truth and take from the children of men the privilege of calling a human mother the Mother of God.

Pope Celestine I, thus honored by a general council, received the tribute *in absentia*. Pope Paul VI, while honored by nothing like so important an assembly, did of course have the satisfaction of being present at St. Peter's when his audience applauded him and chanted out their joy to him as the custodian of the everlasting Faith. The parallel between the two demonstrations has contrasts. But the motivation was the same in both. The triumphal outbursts at St. Mary's in Ephesus and at St. Peter's in Rome sprang of the same jealous love of the truth in jeopardy.

The supreme teaching authority of the Holy See, infallible in its decrees *ex cathedra,* is a dogma of faith. It transcends the status of a mere opinion, a theory, a hypothesis. Deny it, if once you believed it and understood it, then whatever else you remain, are you still a Catholic? No sooner had the First Vatican Council defined Papal Infallibility, which the Second confirmed, than the warning followed: "But if anyone — which may God avert — presume to contradict this our definition, let him be anathema."[7]

Father Raymond Brown in his *Biblical Reflections on Crises Facing the Church* questions the authenticity of the scriptural text which gives to Peter the primacy. He questions the Rock on which the Church has been built. But that does not remove it. His attitude has led Paul H. Hallett to say what needs to be said: that whatever is in crisis, it is "not the teachings of the Church."[8] There is nothing dissolvable about her Rock of Authority. It is permanent. So the most recent of ecumenical councils declared. "He," its *Dogmatic Constitution* records of Christ, "placed Blessed Peter over the other apostles and instituted in him a permanent . . . foundation of unity of faith."

The unique jurisdiction of Simon Peter, passed on to his successors in the See of Rome, remains. It shall remain. What the Founder of the Church established and the doctors of the Church sanctioned and the councils of the Church acclaimed, all this modern nonsense about an on-going revelation cannot undo. "The powers of death shall not prevail against it."[9]

As time wears on the faithful may well look back to his turbulent reign to say of Paul VI: "There, in his slight but resolute figure, walked one of the Church's most abused and most valiant popes. Short of using the anathema within his power, he still repudiated the errors of modernism. He did not keep an indolent silence when the outraged truth demanded of him a statement. Against a magpie chorus of outcries to change the matrimonial code, he issued his stand-pat encyclical on *Human Life*. Against the whole rigmarole of doctrinal deviations, he proclaimed to the world his *Credo of the People of God*. Mercilessly blamed for not yielding, he seldom lost his temper and never his courage. He suffered, if at times tearfully, always confidently. He did not waver."

The appraisal could be summed up in a sentence: "Pope Paul VI lived out his difficult reign a martyr to the Faith."

Notes

1. The Holy Year opened for Rome at St. John Lateran Basilica, Nov. 10, 1973. The New York Times two days later reported the ceremony, running a feature article under the title: "Pope Expresses Anguish over Defections of Priests."
2. Cf. Bishop William L. Adrian, D.D.: "The Pope Explains Collegiality." *The Wanderer,* Nov. 27, 1969.
3. Ibid.
4. Council of Chalcedon, 451, and Third Council of Constantinople, 680-681.
5. Cf. Reuben Parsons: *Studies in Church History,* Vol. I, Ch. 26. Also: Mansi IV, V, and Hardoin I.
6. Homily 4: P.G. 77, 991. 995-996.
7. Denzinger 1840.
8. Paul H. Hallett: Review of *Biblical Reflections on Crises Facing the Church* (Paulist Press, 1975) in National Catholic Register, Nov. 16, 1975.
9. Mt. 16:18.

19.
That They May All Be One

THE confederacy of evil would seem to be getting the world ready for a showdown. The symptoms are there. Decency is ridiculed. Debauchery prevails. Violence stalks the street. Divorce threatens the home. The atrocity of abortion goes unimpeded. The expulsion of God from the schools in most countries has been legalized and ignorance of his law dominates education. Far too few protest. The cruelty of brainwashing, the slave-labor camp, the murder of nations cause no great alarm: the dignity of the individual citizen has ceased to count in a society without God. For that matter, the atheist conspiracy has already overthrown half the governments and fully intends to subdue the others to its lone domination. And it is all pretty much taken for granted. In such an age what believer in Christ but must regret the disunity of Christians which can only be aiding the totalitarian advance of evil? The reunification, however, if it should come and were to pose an adequate counterforce, would have to come on God's terms. It would have to meet his demand. The restored unity of faith would have to include the entirety of his revealed truths.

That is what Pope John evidently had in mind when he convened Vatican Council II. He spoke his mind clearly at its opening session. "Men," he said, "without the assistance of the whole of revealed doctrine cannot reach a complete and firm unity." He encouraged the divided Christians to talk things over: to rejoice in their doctrinal agreements, correct their misunderstandings, iron out their accidental differences, pray together for guidance, and then wait hopefully until in God's time his influence upon so many diverse followers of the Gospel would bring harmony out of the honest discord. Nor did her supreme pontiff fail to remind non-Christians that "the Catholic Church, raising the torch of religious truth by means of this Ecumenical Council, desires to show herself to be the loving mother of all."

But nowhere, positively nowhere, in his introductory address to the assembly of bishops and delegates and collaborators and observers did "the latest and humble successor to the Prince of the Apostles" betray the sheerest hint that a single doctrine of the credenda would be compromised to secure unity at such a price. On the contrary, he found it of utmost importance to insist on "all the teaching of the Church in its entirety and preciseness, as it still shines forth in the acts of the Council of Trent and the First Vatican Council." The Second, over which he was now presiding and for which he was now speaking, "wishes to transmit the doctrine, pure and integral, without any attenuation or distortion." Could words be clearer? They formed the keynote of Pope John's opening speech.[1]

Impartial toward the creed, insisting on all its doctrines, Pope John had the same impartiality in his desire for converts. He saw in "those who follow non-Christian religions" and yet feel some degree of "esteem and respect for the Catholic Church" an incipient affinity which he dared to hope would lead them in. As for the many Christians "separated from this Apostolic See" the jovial pontiff apparently had no doubt that efforts at reunion would after some future turn of events bring it about and restore to the partial believers their full heritage. Clearly his idea of unity in the undiminished truth sprang from that resolute benevolence which the world associates with Pope John. His own enrichment from the Faith, not just a part but the whole of it, he hoped against hope the deprived would come to enjoy with him.

To his way of thinking, which is the Church's way as well, no charitable Catholic who dialogues with non-Catholics would pretend that mere fragments of his creed suffice for them. It would be treating them shabbily, holding them cheaply. To tell a Jewish friend of the Orthodox persuasion that, since he already acknowledges the one true God, he need not bother his head about the Triunity of God and by the same token is not expected to believe that the coequal Son of the eternal Father also became the Son of a Galilean mother to appear on earth the long-awaited Messiah of the prophets: to tell him that, in view of the ennobling doctrine of the Incarnation, would be slighting the man. It would assume that the dignity of having Jesus Christ for a brother is not for him.

It would be exposing him to a subtle form of anti-Semitism. It would deny him the proudest distinction of his race, which he may in good faith not admit but nonetheless has the right to be complimented upon. A convert from Judaism once said to a K of C audience: "How many of you gentlemen can boast that the Incarnate Son of God, consubstantial with the Father, is of your blood? Well, I honestly can. He is of mine." What matters theologically is that the Babe in the manger, who had a crowded sky of angels singing of his birth, came to us from his Father through a human mother. But the particular fact remains, and in ecumenical dialogue with the sincere Judaist should be sincerely put forward, that this human mother was in all her sublime loveliness a Jewess.

Early in this book a reference was made to a clique of

so-called Catholic theologians who were hacking away at the deposit of faith. But are the more typical of them really hackers? The term connotes a directness which their method does not have. It is rather one of innuendo. They prefer to question than deny. Their suavity does not challenge, forces no argument, and proves the more insidious on that account. They do not so much assert as propose, raising doubts in many an unsuspecting mind and taking from it its certitude.

"Is it not feasible to say," an audience of nuns was typically asked, "that while we must believe Mary a virgin at the time of Christ's birth, she need not have remained one after that?"

"No!" shot back an intrepid Josephite. "It is not feasible. It is heretical."

"Oh, but please don't be so perturbed, dear," she was softly told. "I did not assert. I merely raised a question."

A question loaded with mischief it was. Whether the coordinator of the workshop knew it or not, his negative question (is it not?) automatically implies an affirmative answer. So his rebuke was on target. He had asked for it.

Quibblers like him, at first claiming to have been implementing the conciliar decrees, thus found a convenient cloak under which to hide from the unwary their purpose. Under pretext of supplying new insights into the authentic teaching of the Church, they argued away whatever of it did not meet their modernist approval. Their kind of dialogue with the sincere Protestant, one can imagine, could only have deepened the misunderstanding instead of offering a genuine effort toward clearing it up. If "the Catholic Church has been endowed with all divinely revealed truth" — which is what the council stated — then he is an unreliable spokesman for her body of doctrines who rejects any single dogma of it.

Right here lies the bitter irony of the farce. If in the spirit of compromise a dialogist insinuates to a Protestant group that neither do Catholics have to believe in the Immaculate

Conception or in the Assumption of Mary the Mother of God, he has not drawn his audience closer to an understanding of Catholic doctrine but has simply announced his own estrangement from it. Whatever he is in, if his concession involves a knowing denial of the dogma, it is not the Church. He has excommunicated himself.

Pope Pius XII with the consent of 98% of the episcopate defined the Assumption of the Virgin Mary a dogma, and immediately attached a significant warning to his definition. It reads: "If anyone, which God forbid, should dare wilfully to deny or call into doubt that which we have defined, let him know that he has fallen away completely from the Divine and Catholic Faith." The same applies to the denial or calling into doubt of any other dogma, if wilfully done. It presupposes a complete loss of confdience in the Church of God as the unerring and unerrable teacher of his revealed truths.[2]

Without papal guidance, unity of doctrine has proved an impossibility. Every sectarian break from the Holy See did not remain united but disrupted into fragments of additional sects. This fact of history, too obvious to need pointing out, should in any honest dialogue with the non-Catholic Christian be touched upon only to show the necessity of a supreme unifying authority on earth. It was a lapsed Protestant by the name of Stevenson who wrote: "While Calvin is putting everybody exactly right in his *Institutes,* and hot-headed Knox is thundering in the pulpit, Montaigne is already looking at the other side of his library in Perigord, and predicting that they will find as much to quarrel about in the Bible as they found already in the Church."[3]

It has always been so. Nestorius, not content with the Arian denial, denied the Divinity of Christ a different way. Pope St. Celestine warned him, through the mediation of St. Cyril of Alexandria, to recant his error of dividing the Son of God and of the Virgin Mary into two persons. It did not avail. The patriarch of Constantinople started yet another sect.

But none fought the twin heresies of Arianism and Nestorianism with truer zeal than the monk Eutyches — until his zeal turned false. Had he taken the *monitum* of Pope St. Leo, he would have held his balance. But the zealot thought he knew better. He thought his mind could understand the intricacies of the Incarnation without aid. His logic ensnared him. He concluded that, since Jesus was but one person, a Divine Person, therefore he had but a Divine Nature. This founder of the Monophysites became every bit as headstrong in denying the humanity of the God-Man as ever Nestorius had been in denying the union of his two natures in one Person.

Newman wrote in his *Apologia,* with presumably a twinkle in his ascetic face, "who would have thought of going to the sayings and doing of old Eutyches . . . in order to be converted to Rome!" Yet so it happened. He did go to "that *delirus senex*" — that defier of the Holy See — to learn a lasting respect for it. Reading deeply into the Monophysite controversy, as he had done with its Nestorian counterpart, the Anglican scholar received a shock to his complacency. He saw in a flash of enlightenment for the first time the need of a predominant authority on earth to check these wild misinterpretations of revealed truth so as to keep every particle of it in close harmony with the whole. Why had he not noticed the obvious before? The Holy See had always been performing that role, and would so continue, in a long sequence of battles with heresy. But it took defiant old Eutyches and "the enormities of the unprincipled Dioscorus" to awaken his dormant mind to it.[4]

From now on, at first timidly, then ever more resolutely, John Henry Newman believed the papacy a unique provision of God's mercy to restrain human freedom from "its own suicidal excesses" — from deviating into error away from the truth that counts most. The mind at liberty, in it-

That They May All Be One

self a noble reflection of the Omniscient, yet on account of its original misuse bears the curse of its present enfeeblement. It is so easily prone to misunderstandings of a revelation beyond its natural grasp. Accordingly, against its erratic tendency and even delusions of self-sufficiency, the mind in matters of the Faith requires guidance. This it has from the voice that speaks *ex cathedra* by the authority and in the name of Jesus Christ, who established the Chair of Peter for no other reason.

While the council was still in session Pope Paul issued the encyclical, *Ecclesiam Suam,* in which he states anew the same cherished objective. But the prospective reunion of the non-Catholic and the Catholic Christian, or a better understanding between Christian and Jew, must as a first step be wanted by both sides. They must mutually open their minds to its desirability, pray for its realization, and in the meantime have patience. An impetuous haste to settle differences by simply assuming there are none, so the encyclical warns, would impede any advance toward genuine unity. It would make a farce of dialogue. Rabbi Israel Mowskowitz was only showing a sense of humor, and a laudable honesty, in ridiculing the instance "when a Jew who does not believe in Judaism meets a Christian who does not believe in Christianity and they find they have much in common."

Pope Paul lost no time carrying into action his plea that a predisposition of friendliness break down the barriers of distrust to open the way. During an interim between sessions of the council he made a pilgrimage to the Holy Land in order to meet the foremost dignitary of the Greek Orthodox Church in Jerusalem and with him exchanged a liturgical kiss of peace. In the Basilica of the Holy Sepulchre they recited the verses, alternately, from the Last Supper prayer of Jesus for unity among his followers. It set a precedent. It set the world an example.

Nor was it their last meeting. After the council each visited the other at his residence: Paul VI went to Istanbul,

Athenagoras I returned the courtesy by showing up at the Vatican. On the earlier occasion the Eastern dignitary announced in his crowded cathedral: "Here, contrary to human expectation, we see in our midst the Bishop of Rome, who has the primacy of honor, who presides in love." And later at St. Peter's in Rome an applauding congregation watched the two walk side by side through the nave to a spot right above the apostle's tomb. There, at that sacred spot, the bearded patriarch of Constantinople placed a bouquet of nine red roses. Why nine of them? To betoken his sorrow over the nine regrettable centuries of division. He said he had come as a brother to his brother, whose apostolic see he again acknowledged "the first in rank in the organization of the Christian Church." Pope Paul, with a humble nod, took the reference to his supremacy as the truth, the irreformable truth, the dogmatic truth.

He had been no less happy and gracious a host on a like occasion the year before. In March of 1966 he welcomed the Anglican Archbishop of Canterbury to the Vatican, embraced him, and in the Sistine Chapel compliantly heard him ask their heavenly Father "to enable us to feel the pain of our diversion." They both did indeed feel it. Each also felt privileged by the other's presence Together, as a climax to the historic visit, they conducted a service in St. Paul's Basilica beyond the city wall in an ecumenical plea for unity in the end.

Dr. Ramsey left Rome with a rare keepsake. It was given to him by his host. To his dying day in England he would treasure it. It was the ring that Archbishop Montini of Milan had worn before he became Pope Paul VI and laid it aside to put on the Fisherman's ring.

Other denominationtal dignitaries, Bishop Carson of the Methodists, Metropolitan Nicodemus, the Armenian Vasken I, the Brothers of Taize, the Secretary-General of the World Council of Churches, Marc Boegner and Oscar Cullmann and Karl Barth and their like, all met a warm welcome at the Vatican. Their host made it a point, whenever feasible, to return the visits. Where did he not go, if invited, and if going there could promote the cause of unity? He stopped at nothing within his power to aid the present advance toward a better understanding. What he had not the power to do he did not pretend he had. He could not change, he dared not deny, the immortal dogmas of revelation as defined by the Catholic Church. But he did not flaunt them. He presented them amiably, appealingly, "speaking the truth in love," as his patron saint recommends.[5]

Pope Paul wrote his *Credo of the People of God* to caution them to resist "the passion for change and novelty" and to remain firm of faith. to give up none of the doctrines, which their supreme custodian then enumerated. In the process he did not forget about his separated brethren. He showed in the writing the same zealous charity of his predecessor for all partial believers. He would not have felt right if he did not include, which he did, his expression of "hope that Christians who are not yet in full communion with the one only Church will one day be reunited in one Flock with one only Shepherd."[6]

Nor did his next two successors deviate from Pope Paul's or Pope John's policies as enunciated in the *Documents of Vatican II*. It was no accident that John Paul I and John Paul II adopted the pontifical names of their predecessors. Both dedicated themselves to the promotion of an ecumenical unity among divided Christians and to exerting every effort to bring straying infidels into the fold under one shepherd. Beyond the shadow of a doubt in his extensive travels the present Holy Father has never failed to lament the disunity of Christians — and of humanity.

No sooner had Pope John Paul II kissed German soil in November of 1980 than the large welcoming crowd at the Cologne-Bonn Airport broke into cheers, and then went silent to hear his mirthful greeting, and then, though standing in the rain, listened avidly to his apostolic appeal: "May here, where the Reformation had its start, be redoubled the effort to do, in fidelity to the Lord, whatever is humanly possible to fulfill the desire of his heart, that *all may be one.*"[7]

Years earlier Pope Paul had recited with Patriarch Athenagoras the Last Supper discourse in which Jesus prays aloud to his Father that the apostles and disciples "may be one even as we are one."[8] Taking confidence from so divine a petition, and acknowledging in his *Credo* that "the divine design of salvation embraces all men", including the heathen, Pope Paul had hoped for the day of days when on earth the divided human race will at last find harmony in an undivided Church. For that he prayed.

In his public addresses Pope John Paul often has the same prayer on his lips, yearning with the Sacred Heart of Christ that" they may all be one." During the 1981 Church Unity Octave at St. Peter's, in the Sistine Chapel, he reminded the Roman Curia in a prepared homily that the unification of divided Christians is to be most ardently hoped for and prayed for and worked for. "If we are not one," he said, "as the Father is one with Christ, and as Christ is one with the Father, the world will not believe." The world, he went on to say, finds the division a mockery. "Christ the Lord established one Church and one Church only. Many Christian communions present themselves as the true inheritors of Jesus Christ: all indeed profess to be followers of the Lord but differ in mind and go their separate ways, as if Christ himself were divided. This contradicts the will of Christ, scandalizes the world, and does damage to the holiest of causes, the preaching of the Gospel to mankind."[9]

One would have to be slow at catching a hint not to catch, in the same homily, insinuations against the current discord within the Church quite as much as the denominational discord without. Pope Paul often complained of this "self-destruction" from within. It were as if "the smoke of Satan," he once said, had sneaked into the post-conciliar Church to

That They May All Be One

becloud the dissenter's mind. He considered the internal rebellion against doctrine the worst drag on efforts to achieve the ecumenical unity so ardently cherished by Vatican II. Pope John Paul agrees.

The scandal of dissent from theologians or biblicists, who claim a Catholic identification, has became a hindrance to heaven knows how many of the well disposed. Malcolm Muggeridge admitted to a correspondent that "Kitty and I had once thought of ending up in the Church of Rome." What kept the two out? Why did Mr. and Mrs. Muggeridge lose faith in their joint resolve? I wish that what now has to be said were not true, but it is. The effrontery with which an ill-advised clique of priests attacked *Humanae Vitae* and thereafter continued to defy the Holy See, is what shocked the Muggeridges into a change of mind. It drove them to the conclusion that the Catholic Church, "this last bastion" in a dying civilization, "was going the way of the whole modern world."[10]

Years later, November 29, 1982, Malcolm Muggeridge at the age of 79 went into the church of St. Mary Help of Christians in Sussex to embrace the Catholic Faith, all of it, every doctrine of it. It was for him a joyous occasion. He indeed called it a homecoming. The scandal of a group of self-appointed dissidents, who spoke with an authority not theirs, could no longer delay his decision. By the grace of the Holy Spirit he had finally come to see that it was not they who determine the truths of the Catholic Church. They are not her teaching voice. The Supreme Pontiff, the successor of St. Peter, and the bishops under his jurisdiction and in accord with him, these are.

* * *

Notes

1. *The Documents of Vatican II*. Appendix: "Pope John's Opening Speech." The Walter M. Abbot, S.J. Edition.

2. Apostolic Constitution, *Munificentissimus Deus*, A.A.S., Vol. 42, 1950, p. 770.
3. "Crabbed Age and Youth" from *Virginibus Puerisque*.
4. *Apologia Pro Vita Sua*: "History of My Religious Opinions from 1839 to 1841."
5. Eph. 4:15.
6. *Credo of the People of God,* June 30, 1968.
7. Cf. *Our Sunday Visitor,* November 30, 1980. "Pope Aims Right at Ecumenical Target on German Trip."
8. Jn. 17:1-21.
9. Cf. *The Pope Speaks* — a Quarterly by *Our Sunday Visitor,* Inc., Huntington, Indiana 46750. Cf. *The Wanderer,* Feb. 12, 1981 — "Pope Reflects on the Scandal of a Divided Christianity."
10. "At Home with Mug" by Hugh Kenner who visited the Muggeridges in their Sussex home. New York Times Magazine, Sept. 12, 1976. Cf. "Malcolm Muggeridge on *Humanae Vitae*" a pamphlet published by The National Committee of Catholic Laymen, Inc., Room 840, 150 East 35th Street, New York, N. Y. 10016.

20.
Pope John Paul II: Man of the Hour

Have no fear. The present Holy Father, out of his love for God and man, has no intention of submitting to the dissenters. He means to preserve the Faith, every dogma of it, to posterity. Strong of character, urged on by the Holy Spirit, he will prove more than a match for them. "One of the remarkable things about dissenters," observes Hitchcock, "is their seemingly-total absence of self-criticism." After a sharp paragraph the analyst of modern trends concludes that "in case after case, the dissenters — on contraception, on women's ordination, on celibacy, on papal infallibility — give their theories a practical infallibility."[1] As formerly they demanded of Pope Paul, so now they demand of Pope John Paul that he surrender his authority to them. And because he refuses, they are showing him their dissent.

Pope John Paul, as all the world knows, has suffered more than the hisses of dissent. He received, from an assailant who did not hate him but hated his office, two bullets from a spray of gunshot. Never had this lover of the human race looked nobler than in his agony of pain. The news media, according him full coverage, rejoiced at his survival. On his fourth day in the hospital he had a message ready for the crowd who had come to the scene of the crime, St. Peter's Square, for the customary noontime prayer — even though the usual leader of the prayer would be missing. His voice, however, was there — a little feeble, yet clear. At the sound of its familiar greeting, "Praised be Jesus Christ," an outburst of applause and cries of relief filled the air.

Taped at his bedside and radioed into the Square, the brief address in Italian lost none of its impact the next day when, having been translated into whatever vernacular, it was printed on the front page of many newspapers. "Beloved brothers and sisters," it began with the warmth of an embrace, and then went on to say how near the patient felt to all who were praying for him — in particular to the two who had been wounded and were suffering with him. "As for that brother of ours who shot me, I have forgiven him." Not a trace of bitterness there.

The next sentence explains why. In it lies the secret of this man's robust serenity amid the cruelties of life. It might be called the touchstone of his grandeur of person. The sentence reads: "United with Christ, priest and victim, I offer my sufferings for the Church and for the world."

Having thus finished with his audience at large, the dedicated sufferer had a final remark to make. Dropping his voice to a confidential whisper so that the crowd in St. Peter's Square could scarcely hear it, he spoke directly to the Mother of God, the Mother of the Church, the spiritual Mother of Mankind. It was nothing new to her. She had heard it from him before. It was his promise to her of long standing, "To you, Mary, I repeat: *totus tuus ego sum.*" *I am all yours* — spoken from the heart of a trusting child, what beautiful words in any language![2] Our Lady of Fatima, predicting in 1917 the terrors that have since befallen the world because of a deficit of prayer and penance, did have

Pope John Paul II: Man of the Hour 237

a reassuring word to add. "In the end," she assured her young visionaries, "my immaculate heart will triumph." When, God knows. For the present, whether or not Providence prolongs the life of Pope John Paul II until the great turnabout, he is in truth heaven's man of the hour.

Four days after he had left the hospital for his first return to the Vatican, the still ailing pontiff demonstrated anew his dedication to the Faith and his desire to share it with all mankind. It was Pentecost Sunday and into St. Peter's Basilica an estimated 20,000 Catholics, Lutherans, Anglicans, Methodists, Greek and Russian Orthodox, and others, had gathered for a common purpose: to attend a Mass of the Holy Spirit for unity. They did not expect the ailing pontiff to be present. They themselves were there, many dignitaries among them, to celebrate the 1,600th anniversary of the Council of Constantinople which in 381 defined the doctrine of the Divinity of the Holy Spirit. They had come to pray for a reunification of divided Christians.

No sooner had the Mass ended than the voice of John Paul II sounded through the basilica to announce his unexpected presence in a rear balcony and to draw an instant turning around of 20,000 heads. The crowd now stood facing him, cheering him, waving to him. "I want to be with you," he said, forcing some of its former strength into his voice. He told them why: "to reconfirm our common faith in the Holy Spirit." It was an unforgettable experience to see all those heads bowed in silence as the Holy Father implored the Spirit of Love to bring about out of the discord a perfect unity.[3]

Charles W. Bell, who followed the itinerary of the Holy Father in the United States, kept a diary of the seven days. He had a significant entry to jot down under the date of October 6, 1979. In the International Inn, Washington, D.C., he was having lunch that morning with fellow journalists, when one of their craft from New York walked over to them with the spicy remark: "You guys have lost all critical judgment. You're not reporters, you're groupies. This guy's just a priest with a lot of fancy titles. Your copy looks like it was written by the Vatican."

The entry goes on to add that some hours later the critic, after attending Pope John Paul's Mass on the mall, returned to the inn and to the same table of fellow reporters to give them a different story: "The man's a saint. A living saint, I tell you." In response to which, the diarist closes his entry for the day with his own comment: "Now everybody's a groupie. We can't help it. JP is the real thing. Talent. Goodness itself. And no fake."[4]

Pope John Paul II has won a new respect for the Church, creating in country after country a predominant climate of willingness to listen to him. He has even gone behind the Iron Curtain to preach the rights of mankind to freedom of worship and the supernatural dignity accruing to mankind from Jesus Christ. Such apostolic talk drawing uncountably large audiences within the boundaries of Soviet domination, and televised to the world, had been unknown before. An astute observer calls it "a break in the Iron Curtain which may be impossible to close."[5]

Pope John Paul charmed Britain during his six-day visit of England, Scotland and Wales. Upward of two million people came out to welcome and applaud him, to pray with him and laugh with him. As usual, he won the approval of babies no less than older children, exchanging looks of mirth with them, when not caressing them to their happy astonishment. He kept the news media busy showing or reporting the popular reaction, from the prolonged chanting and cheering and waving of flags by teen-age crowds to the casual remark of individuals. *Time* quotes one such remark from a densely packed sidewalk on London's Victoria Street: "I'm not a Catholic, but I believe this is my only chance to see an authentic saint."[6] An apostle of love, and the peace that comes of love, is the impression he conveyed.

This man of God, soon after his arrival on English soil,

expressed the hope "that my visit may serve the cause of Christian unity."[7] From what they knew of him, his audience must have known that he meant a unity without compromise in Catholic doctrine; though in non-essentials, yes, if need be. That is why, in the two Anglical cathedrals, the Communion Service was omitted from the ecumenical program. During the reign of little Edward VI the Blessed Eucharist was reduced to just a sacrament when Archbishop Cranmer removed every reference to a sacrifice from the Book of Common Prayer and then in 1552 had Parliament ratify the change. Accordingly, the Anglican ritual for Holy Orders eliminates from the functions of the priest his offering the immemorial Sacrifice of the Mass. Will there eventually be a breakdown of such barriers to reunion?

A growing party of High-Church Anglicans fervently hope so. God alone knows how many Britons of other denominations also hope, if only subconsciously, for a return to unity. It would seem to be an enormous number. Richard N. Ostling, getting his report from Mary Cronin on the scene, had this to say of a London crowd while His Holiness spoke to them on the subject: "The eyes of his audience welled with emotion and tears."[8] In Glasgow 300,000 gathered into Bellahouston Park to greet their visitor with cries of welcome as the Popemobile rode him up and down the lanes for all to see. Afterwards, during his Mass, their hilarity gave way to a devout silence. In Wales it was no different. At Pontanna Fields 100,000 filled the air with jubilee until the Holy Father began his Mass and then they quieted down to follow as best they could a ceremonial many of them may not have understood. It was the largest religious turnout ever in Cardiff.

Go where he would, go where he did throughout the six-day tour, there prevailed between Pope John Paul and the people an unfailing spirit of unity. In the cathedral at Canterbury a blare of trumpets announced a welcome as he entered through the west portal and walked in procession to the sanctuary. Early during the ecumenical service the Canterbury Gospels were carried to the lectern as a gesture of good will since Pope Gregory I had donated the precious volume to the first occupant of the see, St. Augustine, who had himself been sent from Rome by the same Holy Father to Christianize pagan Britain. But first, the present Archbishop of Canterbury embraced the present Pope with the word "Your Holiness, my brother in Christ," while the packed pews of onlookers broke into applause. When his turn came to speak, the honored guest began with the greeting which set the tone for his homily: "My dear brothers and sisters of the Anglican Community whom I love and long for."[9]

That His Holiness felt the same yearning for the Presbyterians in Scotland and the Methodists in Wales he made unmistakably clear. By word and action he expressed their endearment to him. Nor did he fail to visit a Jewish settlement in England to assure these descendants of Abraham face to face that, of the animosity they may be suffering, there is none in *his* heart. London's reputable *Sunday Times,* finding him the most loving and lovable of tourists, named Pope John Paul "the first citizen of the world." Dr. Kenneth Greet, secretary of the Methodist Conference, found him a humane dignitary who killed the prejudice in Britons toward his high office. In thinking of the supreme pontiff, no more do they have "the image of a proud prelate wearing a triple crown" in token of his unrestrained dominance. They know better now. In Pope John Paul they recognized "a man of devotion wearing a crown of thorns."[10] And how did Brian James conclude his New York *Daily News* report on the need of religious unity in a chaotic world and the corresponding need of a leader to bring it about? He said that, since the six-day papal visit, "there no longer is any doubt in Britain who that leader should be."[11]

Not that the papal motorcade did not meet with stiff opposition from organized protesters; here and there it did;

but not only did the police control them, the crowd booed them. Better still, as could be seen on TV, an incdient showed off to perfection John Paul's charisma. In passing by a boisterously hostile group as he stood in the Popemobile, the white-robed figure raised a hand and with a quick cruciform gesture and a smile on his face threw a blessing down to ringleader Ian Paisley on a side street.

Reverend Paisley in his vituperative rage brandished a Bible at "this Antichrist in our midst." A renegade priest at Fatima just two weeks before ran toward him with a drawn bayonet. The would-be assassin was stopped short, for which the Holy Father thanked the security guards — and Our Lady right there at her shrine. He had come to the shrine precisely for the purpose of thanking her in public for having preserved his life from an attempt on it a year ago to the day and for the additional purpose of consecrating the nations to her immaculate heart. The date is sacred to him for personal reasons to be sure, but mainly because it was on the 13th of May in war-saddened 1917 that Our Lady of Fatima first appeared to her three young seers to give them heaven's peace plan and to predict the world's present chaos if it failed to heed her plea for prayer and penance.

The future may well prove May 13, 1982 a turning point in history. For after his Mass in the Cova da Iria, Pope John Paul did what Pope Pius XII had done twice *in absentia*. Right there on the scene of the apparitions he consecrated the world (which of course includes Russia) to the Immaculate Heart. "We have recourse to your protection, holy Mother of God," her foremost client on earth began the act of consecration. His use of the plural *we*, by his own admission, included the whole college of bishops in union with him as the other apostles were with Peter.

This is significant. Pope Pius had acted alone, whereas Pope John Paul first obtained from the hierarchy their consent to make his prayer to Mary theirs as well. The collegial effort Our Lady of Fatima has repeatedly made a prerequisite for the conversion of Russia and peace in the world. We have the insistent word of Sister Lucia for that.

The Vicar of Christ, in his appeal to Mary, never for a moment forgot whose Mother she is. Take a look at his words of praise for "all those who day after day, with undiminished generosity, obey your plea, O Mother of God, to do what your Jesus tells them to do."

With nuclear annihilation threatening our sin-ridden world, the robust man of faith could not hold in an anguished cry. "Oh, how deeply we feel the need of consecration on the part of the world — our world." The collegial consecration ends on a note of beseeching confidence: "Accept, O Mother of Christ, this cry laden with the sufferings of all individual human beings, laden with the sufferings of whole societies. Let there be revealed, once more, in the history of the world, the infinite power of merciful love. May it transform consciences. May your Immaculate Heart reveal for all *the light of hope.*"[12]

What the future holds in store for Pope John Paul we do not know. We do know that he has magnanimously followed the lead of his predecessors toward a hoped-for unity among Christians and the conversion of infidels. Should he suffer a martyr's death from the forces of evil, let us not forget that this would not defeat the cause so dear to his heart. St. Stephen, while being stoned to death, prayed for his killers. The prayer did not go unanswered. The ringleader of the persecuting gang was thrown from his horse by a sunburst of enlightenment and, so divinely stunned, rose from the ground the Apostle Paul.

Lord Macaulay in reviewing Von Ranke's *History of the Papacy* could not but see that it was her early popes who stabilized the Catholic Church through her first centuries in the catacombs, and that her later popes continued to promote her stability. "She saw," he wrote only a century ago, "the commencement of all the governments . . . that now exist in the world; and we feel no assurance that she is not

Pope John Paul II: Man of the Hour 243

destined to see the end of them all" — as once she witnessed the demise of the mighty Roman Empire. It could not have given a man of Macaulay's bias any special delight to pay the Catholic Church that compliment. But feeling as he did her apparent indestructibility under the guidance of her popes, although he was careful not to call it supernatural, he obviously felt compelled to admit as much as he dared.

A century later his premonition has quite impressively withstood the test of time. Better than two-thirds of the ruling dynasties of Macaulay's day, including those of such notable countries as Russia, Germany, Spain, Austria-Hungary, Poland, China, Japan, are no longer in existence. They have passed. Russia has no Tsar, Germany no Kaiser, Spain no King, Austria-Hungary no Emperor, and so on through the long list of casualties. The Catholic Church, on the other hand, as she has been doing for two millennia, goes right on having one Supreme Pontiff after another.

Nor did she at any time during that long interval have an easy existence. As late as 1860, a hostile Italian government seized the Papal States which the Emperor Charlemagne had donated to the Holy See for the same reason that Maryland donated the District of Columbia to the federal government of the United States. The seizure left Pope Pius IX in his old age a veritable prisoner in the Vatican. He bore the confinement with an intrepid dignity of person, upholding the preogatives of his high office, as in turn his immediate successors did, Pope Leo XIII, Pope Pius X, Pope Benedict XV, Pope Pius XI. For some sixty years the supreme pontiff, whoever he was, remained the prisoner of the king and did not dare to leave the Vatican grounds.

Then in the 1920's Benito Mussolini, whose dominance had by now nullified the royal power, restored to the Holy See at least a portion of its former territory, which left Pope Pius XI free to govern unmolested from Vatican City, now itself an autonomous seat of authority both civil and spiritual. The concordat brought to an end the political squeeze on St. Peter's to prove once again that the Catholic Church, inured to crises, never fails to survive. Macaulay, no lover but admirer of hers, has had to admit: "When we reflect on the tremendous assaults she has survived, we find it difficult to conceive in what way she is to perish."

When feudalism collapsed, the Church, the custodian of the eternal truths, learnt to get along without it. She outlived it as she outlived the later economy of the guilds. If now capitalism should go and communism takes over the world, let not the Communists think they will have the world all to themselves. They will find there, coexisting with them, the Catholic Church. The wild jubilation of the crowds pressing around Pope John Paul II has already served notice on even the atheistic governments of the world that, in spite of their persecutions, the old Church still has plenty of life in her and intends to go on having plenty of life in her.

Were it not for the papacy, the continual assault upon the Faith — first upon this doctrine, then upon that — would have long ago prevailed. Jesus of Nazareth would have been reduced to a mere man, the Blessed Trinity to a nonentity, Holy Scripture to an anthology of fairy tales. The angels would be accepted as only figments of the imagination, and the saints as so many decomposed corpses of nothing at all. No power on earth but that invested in the supreme pontiff has been able to withstand the fury of one wild heresy after another. Its very durability through the turbulent centuries proves the Holy See to be the unique instrument of Providence for preserving the Faith.

Of that Pope John Paul is firmly convinced. His words say it. His actions prove it. He has dedicated his pontificate to preaching, to cherishing, to preserving the eternal truths.

The separated who have retained from the Catholic Church not a few of her doctrines have had from the papacy a strong, if indirect, encouragement. Through the good will of these, of Christians at large, of all the potential Christians, may the harmony of a common creed be achieved at last. After our permissive society will have become a hate-ridden hell of anarchy, may the disillusioned everywhere recognize, amid the chaos, the voice of the Lord in the only voice on earth that speaks with his kind of authority, the voice of his vicar. May they obey its call to a restored unity of faith, to a safe refuge from the turmoil, coming by the light of the Holy Spirit into one Fold under one Shepherd.

* * *

Notes

1. James Hitchcock: *Pope John Paul II and American Catholicism.* Published by The National Committee of Catholic Laymen, Inc., Room 840, 150 East 35 Street, New York, N. Y. 10016.
2. *New York Daily News,* Monday, May 18, 1981.
3. "Pope Delivers Talk in St. Peter's Basilica on Pentecost" in *The Star-Ledger,* Newark, N. J., Monday, June 8, 1981.
4. *New York News Magazine,* November 25, 1979. "Saturday, October 6."
5. Alexander Haig, so quoted in *Laywitness,* November, 1979.
6. *Time,* June 7, 1982.
7. *Newsweek,* June 7, 1982.
8. *Time,* June 7, 1982.
9. *Newsweek,* June 7, 1982.
10. Kristina Cooper, staff writer for the *Universe.* Cf. The National Catholic Register, June 20, 1982.
11. *New York Daily News,* Sunday, June 6, 1982.
12. *The Remnant,* May 31, 1982.

Index

Adam, incurred the Fall, 14-23; 28, 110; father of human race, 138
Aeneas, 51
Alexander of Alexandria, St., 64, 88, 90ff, 101
Alexander of Constantinople, St., 100ff
Ambrose, St., 22, 68, 155, 159
Ananias, 28f, 52
Anaxagoras, 39
Andrew of Crete, St., 185
Angels, excluded from modernistic catechisms, 151ff; acknowledged as a doctrine of faith by five councils, 154; most Fathers and the exegetes of the Torah think they operate the universe, 156ff
Apollinaris, bishop of Laodicea, 76ff, 79, 81, 83
Apollinarianism, denial of Christ's human soul, 77; condemned by Pope Damasus and Constantinople I, 78; 80
Aquinas, St. Thomas, 39ff, 43f, 128, 133, 156, 164f
Aristotle, 39ff, 115, 132f, 157f, 205

Arius, 77, 83, 87ff; his sensational death, 97; 101ff, 134
Arianism, denial of Christ's Divinity, condemned by Pope Sylvester I and Nicaea I, 91; Semi-Arianism condemned by Pope Julius I, 88
Arsenius of Meletia, 94
Assumption, 227
Athanasius, St., 66, 68, 76, 80, 91ff, 97ff, 134, 186, 218
Athenagoras, patriarch, 230, 232
Atomists, 37
Atzert, Father Edward P., 184
Augustine of Canterbury, St., 240
Augustine of Hippo, St., 19, 22, 34f, 44, 67f, 128, 132ff, 154, 159, 166, 193, 209
Averroes, 39, 130
Avignon, 59ff

Bacon, Francis, 204
Barlaam, St. 189
Barnabas, St., 52
Baronius, Cardinal, 191
Basil, St., 22, 67, 77, 99f, 189
Basilides, 48

Bauer, Ferdinand Christian, 129
Bell, Charles W., 237
Bellarmine, Cardinal, 206, 209 ,
Belloc, Hilaire, 44, 147
Black Mass, 175f
Book of Common Prayer, 239
Bounoure, Louis, 141
Brahe, Tycho, 204
Brown, Kim, 176
Brown, Father Raymond, 117, 221
Buddha, Guatama, 37

Calvin, John, 77, 84, 120, 227
Canterbury Gospels, 240
Catechisms, deficient in doctrine, 122, 151ff; General Catechetical Directory from Holy See, 170; CCD teacher resigns, 171ff
Carpocrates, 48
Catherine Labouré, St., 161
Catherine of Siena, St., 59-61, 72, 218; patroness of Holy See, 61
Cecilia, St., 35; incorrupt in tomb, 191f
Cerinthus, 109
Chair of Peter, 45, 65f, 68, 134, 229
Charlemagne, Emperor, 243
Chesterton, G. K., 41, 84, 119, 130f, 200
Christian Science, 84
Church, institutional, 47ff, 52ff, 123, 134, 214; indestructible, 242ff
City of God, The, 132
Claudel, Paul, 159

Coelestius, ally of Arius, 19f
Cohen, Morris R., 207
Coleridge, Samuel Taylor, 131
Collegiality, 227, 241f
Communism, atheistic, 32, 43, 128, 146, 148, 223, 244
Confessions of St. Augustine, 135
Confucius, 38
Constantia, sister of Emperor Constantine, 93
Constantine I, Emperor, 63, 70, 76f, 90ff, 97ff, 102, 193
Constantine II, Emperor, 102
Copernicus, Nicholas, 205f
Cornelius, 51
Councils: Brago, 54; Carthage, 20; Chalcedon (Ecumenical IV), 68, 70, 75, 81ff; Constance (E XVI), 61; Constantinople I (E II), 68, 78f, 193; Constantinople III (E VI), 69, Ephesus (E III), 68, 79ff, 217ff; Florence (E XVIII), 34, 154; Jerusalem, 51, 52, 129; Lateran IV (E XII), 154; Lyons II (E XIV), 154; Nicaea I (E I), 63, 68, 75, 77, 91ff; Orange, 21; Sardica, 68; Trent (E XIX), 21, 119, 154; Vatican I (E XX), 30, 66, 68, 117, 154, 224; Vatican II (E XXI), 7ff, 49, 69, 221, 224ff

Cranmer, Thomas, archbishop of Canterbury, 239
Creation Research Society, 144
Credo of the People of God,

Index

21, 111, 120, 154, 221, 231f
Cronin, Mary, 239
Cyprian, St., 22, 65
Cyril of Alexandria, St., 67f, 68, 79; genius of Ephesus council, 218f; 227f

Damascene, St. John, 187
Danielou, Cardinal, 118
Dante, 204
Darwin, Charles Robert, 139, 140ff
Das Capital, 128
Dawson, William, 141
Decline and Fall of Radical Catholicism, 105
Delage, Yves, 142
Democritus, 37
De Quincy, Thomas, 131
Derrick, Christopher, 127
De Rosa, Peter, 122
De Rossi, archaeologist, 65
Descartes, René, 40f, 204
Descent of Man, 146
Development of Christian Doctrine: only from implicit to explicit, 117f
Devil, the, *see* Diabolism
Dewar, Douglas, 139f, 145
Dewart, Leslie, 147f
Diabolism, 30, 169ff
Dialectics, Hegelian, 43, 128ff
Dialogue, false, 109ff, 226ff
Dialogue with Trypho, 48
Dioscorus, 228
Dissenters, Neo-Modernist, 8ff, 47, 55f; self-appointed popes, 105ff; 112f, 206, 210, 213ff, 218
Dotsenko, Boris P., nuclear scientist, 157
Dwight, Thomas, anatomist, 121; Ibid. 139

Eames, Stanley, 182
Ecclesiam Suam (Paul VI encyclical), 229
Ecclesiastical History (by Bishop Eusebius of Caesarea), 63
Ecumenism, 9, 70f, 112, 224ff, 239
Edict of Milan, 93
Edward VI, King of England, 239
Einwaller, Sister Arlene, 122f
Eleatics, 37
Elymas, 52
Empereur, Father James, 116
Engels, Friedrich, 146
Epiphanius, St., 89
Eucharist, 53ff, 118ff, 199, 239
Eusebius of Caesarea, historian, 63f, 90ff
Eusebius of Dorylaeum, 81, 134
Eusebius of Nicomedia, 89ff, 100
Eusebius of Vercellae (Vercelli), St., bishop, 98
Eustanthius of Antioch, 64
Eutyches, 65, 70, 80f, 83, 134, 228
Eutychianism, *see* Monophysitism
Eve, 15, 110; her body created from Adam's, 138
Evolution Protest Movement, founded by Sir Ambrose Fleming, inventor of the thermionic valve, 141, 145f
Evolutionism, 115ff, 121,

130, 135; a fairy tale for adults, 137ff; 151ff
Existentialism, 42

Fabian, St., 53
Fall, the, *see* Original Sin
Fatima, Our Lady of, 31ff 213, 236, 241
Faucolt, astronomer, 209
Ferrier, James Frederick, 131
Flaubert, Gustave, 14f
Flavian of Constantinople, St., 80f, 134, 213, 236, 241
Fleischmann, Albert, 142
Fleming, Ambrose, 141
Fossil Record, 144
Francis of Assisi, St., 161
Francoeur, Robert, 152
Fuller, Edmund, 155, 158

Gabriel, archangel, 152
Galileo, Galilei, 206; his case at court, 203-214; accused the Bible of error, 204; most scientists, scholars, philosophers and literati opposed his theory, which his judges allowed him to hold as a working hypothesis, 204, 208; Einstein's relativity nullifies it, 207; but his judges unnecessarily interpreted the biblical texts literally, 204, 208; neither of the popes involved signed the condemnation, 109f; three of the ten who formed the tribunal also refused to sign, 210
Garaudy, Roger, 148
George of Cypress, St., 187
Germanus, St., patriarch of Constantinople, 185ff
Gertrude, St., 33
Gibbon, Edward, 97
Giese, Tiedemann, bishop, 205
Gnostics, 48, 55, 80, 84, 109, 113
Gorgias, 38
Gray, James, 141
Greet, Dr. Kenneth, 240
Graeco-Slav Liturgy praises Pope Sylvester I for condemning Arius, 67
Gregory Nazianzen, St., 98
Gregory of Nyssa, St., 22, 98

Hallett, Paul H., 132, 159, 221
Hazlitt, William, 16f
Heaven, 123
Hegel, George Wilhelm, 40, 42f, 127ff
Hegelianism, 43, 128ff; condemned by Pius IX, 131f
Heidegger, Karl Wilhelm, 42
Heraclitus, 37f, 115f, 128, 133
Heresy, apostles did not tolerate it, 54, 108; nor did Christ, 107; 76f, 79f; John Paul II pleads with bishops to correct it, 112f
Heresies, Against (by St. Irenaeus), 63
Higher Criticism of Bible, 129
Hilary, St., 98
Historicism, 129f, 148
Hitchcock, James, 105, 233
Hosius of Cordova, bishop 64; presided over Nicaea I as papal delegate, 90; proposed the key word *con-*

Index

substantial at Nicaea, 91
Humani Generis, 121, 138, 145, 146
Humanae Vitae, 113, 214, 221, 233
Huxley, Julian, 142, 146f
Huxley, Thomas, 142, 208
Hymenaeus, 109
Hypostatic Union, 82ff

Iconoclasm: Pietà at St. Peter's attacked, 181; recurrent outbreaks heretically motivated, 184f, 191; condemned by Gregory I, 187f, by Gregory II, 186, by Adrian I, 187, by Paschal I, 191, by Nicaea II, 187, and by Constantinople IV, 188, and still again by Trent, 189; catacombs replete with images of Jesus and his mother, of angels and saints, 189; artistic churches recommended by Paul VI, 186, 201; by Vatican II, 191, 195; Solomon's Temple with its angels of art had God himself for its architect, Arc of Covenant by God's command overlaid with gold, 196-198
Ignatius of Antioch, St., 65
Infallibility of Pope, 8, 10f, 45, 72, 75-85, 134f, 220f
Infant Baptism, 19-22
Irenaeus, St., 22, 62f, 80, 109
Irene, Empress, 187

James, Brian, 240
James the Less, Apostle, 63
Jansenists, 56

Java Man, 140, 146
Jerome, St., 22, 67, 88, 156
Joachim of Flora, 49
John, Apostle, 50, 51, 109
John Chrysostom, St., 22, 67f, 186
John of Monagria, abbot, 185
Judas Iscariot, 28, 49f, 51, 103, 112
Julian the Apostate, 103
Justin, St., 48

Kant, Immanuel, 38, 42, 127, 130
Keppler, Johannes, 156, 159, 203f
Kerkut, G. A., 144
Kersten, John, 119
Knox, John, 119, 227
Knox, Monsignor Ronald, 73
Küng, Professor Hans, 72

Labbe, Father Philip, S.J., 69
Lactantius, 90
Lamarck, Jean Baptiste, 143
La Vey, Anton Szador, 30, 169
Lawrence of Rome, St., 33
Leibnitz, Baron Gottfried Wilhelm, 41
Lemoine, Paul, 141, 147
Lenin, 128
Leo III, the Isaurian, Emperor, 184, 186f
Leppershey, Dutch optician, 203
Leucippus, 37
Life of Constantine (by Eusebius of Caesarea), 64
Loisy, Alfred Firmin, 10, 131
Loreto, Holy House of, **7, 70, 72**
Lucia of Fatima, Sister, 242

Lunn, Arnold, 135, 139, 143, 188
Luther, Martin, 205f

Macarius of Jerusalem, 64
Macaulay, Lord, 242ff
Macedonius, patriarch of Constantinople, 78, 79
Macedonianism, denial of the Divinity of Holy Spirit as well as Christ's, condemned by Pope Damasus and Constantinople I (Ecumenical II), 79
Machan, Arthur, 10
McKenzie, Father Leon, 122
Madame Bovary, 14ff
Madame Delamarre, 15
Maderno, sculptor, 191
Male, Emile, 189
Manichaeism 29; condemned by Pope Eugene IV and council of Florence and again by Pope Pius IX and Vatican I, 34
Marcian, Emperor, 70
Marcion of Sinope, 48, 65
Maritain, Jacques, 109f, 123
Mark the Evangelist, 63
Marx, Karl, 128, 146
Mary, Virgin Mother of God, 7, 67f, 70; dedication to her, of John Paul, I 71; miraculous medal, 161f; Fatima, 213, 236, 241f
Mary Magdalene, 29, 197
Mateo, Father, apostle of Sacred Heart, 175
Maugham, Somerset, 131
Maxentius, Emperor, 193
Medawar, Peter, Nobel prize winner, 141
Melanchthon, Philipp, 206

Mendel, Gregor Johann, 142, 146
Michael, Archangel, 194, 201
Miller, Leo F., 43
Millikan, Robert, Nobel prize winner, 141
Mivard, St. George Jackson, 208
Modernist Theology, 8, 10, 43, 72, 87, 105ff, 127ff, 219, 226
Molnar, Thomas, 56, 196
Monophysitism, denial of Christ's human nature, 80f, 228; condemned by Pope Leo the Great and by Chalcedon, 81
Montaign, Michael, 204, 227
Morris, Henry, 144
Moses, 62, 66, 106f
Mowskowitz, Rabbi Israel, 229
Muggeridge, Malcolm, 233
Murray, Desmond, 143
Mussolini, Benito, 243
Myers, Edith, 151ff
Mysterium Fidei (Paul VI encyclical), 120
Mystical Body of Christ, 123

Naturalism, 32, 113, 144, 152, 181, 198
Neanderthal Man, 147
Nestorius, patriarch of Constantinople, 67ff, 79, 83, 216ê, 220, 227
Nestorianism, the heresy that Christ is two persons, condemned by Pope Celestine I and Pope Sixtus III, and by the council of Ephesus, 79, 228
Newman, Cardinal, 15, 45,

Index

49, 66, 88, 95, 97, 102, 133f, 159, 160, 165f, 210, 228
Nicene Creed, drawn up at council of Nicaea I, 91; then enlarged at Constantinople I to include salutation to the Holy Spirit, 79, 105, 220
Nihilism, 38
Nilsson, H., 142

Oath against Modernism, 117
O'Connell, Father Patrick, 145f
Olivier, Father, historian, 67
Ordination to priesthood in early Church, 52f
Ostling, Richard N., 239
Original Sin, 14-23, 28, 35, 40, 42f, 110, 122, 148
Origin, 22, 156, 159
Origin of Species, 146

Paisley, Rev. Ivan, 241
Pantheism, 38, 128, 132, 160, 166
Papacy, History of the (by von Ranke), 242f
Parmenides, 37
Pascal, Blaise, 204
Paul, St., 29ff, 52f, 242
Paulicians, Manichaean iconoclasts, 185
Paulinus of Nola, St., 189
Peking Man, 147
Pelagianism, denial of the Fall and of death as a curse, condemned by Pope Innocent I and Pope Zosimus, and by the councils of Carthage, Orange, Trent, 20ff, 28

Pelagius, 18-23, 28, 67, 134
Peter Chrysologus, St., 65
Pharisees, 37, 107ff
Philetus, 109
Philosophy, needs help, 37ff; suffers mental breakdown, 48
Piltdown Man, 140, 147
Plato, 39f, 132f
Polorization, 106-114, 107f, 113f
Polycarp, St., 63
Polygenesis, condemned by councils of Carthage, Orange, Trent, and by Pope Pius XII in *Humani Generis*, 138
Popes: Agatho, 69; Alexander, 62; Benedict XV, 243; Celestine I, 67ff, 220, 227; Clement, 62, 64; Cletus, 62; Damasus, 67, 77f; Dionysius, 67; Eleutherius, 62; Eugene IV, 34; Evaristus, 62; Fabian, 53; Gregory I, 154f, 159, 240; Gregory II, 186; Gregory XI, 218f; Innocent I, 20, 67; John III, 154; John XXIII, 7ff, 70, 72, 224f, 231; John Paul I, 76, 111, 231; John Paul II, 7-11, 21f, 45, 56, 61, 71f, 75, 111ff, 201, 203f, 210, 231, 235-245; Julius I, 88; Linus, 62, 65f; Leo I, 68, 70, 81f, 228; Leo XIII, 243; Paschal I, 191; Paul III, 205; Paul V, 209; Paul VI, 7, 9f, 21, 56, 70f, 72, 105, 111, 113, 115, 120, 154, 182; lived and died a martyr, 213-221; 229; Pe-

ter, 8, 11, 49f, 59f, 62f, 65f, 68f; Pius IX, 34, 131, 243; Pius X, 10, 117, 138, 243; Pius XI, 243; Pius XII, 121, 138, 146, 227; Sixtus III, 79; Sylvester, 64, 67, 77, 88, 90f; Urban VI, 60f; Urban VIII, 210

Primacy of Holy See, 47-73, 134, 213ff, 218f, 221f, 242ff

Process Theology, 10, 43, 108, 115-124, 127ff, 137ff, 221

Protagoras, 38

Ptolemy, 205

Purgatory, 123

Pythagoras, 205

Ramsey, Dr. of Canterbury, 230

Raphael, Santi, 194

Rationalism, 40

Raymond Penafort, St., 35

Reconciliation, Sacrament of, 53f

Reinke, expert botanist, 142

Relativism, 110f

Resurrection, of Jesus, 118, 129; of the human body, 123

Robinson, Carol Jackson, 130

Rostand, Jean, 141

Sacrament in early Church, 52ff

Sadducees, 37

Sanders, Ed, 177

Sartre, Jean Paul, 42

Satan, 27ff, 109f, 113; created a good angel who fell, 154; 164, 169ff, 194

Satanism, *see* Diabolism

Saturnillus, 48

Schillebeeckx, Edward, 118

Schomberg, Cardinal, 205

Schopenhauer, Arthur, 131

Scott, S. Herbert, 67

Sedgwick, Professor, 143

Serenus of Marseilles, bishop, 188

Shakespeare, 38

Sheed, Frank, 8, 120

Shelton, H. S., 139

Simpson, George Gaylord, 142

Smith, Sydney, 131

Socrates, historian, 97, 99, 102; philosopher, 39f, 132f

Soul, human, created directly by God, 138, 140f

Spencer, Herbert, 139

Standen, Anthony, author of *Science Is a Sacred Cow*, 139

Stephen, St., 52, 242

Suenens, Cardinal, 217

Syllabus of Errors condemns Hegelianism, 131f

Tabitha, 51

Tassoni, Alexander, 205

Tate, Sharon, 177

Taylor, Sherwood, 208

Teilhard de Chardin, 116f, 121, 123, 144, 148, 166

Temple, Solomon's, God commanded its magnificence, 197

Teresa of Avila, St., 161

Tertullian, 65

Thalia, 89

Thomas of Canterbury, St., 69

Thompson, Francis, 26, 160f

Index

Thompson, W. R., 140, 147
Tinkle, William, 143f
Tome of Pope Leo the Great, 82f
Toth, Laszo, who attacked the Pietà, 182
Tradition, 54
Transubstantiation, 119f
Triumphalism, 68f, 81ff, 84, 92, 193f, 199ff, 215, 220
Truth in crisis since Vatican II, 105- 114; doctrines do not change, 117; truth is objective, not what the mind demands it to be, according to Kant, 127f
Trypho, 48
Tyrrell, George, 10, 131

Unity in Truth: 54, 61, 108; disunity among Christians aids the atheistic advance, 223ff; Jesus at the Last Supper yearned for unity, 229; John XXIII, Paul VI, John Paul I, John Paul II have expressed the same yearning 233; without papal guidance it cannot be achieved, 227

Vernet, Maurice, 141
Vialleton, Louis, 141
Vincent Ferrer, St., 60
Vincent and Vitus (Victor), Holy See delegates at Nicaea I, 64, 92
Von Gebler, biographer of Galileo, 210

Waldenses, 61
Warneke, Michel, 169
Watson, D. M. S., 143

Western Schism, 60ff
Wilhelm, Anthony, 154
World, the: its two aspects, 25ff; its beauty suggests a better world, 25f; 26, 33; its destruction and replacement, 163ff
World Council of Churches, Geneva, 70
Wright, Cardinal, 3f, 155, 159f

Xenaeas of Hierapolis, bishop, a Nestorian iconoclast, 184